Ingemar Johansso

Ingemar Johansson

*Swedish Heavyweight
Boxing Champion*

Ken Brooks

McFarland & Company, Inc., Publishers
Jefferson, North Carolina

ISBN 978-0-7864-9847-5 (softcover : acid free paper) ∞
ISBN 978-1-4766-2023-7 (ebook)

LIBRARY OF CONGRESS CATALOGUING DATA ARE AVAILABLE

BRITISH LIBRARY CATALOGUING DATA ARE AVAILABLE

Front cover: Ingemar Johansson, 1958 (Kurt Durewall)

Printed in the United States of America

*McFarland & Company, Inc., Publishers
Box 611, Jefferson, North Carolina 28640
www.mcfarlandpub.com*

To my son Ty, and
to Barbara, Lucy and Anna Waldrop.
Thanks for being there.

I am the God Thor,
I am the War God,
I am the Thunderer!
Here in my Northland,
My fastness and fortress,
Reign I forever!

Here amid icebergs,
Rule I the nations;
This is my hammer,
Mjölnir the mighty;
Giants and sorcerers
Cannot withstand it! …

The blows of my hammer
Ring in the earthquake!
Force rules the world still,
Has ruled it, shall rule it;
Meekness is weakness,
Strength is triumphant,
Over the whole earth
Still it is Thor's Day!
　　　"The Challenge of Thor"
　—Henry Wadsworth Longfellow

Acknowledgments

All quotations in this book come from interviews conducted by the author, as well as magazine, book, newspaper, and broadcast accounts of the day.

My thanks to the following people who granted interviews: Rolf Johansson, Maria Johansson Gregner, Birgit Lundgren Johansson, Edna Alsterlund, Patrick Johansson, Thomas Johansson, Olof Johansson, Paul Gallender, David Ladd, Joe Gallison, Robert Daley, Gene Kilroy, Paolo Roberto.

My gratitude to the following people who contributed their time and efforts; Ove Karlsson, Erik Stenberg, Larry Farber, Paul Gallender, Joakim Berglund, Marja Durewall-Nilson, Tommy Holl, Lucy Waldrop, Barbara Waldrop, Ken Sizemore, Hallman Bryant, Dan Cuoco and the International Boxing Research Organization.

Table of Contents

TABLE OF CONTENTS

Introduction

"If you could stitch together the ideal heavyweight champion, piece by piece, how would he look?"

The question was posed in 1987 to the late Reg Gutteridge, dean of BBC boxing commentators, who'd seen a lifetime of the sport's greatest fighters.

Gutteridge's response: "Larry Holmes' jab, Joe Louis' left hook, George Foreman's uppercut, Sonny Liston's raw power, Rocky Marciano's aggression, Jack Johnson's defense, Ken Norton's physique, Joe Frazier's determination, Jack Dempsey's infighting, Floyd Patterson's hand speed, Muhammad Ali's showmanship, and…"

Gutteridge's final ingredient: "…Ingemar Johansson's right hand."

* * *

I will make no claim here that Ingemar ("Ingo") Johansson belongs on the same tier with Joe Louis, Muhammad Ali, Joe Frazier, Jack Dempsey, or any of the other giants of the game.

His infighting was nonexistent, his jab without sting, his chin suspect, his title reign too short. Boxing historian Mike Casey calls Johansson "one of the most technically lacking of the heavyweight champions," and I won't argue too heartily with that. But Casey adds: "Whatever else Johansson didn't possess as a fighter, I say unhesitatingly that he was one of the greatest natural punchers that boxing has ever seen." It was this singular skill, this gift from the boxing gods, that set Ingemar apart from his contemporaries.

For six days short of a year—from June 26, 1959, when he kayoed Floyd Patterson, to June 20, 1960, when Floyd returned the favor—Ingemar Johansson ruled the world, at a time when the heavyweight champion was among the most heralded men on earth and a title fight was as big as the Super Bowl and World Series combined.

It was quite a ride, however short, for him and for us. He brought dimple-chinned, leading-man glamor to a moribund game and challenged the sport's establishment by refusing to kowtow to mobbed-up promoters. He defied traditional training regimens by flouting the boxer-in-training's vow of celibacy, openly living with a shapely Swedish dish while still married to his first wife. He appeared on the cover of *Life*, was named *Sports Illustrated*'s Sportsman of the Year, hit fashionable nightspots on two continents, and charmed hardened sportswriters as easily as he did Hollywood starlets. Journalists hailed him as the best thing to happen to boxing since bareknuckle Boston strong boy John L. Sullivan swaggered from bar to bar boasting, "I can lick any man in the house."

In retrospect, one could be excused for dismissing Ingemar as a lucky one-shot champ, one of those ignominious few—among them Jack Sharkey, Buster Douglas, and Leon Spinks—who won the heavyweight title only to lose it in their first defense.

Once a champ, always a champ (*Kurt Durewall*).

But there is so much more to the Ingemar Johansson story, for beyond his fistic exploits, and there were many, lies a tale of ultimate redemption, and of enduring love.

* * *

First, the redemption: disqualified for "passivity" while fighting for the gold medal against the American Ed Sanders in the 1952 Olympics, Ingemar, just 21, was branded a coward, a pariah even in his own country—*especially* in his own country. "For shame, Ingo," read a typical

Swedish headline of the day, and editorials called for the young man to give up the game for good. But Ingemar was made of stronger stuff than anyone knew, and by turning professional, by fighting his way through the ranks, and by gaining sport's ultimate title, he proved it.

And then there is the story of the boxer and the hometown girl for whom he fell, and fell hard, in 1954—he a 22-year-old Göteborg boxer, she a 17-year-old brunette beauty. During their three years on the heavyweight title stage, from 1959 to 1961, Ingemar Johansson and Birgit Lundgren were the sporting world's answer to Liz and Eddie. (Or was it Eddie and Debbie? Liz and Richard? *Eddie and Richard?*)

Ingemar and Birgit were boxing's First Couple. They lived together, traveled to America together—thoroughly modern exemplars for the looming sexual revolution. However brief his reign, Ingemar heralded the coming of the Sixties' Swingin' Jock, the prototype Namath/Belinsky, a bridge from the ho-hum Eisenhower era into the hip Kennedy years. Ingemar and Birgit eventually married (in 1963) and divorced (in 1983), and remained friends through the years.

Ingemar was an inveterate romantic and in 1979 he fell again, sparking a 24-year relationship with Swedish journalist Edna Alsterlund. The two married in 1996. It was a loving and successful union, but when the complications of Ingemar's dementia caused the couple to split, there was Birgit to carry him through his final round.

*   *   *

There are full-length biographies of nearly every heavyweight champion, including *four* books on the life of Floyd Patterson, the Ali to Johansson's Frazier. Yet there exists not a single prior full-length book on Ingemar, a boxer whose accomplishments have been sadly overlooked. Perhaps this is understandably so, for less than a year after Johansson's final fight—against Brian London in April 1963—the world had a new heavyweight champion in Muhammad Ali, a man whose prodigious talent and personal magnetism proceeded to overshadow everyone in his wake.

Ali's three fights against Frazier (1971, 1974, 1975) are unarguably at the top of anyone's list of epic heavyweight trilogies. But it would be just as hard to deny that Patterson-Johansson (1959, 1960, 1961) ranks second. Ardent modern-day fans might argue for Evander Holyfield-

Riddick Bowe (1992,1993,1995), but they were products of a new age, long after boxing had ceased to be part of the global conversation and had faded, inexorably, into the dreaded obscurity of "niche sport."

Ingo was no Ali. Then again, who is? When Muhammad met the Beatles in Miami in 1964, while training for the first Liston fight, it became an iconic cultural event we are still talking about. When Ingemar met the Beatles in 1963, at a party during the group's tour of Sweden, no one took notice, least of all Ingemar, who ignored them totally. He didn't have a clue who they were. Sinatra was more to his taste.

Still, Ingemar possessed a charisma uniquely his own. During Ingo's reign as champ, Harry Grayson, sports editor of the Newspaper Enterprise Association (NEA), described it thusly: "The 26-year-old Swede with the toonder and lightning has the quiet elegance of James J. Corbett, the animal magnetism of Jack Dempsey, the studious determination of Gene Tunney, [and] the simple sincerity of Joe Louis."

* * *

For those fans too young to remember Ingemar, or for those who have simply forgotten, a brief mention of the man's accomplishments are in order:

From 1950 to 1976, the diamond-encrusted, gem-studded Hickok Belt was awarded to the year's top professional athlete. The 1959 winner, by an overwhelming vote of over 300 American sportswriters, was Ingemar Johansson. The final Hickok was awarded in 1976 and over the years the belt's significance has become lamentably forgotten. "The Hickok Belt was the crown jewel of American sports," explains Anthony Liccione, president of the Rochester Boxing Hall of Fame, "bigger than any MVP, bigger than a Lombardi, bigger than a World Series ring, bigger than a green jacket, because it honored the best professional athlete across all sports, not just in one." Previous winners included Willie Mays, Ben Hogan, Rocky Marciano, and Mickey Mantle. Nice company.

The Associated Press began choosing their Male Athlete of the Year in 1931. In over 80 years, only four boxers have claimed the honor: Joe Louis (1935), Ingemar Johansson (1959), Muhammad Ali (1974), and George Foreman (1994).

Sports Illustrated began anointing its Sportsman of the Year in 1954. In 1959, Ingemar became the first boxer ever selected. In six decades since, Ali (1974) and Sugar Ray Leonard (1981) have been the only other prizefighters chosen.

Perhaps Ingemar's most impressive accomplishment is, sadly, his most overlooked and underappreciated feat. That would be his back-to-back knockout victories against both the number one contender (Eddie Machen, in 1958) and the reigning heavyweight champion (Patterson, in 1959). It took Ingemar less than four total rounds, and he did it in brutally savage fashion. In the history of the sport, it is difficult to find another heavyweight champion with a similar pair of devastating consecutive kayos against top-ranked foes.

You have to go back to 1933–34, when Max Baer beat Max Schmeling and Primo Carnera in succession. And it took Baer 21 rounds: 10 to stop Schmeling, 11 to stop Carnera. Safe to say Ingemar's feat is the more dazzling.

In 2002, Ingemar was accorded the sport's highest honor: induction into the International Boxing Hall of Fame in Canastota, New York.

* * *

As a young developing boxer, Ingemar was constantly thrown into the ring with more experienced men. In 1955, in just his twelfth pro bout, the young Swede faced a former European champion, the German giant Hein Ten Hoff, whose record was 32–6. Two and a half minutes later, Ten Hoff was 32–7.

A year later, in his fifteenth pro start, Ingemar kayoed the world-ranked reigning European champ, Franco Cavicchi of Italy, whose record was 43–3.

All of which led to his match with the world's number-one contender. To put Ingemar's destruction of Eddie Machen, in 2:16 of the first round, into perspective, consider that after rebounding from the loss in Göteborg, Machen managed to go the distance against two of the deadliest hitters in fistic history: Sonny Liston and Cleveland Williams. (Machen lost on points to Liston in 1960, and fought Williams to a draw in 1962.) In 1966, towards the end of his career, Machen lasted ten rounds with Joe Frazier.

Here's another impressive nugget: In his entire career as a professional, Ingemar faced not a single opponent with a losing record. In over 120 years of heavyweight championship history, only one other titleholder can make such a claim. That would be Gentleman Jim Corbett, who knocked out bareknuckle champ Sullivan in 1892, in the very first championship bout under the modern Queensberry Rules.

Sports fans who put their faith in stats will be interested to know that Ingemar's knockout percentage of 61 percent (17 knockouts in 28 fights) compares favorably with those of Jack Dempsey (59 percent), Floyd Patterson (62 percent), Muhammad Ali (61 percent), and Larry Holmes (59 percent). And it beats the heck out of Ezzard Charles (44 percent), Jersey Joe Walcott (45 percent), and Evander Holyfield (51 percent).

Ingemar's win percentage of 93 percent (26 wins in 28 fights) also stacks up against some big names: Sonny Liston (93 percent), Jack Dempsey (90 percent), Muhammad Ali (92 percent), Mike Tyson (89 percent), Joe Frazier (89 percent), and Larry Holmes (92 percent).

* * *

So why is Ingemar so little remembered today?

The answer lies, perhaps in part, in the egalitarian nature of the Nordic personality. From childhood, Swedes are taught to be humble and that shyness is a positive trait. It is a culture that values cooperation over competition, where no child is raised to believe he is more special than the next. Ingemar never sought the fame or adulation heaped upon him, nor did he become addicted to it.

Boxing was never his lifeblood, the way it was for Ali. Rather, it was a way to make money, more than a Göteborg stone paver could expect to make in a hundred lifetimes. It's just that a funny thing happened along the way: he not only beat everyone in Europe, but America's top-ranked challenger, and then the reigning world heavyweight champion too. Once Ingemar had secured his family's financial future, he was content to live his life far from the lights and the action and the cameras.

Swedish sports historian Olof Johansson (no relation) thinks Ingemar's style of boxing is to blame for his modern-day obscurity: "During a fight, he'd often go long stretches without doing much, just pawing with the left, waiting for an opportunity to throw the right. It wasn't a style that was popular with fans, especially in America."

Then there is the matter of Ingemar's short reign—356 days, to be exact. "If Ingemar could have won the second or third fight against Patterson," says Rolf Johansson, "my brother would be better remembered today. Or maybe if he had fought Sonny Liston." Rolf has always believed Ingemar could have beaten Sonny. And who's to say he wouldn't have? At the very least, Ingemar would have had what boxers call "a puncher's chance."

*   *   *

Fate cast its curiously random benediction upon this big Swede, and for a time anointed him custodian of the Right Hand of the Gods, possessor of a punch whose mystic powers inspired reams of prose in countless periodicals, not to mention a mythic sobriquet ("The Hammer of Thor"), and even a song (Dutch pop star Johnny Lion's 1959 single, "Ingemar Johansson").

But there was more to the man than the game's mightiest right. The time has come to more fully appreciate boxing's most overlooked and underappreciated champion.

Hopefully, this book is a start.

1

Roots

The tiny fishing village of Grundsund sits on Sweden's southwestern rim, where the Atlantic Ocean meets the rocky outcrops surrounding Göteborg, the country's second largest city. For hundreds of years the men of Grundsund have worked the sea, some trawling for herring and cod, others loading and unloading giant oceangoing vessels that for generations arrived and departed daily for the great ports of Europe, Asia, and the New World.

In the early 1920s, Grundsund native Evald Karlsson found work aboard a vessel bound for America—the SS *Drottningholm*, a steam-turbine transatlantic liner with a rich history. In April 1912, sailing under the name SS *Virginian*, she provided iceberg warnings to the RMS *Titanic*, one of the few ships in radio communication with the doomed vessel. During World War I she served as a troop transporter. Sold to the Swedish-American Line in 1920, she was rechristened the *Drottningholm*; when the ship was dismantled in 1955, it was the world's oldest transatlantic liner still in operation.

It had always been Evald Karlsson's dream to settle in America. The *Drottningholm* had brought him to the docks of New York City. The plan was to earn enough money to send for wife Hulda and their nine children back in Grundsund. In downtown Manhattan, with skyscrapers sprouting like sunflowers, Evald obtained work on construction crews where his powerful arms and straight back found currency.

On a July 4 weekend in the early 1920s, however, Evald and a pal left the city for Niagara Falls to hoist a few ales in celebration of America's big day. The boozy hoopla attracted the attention of local police, and Evald was sent back to Sweden on the first available boat.

Hulda shared her husband's dream. She too had lived briefly in America, working as a housemaid for a prosperous New York family. She even rebuffed a marriage proposal from one of the family's sons. Instead, Hulda returned to Sweden to marry Evald.

9

The couple had just missed the Great Swedish Migration of the late 1800s and early 1900s, when nearly one fifth of the nation's population emigrated, mostly to the United States. Stricken by poverty sparked by massive crop failures they took refuge in the farms of America's Upper Midwest. Göteborg, 70 miles south of Grundsund, served as Sweden's emigration hub, the last sight of homeland for most emigres. (Today, it is home to an emigration museum and genealogical research center.)

Unfortunately for Evald and Hulda, the Great Migration was over by the 1920s, halted by America's newly tightened immigration restrictions. Back in Grundsund with a family to feed, Evald bought a boat and hauled feldspar to foundries on Sweden's west coast. He named his boat *Champion*.

* * *

When Evald and Hulda's daughter Ebba completed high school, she was sent to Goteborg to work as a housemaid, a common career path for young women of the day. Göteborg's community gathering spot was a collection of shops, booths, cafes, and dance halls known as the Iron Market. It was here that Ebba Karlsson, 18, met Jens Johansson, 23, a powerfully built, hard-working stonemason—one of 11 children of a stonemason.

Jens and Ebba soon married and rented a second-story apartment above a grocery store in Johanneberg, a working-class suburb of Göteborg. The family grew—three boys: Henry, Ingemar, and Rolf, and a girl, Eva. Ingemar was born in 1932, during the depths of Sweden's economic depression, and Jens found himself unemployed for long stretches. The family scrimped by.

By 1935 Jens was working as a street paver and was able to send Ingemar to preschool, a luxury not readily available to most depression-era Swedish families. Although most of his day was spent playing, Ingemar received a head start learning letters and numbers.

Ingemar's favorite childhood story was "Three Billy Goats Gruff." Ebba would no sooner finish the story than he'd want to hear it again—and again. In the fable, a carnivorous troll is tricked into letting three goats pass safely over his bridge. The moral, that cunning trumps brutish strength, must have resonated with young Ingemar, who, despite being the Johanssons' middle son, established himself as their leader. The oldest, Henry, suffered from epileptic seizures and was slow-functioning,

10

Family portrait, 1939. Left to right: Jens, Ingemar, Henry, Ebba, and Rolf. Henry was older by one year, but Ingemar, always large-framed, was the larger of the two (*Kamerareportage*).

while Rolf was four years Ingemar's junior. Throughout their childhood Ingemar looked out for them both.

At age seven, Ingemar entered public school. He was not a good student. Preternaturally stubborn and disdainful of rules and authority, he took an instant dislike to teachers, and from all accounts, teachers were less than enamored of him. Teachers enforced classroom discipline with a sharp

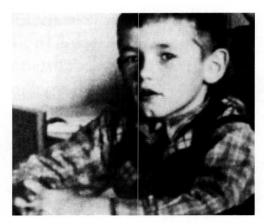

Ingemar, age 8, in 1940 (*courtesy Thomas Johansson*).

rap across the knuckles with a ruler. Invariably, Ingemar would pull his hand away at the crucial moment.

A relative of Ingemar's used to joke that the boy came by his stubbornness naturally. He was, after all, from a long line of stonemasons, and Ingemar's head, it was said, was as hard as the granite cliffs along Sweden's western shore. "My parents can testify I was not God's best child," Ingemar told boxing official Oscar Söderlund in 1959.

Ingemar may have hated school, but he was far from stupid. He displayed a particular facility for mathematics. Still, when asked by a teacher, "What do you want to be when you grow up?" Ingemar answered, "A street paver, because I can do that without having to read books."

About this time an incident occurred in the Johansson home that left a deep and lasting impression on Ingemar. Jens, eager to move his family out of their cramped apartment, discovered a generous lot for sale in a better neighborhood. He phoned a business-savvy friend for advice, a former co-worker who had come up in the world. The man's advice: "Don't ever call me at home and bother me about such things!"

Ingemar remembered his father's expression and the hurt, humiliation, and anger he must have felt, and how his father turned to his boys and said, "Remember this: no matter where you get in life, never feel that you are better than others. *Never be haughty.*"

For a brief time Ingemar attended Sunday school. When he lost interest, his parents didn't object. The Johanssons were not a particularly pious bunch. And while neither parent believed in spanking, at home Ebba was the disciplinarian. "My mother required discipline from me which my pals' mothers didn't demand from their boys," Ingemar recalled in his 1959 memoir *Sekonderna lämnar ringen* (*Seconds Leave the Ring*). "Mother was strict about that."

At age 11, at Ebba's insistence, Ingemar worked after school as a delivery boy for a local grocer. He earned $1.75 an hour, most of which went back into the family till. Later in life, Ingemar would credit his mom for what he called "her inheritance to me ... [which was] learning the value of money."

Jens and Ebba sent Ingemar to summer camp once, but he longed to return home. "I was homesick for my parents and siblings something crazy," Ingemar recalled. A fiercely protective loyalty to Jens, Ebba, and his siblings would characterize Ingemar for the rest of his days.

In his preteens, soccer was Ingemar's sport of choice. He was good but not the standout brother Rolf would become. More than anything, Ingemar loved to watch the city's pro soccer team, his beloved Göteborg Mackerels, at Ullevi Stadium. There was often more action in the stands than on the field, with Ingemar frequently in the thick of it.

Large for his age, Ingemar earned a reputation as an enforcer among his friends, and word got around—*don't mess with that Johansson boy.* Most of his scrapes ended after a punch or two.

The Mackerels would win their first and only Swedish national championship in 1942, an event that sent Göteborg ga-ga. The next time the city went ga-ga, in the early morning hours of June 26, 1959, Ingemar was no longer in town. He was in New York City, and he had just knocked out Floyd Patterson.

*   *   *

Ingemar was 12 when he attended his first live boxing match. He went alone and stood at the entrance to the Göteborg auditorium, mesmerized by the crowd, the lights, the blows: "The theater and drama had me spellbound and I realized I too wanted to be one of those figures caught in the beam of lights."

Over the next year, Ingemar attended as many matches as he could afford on $1.75 an hour. In the fall of his 13th year, Ingemar learned that Göteborg's Redbergslid Boxing Club (RBC) was accepting memberships. He asked his parents for permission to join. His father was hardly in a position to say no, for in his youth Jens was known to throw a fist or two in a crowded dance hall on a Saturday night.

The next day, Ingemar walked to the old fire station that had been converted into a gym. There was a sign-up sheet and Ingemar added his name. He was now a member of—a *gymnastics* team? Seems he had turned up on the wrong night. Or maybe he'd turned left instead of right. Reading was never Ingemar's thing.

When Ingemar finally arrived on the correct night, it was a transformative experience: "The first time I heard the smatter of the skipping-rope, the thumps and pants of sparring, and the smell of sweat and dust I knew it suited me down to the ground."

2

Breakthrough

Redbergslid club rules dictated that a member had to be 15 years old in order to box competitively, but that hardly deterred Ingemar. The kid displayed an endless capacity for roadwork and loved to train—to skip rope, hit the bag, spar. In the ring he learned how to punch, block, move.

Thirteen years old and already a solid 145 pounds, over the next 18 months Ingemar would gain another 40 without losing speed. Sparring with older boxers, he earned a reputation for packing a punch and being hard to hit. The kid was a comer.

If Ingemar's new passion needed validation, it arrived at the old firehouse in 1946 in the person of Gunnar Bärlund.

The name may mean nothing to American fans, but the 6'1", 210-pound "Fighting Finn" was, and remains to this day, a Scandinavian legend, a former European amateur champion who pounded Buddy Baer into a TKO submission at Madison Square Garden in 1938. That year Bärlund rose to #2 in the pro rankings, made the cover of *Ring* magazine, and was set to meet champ Joe Louis for the title when an injury to the Finn put negotiations on ice.

Bärlund's career careened off track in 1941 at Chicago Stadium in a bout against Billy Conn. After seven rounds, it was a competitive fight with neither boxer at a clear advantage. When the bell rang to begin the eighth, Bärlund's trainer inexplicably threw a white towel into the ring—boxing's universal symbol of surrender. Against Bärlund's protests, the fight was stopped and Conn was awarded a TKO victory.

The Illinois Athletic Commission smelled a fix and impounded Bärlund's purse, then meted out a year's suspension to both fighter and trainer. To the end of Gunnar's days—he died in 1982 of complications of Parkinson's—he believed his trainer had double-crossed him for profit. Today, a statue of Gunnar Bärlund sits in a park outside a church in Helsinki.

In 1946, when Bärlund showed up at the Redbergslid Boxing Club, it was like Rocky Marciano walking into a makeshift Boys Club gym in Peoria. Sure, Barlund was 35 years old and a step slower, but he was still a professional. The big Finn was training for a comeback and in need of a sparring partner. Ingemar volunteered.

When the bell rang Ingemar began circling the ring, staying out of range of Gunnar's punishing body blows. The kid bounced a series of lefts off Bärlund's nose and followed with a powerful right. An angry Bärlund grabbed Ingemar in a clinch and the two wrestled furiously along the ropes until an RBC coach pulled them apart.

Here was Ingemar, just 14 and holding his own against an honest-to-God professional. "After that," Ingemar said, "I knew that not every heavyweight could floor me inside three rounds."

*   *   *

The year 1947 was momentous in the life of Ingemar Johansson for a number of reasons. He quit school. He turned 15 and was finally allowed to box competitively. He received his first press notices. And he met Edwin Ahlquist, the journalist and promoter who would eventually become Ingemar's most trusted advisor.

Ingemar's decision to quit school was one of the few times in his life that he defied Momma Ebba. But Ingemar was interested in making money. Feeling school no longer had anything to offer, he took a job as an apprentice street paver.

Ingemar's first competitive bout came at the RBC club championship, a win over the club's top middleweight. The next day's newspaper included the following: "Most promising was 15-year-old Ingemar Johansson. Maybe we ought to keep that name in mind. In a few years that boy will be in the center of big things."

Three months later, Ingemar entered the Göteborg District Junior Championships and won the heavyweight division. His performance attracted the attention of Ahlquist, one of Sweden's most influential sports personalities, founder and publisher of *Rekord*, the country's most widely read sports magazine, and a local promoter of boxing and wrestling matches. He also managed a stable of boxers and kept an eye out for promising talent.

"The first time I noticed Ingemar, at the tournament in Göteborg, he met an opponent several years older than himself," wrote Ahlquist, in his memoir *Må Bäste Man Vinna*:

> I felt sorry for [Ingemar]. The match started and his opponent rushed at him as if he was going to wipe out the kid. The kid danced away. Then it happened! Ingemar stopped retreating and threw a right with lightning speed. The ref counted to ten. When the big guy came to, he asked who threw in the towel. He didn't know what hit him. Ingemar was not yet sixteen but I knew at that moment he was something special, [that] he had something that our former top heavyweights were missing.

In the fall of 1948, Ingemar experienced his first defeat in a boxing ring, a three-round unanimous decision to an older, more experienced fighter, a cop from Svadala. Even so, the newspaper account read: "Johansson, who is considered to be Sweden's next great heavyweight … was tremendously fast for his weight [but] puppyish in

Ingemar, 15, at Göteborg's Redbergslid Boxing Club, 1948 (*Bilder i Syd*).

his movements." The press had tabbed the teen Sweden's Next Big Thing even before he had time to consider the possibility himself.

In 1949 Ingemar fought 11 times, losing only once, a questionable points loss in his opponent's hometown. His most memorable fight of the year was his last, on December 30 against Lars Mörling, a weight lifter of tremendous power. Halfway through the first round, an electrical failure plunged the arena into darkness. Mörling kept swinging, bulling crazily about the ring in hopes of landing a lucky punch. Suddenly the lights came back on and Ingemar stuck out his right, practically impaling the onrushing Mörling, who went down for the count. There may have been electrical problems in the hall that night, but it was Ingo who put out the lights.

* * *

Ingemar called 1950 "the year of my breakthrough." He won 24 of 26 fights, including the Swedish Amateur Championship. He was 17 now, at 187 pounds a full-fledged heavyweight with a right like a wrecking ball, a punch that, in promoter-speak, could put fannies in crannies.

The problem lay in getting the kid to throw the damn thing. The youngster had developed a distinct style: cautious, defensive, pawing passively with the left and keeping his distance until the moment arrived. Then: *the right!* It was a style all his own and not to everyone's taste.

It was not unusual for an impatient crowd—his bouts were now drawing 5,000 and more—to whistle during his fights. (Whistling at a passive boxer during a fight was the ultimate sign of derision; the insult was known as being "whistled out.")

Referees and judges didn't care for the style either. Neither did the press. "Tame" and "unheroic" were adjectives frequently applied to Ingemar's less impressive performances.

A stonecutter from a long line of stonecutters (*Kurt Durewall*).

17

Certainly, Ingemar's cautiousness in the ring reflected his personality. But it was Edwin Ahlquist who convinced his charge to bring that passivity into the ring. Ahlquist could see that Ingemar had huge potential as a professional. "Edwin repeatedly told me to avoid being hit too hard. He told me: 'Your future depends on it.'"

That Ingemar would stick to his style in the face of public opprobrium was a sign of the teen's inner confidence and his ability to remain true to himself. Not to mention that the kid was stubborn to a fault.

Ingemar's career may have been on track, but his social life was an utter disaster. As a local sports celebrity, the young boxer found himself constantly besieged by local females. By the time he was 17 he had already fathered two illegitimate children by two Göteborg girls, with the infants put up for adoption. Then, in 1950 at age 18, he married Barbara Abramson, a predictably short-lived union that produced two children, Jean and Thomas. Not surprisingly, Ingemar was in no mind to settle down, and the couple soon divorced. For a time Ingemar was a familiar face at local saloons, raising hell with a rowdy, brawling bunch. In 1951 he fathered a son, Eddie, out of wedlock, with yet another neighborhood girl. But while Ingemar would remain close to Jean and Thomas throughout his life, it would be 48 years before Eddie and his father would meet face-to-face.

* * *

Ingemar was knocked down for the first time in his career, by Illya Koski of Finland, at an international competition in Helsinki in January 1951. Ingemar was up at the count of nine and won the fight on points. "It was important for my progress," Ingemar said later. "I had won from the floor and now I knew I could rise from a setback."

Ingemar fought 15 bouts in 1951, winning twelve, three by knockout. On March 5 he again won the Swedish Amateur Championship, but not without controversy, which occurred in the semifinals, a three-rounder against counterpuncher Törner Ahsman. "In the first round they were whistled out," the newspaper reported. "In the second [it] changed to a hurricane of booing, and in the last, curses were hurled at both boxers." Ingemar's response to all the fuss was characteristically sanguine: "One day I was the darling of the press and public, the next day catcalls were my music.... I'd gotten used to it."

Winning back-to-back Swedish titles opened an important door. Ingemar was chosen as the heavyweight to represent Europe in an upcoming tournament against Chicago's Golden Gloves winners. The event was to be held in Chicago in late March. It would be Ingemar's first trip to America.

Ingemar and fellow Swede Stig Sjölin, the team's middleweight, flew to London, where the team assembled for their transatlantic flight. The unworldly Swedes were under the impression that America was a land of eternal sunshine, and they had packed accordingly. The plane landed in New York in a blinding snowstorm. The kids from the North Country had never been so cold in their lives.

The team boarded a train for the trip to Chicago. When Ingemar wrote his autobiography in 1959, after winning the world title from Floyd Patterson, he described the 1951 journey from New York to Chicago as "one of my finest memories, [one that] I value more than all my prizes." From Ingemar's *Seconds Leave the Ring*: "I laid down and switched off the light so I could see out. In the bare late winter I looked out at the landscape, alone in the darkness. Occasionally we flashed past a village. I lay awake and relished the journey in a way that I had never done before or since."

Ingemar's memories conjure those of another magical journey by rail, described by Nick Carraway in *The Great Gatsby*: "We pulled out into the winter night and the real snow, our snow, began to … twinkle against the windows, and the dim lights of small stations moved by. [We] walked back from dinner through the cold vestibules, unutterably aware of our identity with this country for one strange hour, before we melted indistinguishably into it again…." This was Carraway's America. "Not the wheat or the prairies or the lost Swede towns," Carraway says, "but the thrilling returning trains of my youth." It may have been Carraway's, but it wasn't Ingemar's. When the team disembarked onto the Union Station platform in Chicago, it was met with stares and laughter. These painfully unassimilated rubes from the old country, with ill-fitting clothes and cardboard suitcases, were apparently a source of amusement to Chicago's workaday commuters. Ingemar felt like he was in a shop window.

* * *

On March 28, 1951, a crowd of 16,000 jammed Chicago Stadium, the historic (and now, sadly, shuttered) "Madhouse on Madison," former home to NHL hockey, NBA basketball, and both the Republican and Democratic national conventions. The event was televised nationwide on ABC.

In the ring the Americans romped, winning all but two weight divisions: flyweight, won by a Finnish lad who, at 108 pounds, billed himself as "the world's smallest blacksmith"; and heavyweight, where Ingemar's powerful blows caused a third-round stoppage.

The performance obviously impressed a *Chicago Tribune* reporter. Under the headline "Europe Loses but Discovers an Idol," the article read: "Europe lost yesterday but one would have thought the visitors from the Old World had won the inter-hemisphere contest. The European team struggled to be the first to slap [Johansson] on the back when he clambered out of the ring, embracing him, cheering him until trainer Sten Suvio, himself over-excited, saw to it that Ingemar got a shower and put his clothes on. Johansson was naturally the happiest young man in the world." The joy was short-lived. It was a victory clouded by controversy—a growing theme in Johansson's life.

Following the event, the Swedish team was scheduled to fly to Washington, D.C., for a match against that city's Golden Glove winners. Ingemar was scheduled to face Norvel Lee, the two-time national AAU Heavyweight Champion. Before leaving Chicago, however, Ingemar's left hand began to throb, and he informed Suvio he would not be able to box in Washington. Suvio summoned a doctor, who found no fractures and deemed the boy fight-worthy.

But Ingemar knew what he knew. The injury—inflamed tendon pressed against bone—had occurred in the past, and rest was the only cure. When Ingemar refused to fight, the International Boxing Association threatened to suspend him. The Swedish press accused him of "being afraid to take a beating" and wondered if the injury wasn't "a sham."

Once again, Ingemar held to his convictions. His instincts were confirmed when, back in Göteborg, doctors discovered nerve damage and placed the left hand in a cast. It would be five months before Ingemar would fight again.

2. Breakthrough

* * *

By August 1951 Ingemar's hand had healed and he was eager to return to the ring. His opportunity arose on August 31 when an all-star team of American amateurs arrived in Göteborg to challenge Sweden's best. The marquee bout: Ingemar Johansson against.... Norvel Lee.

In the days before the match, the press hyped the confrontation as if it were Dempsey-Carpentier. On August 31 over 11,000 fans filed into Ullevi Stadium, only to watch their boys go down 6–4. This time Ingemar was among the losers, out-boxed by Lee, who would go on to win a gold medal in the 1952 Olympics as a light heavyweight. (Lee never turned professional. Armed with a master's degree from Howard University, he forged a career in corrections and education. In 1948, in Covington, Kentucky, Lee was arrested for attempting to integrate the all-white forward section of a city bus, making him one of America's earliest activists. He died in Bethesda in 1992 at age 67).

Following a couple of easy Johansson victories in October 1951, the Swedish press was rife with speculation: was their Golden Boy about to turn pro? Ingemar made no secret he was ready to get paid for his pain. Tired of paving streets, he took a job unloading banana boats at Göteborg harbor. Ingemar hated the job and his boss let him go, but not before giving an inquiring reporter the following scoop: "Ingemar's talent for packing bananas is not very high."

Edwin Ahlquist insisted that his protégé stay clean at least through the 1952 Helsinki Olympics. "You owe that to amateur boxing," Ahlquist told him. In October, Ingemar beat the Italian Aldo Pellegrini for the third time in two years. Clearly, he was running out of credible opponents. Unfortunately Ingemar broke his thumb in the first round when his fist collided with Pellegrini's skull. The injury required surgery, and a pin was placed into the bone. Doctors were uncertain whether Ingemar would ever be fit to fight again.

Just four months later, in February 1952, Ingemar felt ready to return. He tested his thumb in the gym by pounding the heavy bag and felt "nothing but intense joy."

In March, in his first tournament of the year, Ingemar won his third straight Swedish Amateur title with a pair of first round knockouts in Stockholm. He followed that with another pair of first round kayos before losing a highly questionable decision in May to Tomislav Krizmanić of Yugoslavia. Ingemar had hit Krizmanić at will and received barely a blow in return, but apparently the two Yugoslav judges saw it differently. Ten days later, Ingemar bounced back with a second-round knockout of a clearly outclassed German fighter.

The loss to Krizmanić didn't ruffle Ingemar a bit. He had lost interest in the amateur game. His next stop was Helsinki for the Olympic trials. After that, regardless of the outcome, Ingemar was determined to turn pro.

3

The 1952 Olympics

Two weeks before opening ceremonies for the 1952 Summer Olympics, the Swedish Boxing Association sent its seven-man team to a ten-day training session in Sandviken, a small arts community known for its handicrafts and symphony orchestra, located 120 miles north of Stockholm.

Ingemar was miserable from the get-go. "Amateur boxing didn't interest me any longer," he said. "Everybody agreed that I had grown out of it. My mind was on professional boxing."

Worse, he was woefully out of shape, having completely forsaken his roadwork. He hadn't broken a sweat in weeks. The first day in camp, the team ran 10 miles and the next day Ingemar could barely move.

Things didn't improve when Johansson, at age 19 already four years removed from school, learned he was expected to spend two hours a day in a *classroom*, studying boxing *theory*. "Two hours every day we should be sitting," Ingemar told a reporter, "and a man who never had a glove on his hands was talking about what we should do, and we should write it with a pen."

To Ingemar, who hated school, disdained reading, despised teachers, disliked books—well, he simply refused to attend. Swedish officials decided to placate their heavyweight, and he was excused from attending class, but they were beginning to ask: was their erstwhile star a Golden Child … or a problem child?

Ingemar recalled this period of his life with the candor and Zen-like self-knowing that would serve him well throughout his life. "As always, I was in a setback period when people tried to force me against my will," he said, in what would become a familiar refrain. "I am ego-centric and think of myself first and foremost. And God save the boxers who don't. No one else does."

It was during the daily weigh-ins and sparring sessions that Ingemar experienced an epiphany. "I saw ... swollen eyebrows and broken noses ... bashers and sluggers who sought the shortest way to success with long swings and bull-rushes. They let themselves be goaded into slugging matches by elegant terms for stupidity, like 'courage.'" Here was first-hand evidence, if any were needed, that future success in the ring would come only on his terms: Ingo—no bull-rusher, he—would exercise patience and restraint instead.

To his horror, he was about to discover how costly epiphanies can be.

* * *

Opening ceremonies for the 1952 Olympics, officially known as the Games of the XV Olympiad, were held on July 19. Great anticipation gripped the nation of Finland as the torch made its way into Helsinki's Olympic Stadium. Not even a driving rain could dampen enthusiasm as Roaring Twenties Finnish track star Paavo Nurmi set the torch ablaze.

Helsinki had been scheduled to host the 1940 games, and in preparation the city had built an Olympic village for 3,200 athletes. But the games were canceled by World War II and the village became a housing project. When the International Olympic Committee met in the summer of 1947 to choose a host city, Helsinki, the emotional favorite, received three times as many votes as the next city.

For the 1952 games, the Finns built a new complex of five villages to accommodate the largest Olympiad in history. The nearly 5,000 athletes reflected a reshuffled world: for the first time, the Soviet Union, Israel, and the People's Republic of China fielded teams.

All of which probably meant nothing to Ingemar, who drew a bye in his first-round match, which meant *more* sitting around. Johansson's first actual bout was scheduled for July 29 at Helsinki Convention Center, but when the bell rang for the first round, his opponent, Luiz Sosa of Uruguay, was nowhere to be found. Sosa was disqualified, which meant that Ingemar's *next* bout, against Horymir Netuka of Czechoslovakia, would be his first competitive fight in three months.

Netuka was a bull-rushing basher, exactly the type of fighter Ingemar regarded with contempt. Sure enough, at the opening bell Netuka surged forward and was greeted with a left-right combo to the jaw. "From that moment all the fight was out of him," Ingemar said afterwards.

Two knockdowns later, Sweden had its victory, but the bout exposed Johansson's weakness. He had Netuka out on his feet but lacked the stamina to finish him. Olympic bouts are comprised of three three-minute rounds, while most amateur bouts are fought in two-minute rounds. For youngsters not in prime shape, that extra minute stretches out like eternity itself.

Ingemar had 24 hours to recuperate before facing Yugoslavia's Tomislav Krizmanić. Ingo felt "dead tired and irritable," and it showed. Despite his winning all three rounds en route to another win, the fight was a bust, neither fighter showing much inclination to mix it up. "What happened between Johansson and the Jugoslav," one newspaper reported, "wouldn't have disturbed the cocktail party arranged by the Swedish Ambassador on Monday." Still, Ingemar's victory avenged the loss he'd suffered to Krizmanić via split decision 14 months earlier in a three-round bout in Stockholm.

More importantly, Johansson had made it into the semifinals, where victory would mean a chance to fight for the gold. The match pitted

Olympic games, Helsinki, July 30, 1952: Ingemar wins all three rounds against Horymir Netuka of Czechoslovakia (*Kamerareportage*).

25

Ingemar against Ilkka Koski of Finland. The two had met once before, in January 1951. In that fight, Ingo's Bingo (as the press had taken to calling his right) dropped the Finn for an eight-count in the first round, but in the second a cocky Ingo had opened himself up for a right and Koski obliged, knocking the big Swede down for the first time in his career. Up at the count of nine, Ingemar finished strong and earned a split decision.

Now the two would meet again, in the Olympic semifinal. The press favored the bigger, more powerful Koski, calling Johansson "easy to hit," and "lacking killer instinct."

As it turned out, both Johansson and Koski seemed spent, each waiting for the other to attack. As the crowd whistled derisively, the two mostly clinched, and Ingemar eked out a split decision. He'd made the finals.

August 1, 1952: Ingemar on his way back to the dressing room after defeating Finland's Ilkka Koski in the Olympic semifinals (*Bilder i Syd*).

After beating Koski, Johansson remained at ringside to watch teammate Stig Sjölin in his middleweight semifinal against an 18-year-old American from a reform school in upstate New York: Floyd Patterson.

"The first left from the American came flying across and Stig didn't have time to see it," Ingemar remembered. "He fell in the first minute." Sjölin beat the count but, overmatched, grabbed Patterson and wouldn't let go. In the third round the referee warned Sjölin for holding before stopping the fight and awarding the win, via DQ, to Floyd.

Ingemar had another reason to remain ringside. It was an opportunity to scope out the next semifinal, the match that would determine his next opponent, the man who would stand between him and everlasting Olympic glory.

*   *   *

The heavyweight semifinal that evening pitted Andries Nieman, a tricky lefthanded South African carpenter, against Big Ed Sanders, the 22-year-old Navy champion and college graduate from the Watts section of Los Angeles, married, with an infant son.

Sanders was a giant of a man—6'4", 218 pounds—and could hit a ton. The bell rang and Nieman landed a flurry of punches before running into a left hook that shook him to the quick. In the second round, Sanders caught Nieman coming in and threw a right cross that dropped him to the canvas. The South African arose at eight but in no shape to fight. The ref signaled for the end.

Ingemar began formulating a plan. "Sanders was a counter-boxer, just like me," he reckoned, "One of us had to desert his style. I intended not to attack in the first two rounds, to save myself for the last and snatch a points victory."

On Saturday evening, August 2, 1952, Ingemar's moment arrived, an opportunity to achieve greatness, not just for himself, but for a nation starved for heroes. It was all in front of him: money, endorsements, women, escape from a stone paver's life.

For Sanders, too, it was a crossroads moment, for no doubt an Olympic gold medal would jump-start a professional career whose ultimate destination, it seemed likely, was a shot at the heavyweight crown. Indeed, five of the next six heavyweight kings would boast Olympic gold on their resume, a list that includes Patterson, Cassius Clay (Rome '60), Joe Frazier (Tokyo '64), George Foreman (Mexico City '68), and Leon Spinks (Montreal '76). Had the 1952 Olympics been held in Jefferson City, Missouri, site of Missouri State Penitentiary, no doubt Sonny Liston would be on that list, too.

Clearly, two combatants in Helsinki were fighting for more than a medal. But the future is a wheel in spin, and it is more random happenstance than master plan that guides its path. How else to explain the events that transpired? Both men would turn pro. One would become world heavyweight champion. The other would be dead within eighteen months, beaten comatose in the ring. But those events were still in the future, a wheel that had just begun to spin.

* * *

The bell rang and Sanders moved forward, ever forward, waiting for Johansson to throw a punch that never came. Ingemar, true to his plan, merely danced and feigned. The round ended without a meaningful blow amid the whistles and hoots of a disapproving crowd. Between rounds the referee, Frenchman Roger Vaisberg, reprimanded both fighters for inaction, even as Swedish trainer Sten Suvio implored Johansson to keep his distance.

The bell sounded for round two. "Sanders and I stood in front of each other the whole round without moving a glove," Ingemar remem-

Ed Sanders and Ingemar at the 1952 Olympics (*Haynes Archive/Popperphoto/ Getty Images*).

bered. Mid-round Vaisberg stepped between the fighters and issued a warning to the Swede. Deafening boos and whistles reverberated through the building. "Sanders was just as passive and didn't try to attack but Vaisberg [warned] only me," Ingemar complained. "The American expected that I would give him a free chance to counter-box [but] I had neither the strength nor training to attack for three, or even two rounds…. I intended to take my chance in the third."

Ingemar never got that chance. Vaisberg stood with his hands on his hips as the final 15 seconds ticked off the second stanza. At the bell he rushed to Johansson and, throwing his right arm in the air like a baseball ump signaling "out," declared an end to the fight, giving Ingo a final derisive shove towards his corner for good measure. The result would be recorded for posterity as "Johansson—disqualified for failing to show fight."

Ingemar walked back to his corner, eyes cast to the canvas, his expression a half-smile of wan disbelief. Sanders crossed the ring to offer condolences, but a seemingly cordial Johansson did the talking, apparently oblivious to the mess he'd created, no clue that his performance this night would ignite a firestorm of disgrace, his name a sudden synonym for national shame and ignominy.

No clue at all. But he was about to find out.

Ingemar had to be led from the ring by a cordon of cops, such was the intensity of the invective and abuse hurled at him. Back in the dressing room, Swedish national team coach Sven Thoren, purple with rage, banned Ingemar from attending the closing ceremonies and commanded him to leave the Olympic village first thing in the morning, telling him: "You'll never box for the Swedish Olympic team again."

The maelstrom was gathering steam. The next day, a front page headline in a Swedish newspaper, in bold caps reserved for assassinations and earthquakes, screamed: "FOR SHAME, INGO!" In an article headlined "Shame's Cup Filled to the Top," Johansson was described as a "fleeing rat … fleeing in full Negro terror." The reporter added, "I was ashamed to be Swedish."

The *Stockholm Press* piled on: "A professional career is now finished for him. Ingemar is kaput—a chapter completely written off in Swedish boxing. A cowardly boxer should absolutely quit the sport [as] cowardice and boxing don't go together. Johansson was a plain coward and should give up boxing."

Oscar Söderlund, chairman of the Swedish Boxing Association, was quoted thusly: "We Swedes had to creep out of the hall to avoid the scorn. He brought shame to the Swedish name and ended his sports career with the reputation of Herostratus." (For those not fluent in ancient Greek history, Herostratus was a serial arsonist who, in 356 BC, burned down the Temple of Artemis in Ephesus, one of the Seven Wonders of the Ancient World, just for kicks. Torch just *one* of the Seven Wonders and two millennia later they're *still* throwing it your face. What were Ingo's chances of outliving his own personal Artemis?)

The Swedish Sports Association wasted no time in adding their condemnation, wiring a telegram to the International Olympic Committee: "On behalf of itself and the Boxing Association, [we] hereby wish to express our sincere and unreserved regrets regarding the unsportsmanlike manner in which the Swedish boxer Ingemar Johansson conducted himself during yesterday´s final."

Around the world, sportswriters branded Johansson a coward, too frightened of the big American to fight. Paul Zimmerman of the *Los Angeles Times* called Johansson's performance "the greatest retreat since the Allies swept through Germany in World War II."

Could things possibly get worse for Ingemar? Of course they could. At the medal ceremony, officials declared there would be no silver medal awarded for the heavyweight division. As the "Star-Spangled Banner" played, there was Big Ed Sanders atop his pedestal. The adjacent pedestal, reserved for the silver medalist, was empty, but next to it stood a Finnish official holding a balled-up Swedish flag, a symbol of Sweden's disgrace.

A lesser youth would have been crushed, would have slinked back home, a scarlet letter where a medal might have hung, and lived out his years hauling street stones as penance. Which one of us would not?

Ingemar would prove himself no lesser youth. Facing what he described as "a gigantic choir of hate and fury," he never flinched. "I didn't take much notice of the public's anger. If I had done otherwise I wouldn't have come through it. I protected myself as I do in the ring, shut out everything except my own conviction that I had done right and that my only chance had lain in exactly the way I planned."

Ingemar returned to Sweden, to the seclusion of the family abode, where the Johansson clan rallied to him. "Dad took my hand," Ingemar recalled, "and said, 'You did absolutely right. Don't let them get to you.'"

Later, Ingemar would draw an analogy between Vaisberg's imploring him to fight and his grade school interactions with teachers. "It was the same thing as when the old teacher would hit me on the fingertips. I couldn't hold my fingers in something that was wrong for me."

* * *

Who, in the fall of 1953, would have traded Sanders's future for Johansson's ?

Ingemar was the most reviled figure in boxing. Sanders was the sport's Next Big Thing, the first American heavyweight to win Olympic gold since Samuel Berger in 1904 in St. Louis, an achievement all the more impressive considering that in 1904 the field included *only* American boxers. Ed returned to the States a national hero. The city of Los Angeles declared Ed Sanders Day and threw a parade in his honor.

After Sanders's first professional fight, a first round kayo win in March 1954, the sports editor of the *Lowell (Massachusetts) Sun*, George McGuane, called Big Ed a "coming heavyweight champion."

After winning six of his first eight fights, Sanders took on hard-hitting Willie "Cadillac" James, the reigning New England Heavyweight Champion, at Boston Gardens, on December 11, 1954. James began landing heavy blows right from the start. A right uppercut in the tenth nearly put Ed down for good. Sanders shambled back to his corner where his seconds worked to revive him.

As the bell rang for the 11th, Ed told manager Numo Cam, "I'm going win these last two"—his last words, as it turned out. In the opening seconds James landed a series of lefts and followed with a right cross to the head. Sanders collapsed to the mat, landed on his right side, then rolled to his stomach, motionless as the ref counted ten. Ring attendants rushed to his side, removed the gloves and tape from his fists, and placed him on a stretcher. An ambulance was summoned. Ed was laboring to breathe.

At the hospital, neurosurgeons performed a four-hour operation to relieve pressure on the brain, after which Ed was placed in an oxygen tent and packed in ice to control a rising fever. When the end was near, Sanders's wife Mary was summoned to his bedside. At 4:30 p.m. on December 12, Big Ed Sanders, the presumptive next king of the heavies, was pronounced dead at the age of 24.

4

Turning Pro

The art of boxing gave Ingemar's life purpose. Without it, the scruffy ruffian was headed down some very wrong paths. At best the kid faced a future pounding cobblestones into the dirt. Instead, the boxing gods replaced his right hand with a hammer and anointed him Europe's next Great Hope. After five glorious years as an amateur, Ingemar's path to the pros—to a life of fame and wealth and, if Jupiter's moons aligned, a heavyweight title—seemed preordained.

Then Helsinki happened and Ingemar was forced into exile. He even tried convincing himself it was voluntary. "I had to let the storm die first," he recalled. "To hurry would cause more damage than to wait."

Ingemar was through with amateur boxing, that much was certain. Now the question became: would anyone pay to watch him fight? To test the waters, Ingemar and retired boxing legend Olle Tandberg—Sweden's previous Great Hope—embarked on an exhibition tour of their homeland, sparring five two-minute rounds.

The Tandberg name, at least, had never been dragged through the sludge. On the contrary, the 6'3" boxer had been the idol of Scandinavia when Ingemar was still soiling his short pants. Tandberg boxed in the 1936 Olympics (he was eliminated in the second round), then held the European Amateur championship twice, in 1937 and 1939. He turned pro in 1941 and two years later won the European heavyweight title. Tandberg retired in 1949 with an impressive career mark of 23–6. His final fight, a TKO loss to future heavyweight king Jersey Joe Walcott, drew 43,000 fans to Stockholm's Råsunda Stadium, at the time the largest crowd ever to witness a bout in Scandinavia.

The Johansson-Tandberg tour was a disaster. In Sundsvall, an industrial municipality of 50,000-plus, exactly 10 people showed up. Tandberg dropped out and was replaced by Gunnar "Silver" Nilsson. (Gunnar's nickname referred to the silver medal he won as an Olympic heavyweight in 1948.) In nearby Söderhamn, Johansson-Nilsson shared the bill with a traveling troupe of ventriloquists, jugglers, and acrobats. When the show was over, one of them absconded with the money and the boxers didn't see a krona—"a hard blow to Gunnar," Ingemar said, "who had a big family and needed the income."

December 5, 1952: Ingemar makes his professional debut with a fourth round knockout of Robert Masson (*Bilder i Syd*).

* * *

The exhibitions thankfully behind him, Ingemar began training in earnest for his pro debut. Edwin Ahlquist had lined up Frenchman Robert Masson for December 5, 1952. Ingemar admitted he was worried no one would show, but come fight night it was standing room only as 5,500 fans filled Göteborg's Masshallen arena. On the way to the ring Ingemar heard the catcalls—"*coward!*"—but put them out of his mind. Masson, France's fourth-ranked boxer with three wins and three losses, provided scant opposition. Ingemar knocked him down twice before the fight was stopped in the fourth.

Next, Edwin booked former French light heavyweight champ Emile Bentz, France's second-ranked heavyweight, for February 6 at Masshallen. Barely a minute into their fight, Ingemar dropped Bentz for a nine-count. In the second round Ingemar flicked out a left jab, not so much to score as to measure his man for the hammer. The left, his range-finder, penetrated Bentz's guard and was followed, an instant later, by "toonder." Fight over.

A month later Johansson boxed his first six-rounder, a points victory over Jamaican journeyman Lloyd Barnett, a crafty, hard-to-hit lefty.

A week later in Copenhagen, Ingemar squared off against Erik Jensen of Denmark for the Scandinavian heavyweight title. Two minutes into the fourth round, Ingemar sent Jensen to the canvas, down and apparently out, but when the ref got to "nine," the bell rang. Saved by a hometown timekeeper, Jensen survived but lost on points. Ingemar now had his first professional title but it came at a cost: a broken bone in his right hand from a punch thrown in the opening round. It took nine months for the injury to heal.

Ingemar's return was scheduled for Masshallen on December 6, 1953, one day shy of a year since his pro debut. His opponent was another top-ranked French fighter, Raymond Innocenti.

The night before the bout Ingemar lay awake, keyed up and anxious, his once certain future in doubt. At 2 a.m. he shot out of bed and phoned a young lady. The two agreed to meet at an all-night dance hall. Ingemar got home at 6 a.m., fell asleep, and was in fine fettle for Innocenti. "In the second round I made perfect contact with the left," Ingemar said, "and the right followed like a shadow." Fight over. But the legend of

Momma Ebba breaks up a "fight" between Ingemar and Rolf in the family garden in Göteborg, 1952 (*Sipa USA*).

Ingo, the playboy-boxer who trained on fox trots and blondes, had just begun.

* * *

Ingemar's career appeared on track as 1953 wound to a close. Five fights, five wins, and a title—not that "Scandinavian Heavyweight Champion" carried any cachet. Still, the Johansson name was getting around European squared circles. "Swedish boxing fans," wrote one reporter, "[were beginning] to wonder if they had been hasty in their denunciations of their former hero."

Come 1954, however, Ingemar would log more time inside a jail cell than a boxing ring.

The reluctant soldier, 1954 (*courtesy Thomas Johansson*).

He had turned twenty and, summoned to serve his mandatory hitch in the Swedish military, reported to a base outside Stockholm expecting a cushy post leading novice trigger-pullers in calisthenics. He was wrong.

To Ingemar's dismay, he was assigned to the Swedish navy. Oddly, the kid who grew up playing along Göteborg harbor was positively phobic about leaving terra firma. Assignment to a submarine compounded his fears. "I detested the sea," he said. "If they thought they could get me down in a sub, they were in for another thought."

A company officer pulled him aside and said, "You are Johansson the boxer, yes? Then you should be a role model for the other young men."

Ingemar had no interest in being a role model and told him so. Worse, this stubborn snot from Göteborg seemed constitutionally unable—or unwilling—to follow orders. He refused, for example, to wear the protective beret that soldiers wore under their helmet, proclaiming it unsanitary. Unwilling to march in step, Ingemar had to be placed in the rear, where his uneven cadence wouldn't contaminate others. He was marching with his platoon one day when the officer barked, *"Halt!"* Ingemar kept marching, but with an exaggerated limp. His explanation: he thought the officer meant "halt" as in "crippled." The officer wasn't amused.

After flatly refusing to board a sub, Ingemar was assigned to a battleship where his duties included loading an antiaircraft gun. He found the job "intolerable," claiming it left him "physically and mentally sick."

Ingemar demanded land duty. Rebuffed, he went AWOL and escaped to Göteborg for a few days. Upon his return he was sent to a military psychologist for evaluation. Ingemar tried pleading his case: his fear of the sea, his desire to serve in the infantry. When the doctor cut him off, Ingemar pitched a fit and had to be dragged from the building. The result: a charge of insubordination and confinement to the brig.

All told, Ingemar spent 60 days in captivity. "I accepted [the sentence] with relief," Ingemar recalled. "It was freedom compared to service aboard ship." He made the best of it. The exercise area was a cage 25 feet in length and included a punching bag. Ingemar ran wind sprints and hit the bag. With a couple days left to serve, he smuggled in a crystal radio set and listened to it at night. If he had been caught, the contraband would have meant extra time, which, presumably, was the point.

Released from the brig, refreshed and 10 pounds lighter, Ingemar was finally assigned land duty: scraping barnacles off a rusty decommissioned battleship. "I enjoyed it," Ingemar said. "It was a bright end to a dark time." He added, perhaps unnecessarily: "I simply wasn't the military type."

Hard to say who was more relieved when Johansson's eleven-month navy nightmare ended: Johansson or the Swedish Navy.

* * *

Sweden's compulsory military service mercifully behind him, Ingemar returned to the ring in November 1954 with a fifth round TKO of German boxer Werner Weigand. That was followed in January 1955 with a points win over British southpaw Englishman Ansel Adams. A month later, Ingemar scored a fifth-round TKO against Austrian Kurt Schiegl, the number four–ranked European fighter.

Edwin Ahlquist suggested Aldo Pellegrini for the next opponent, but Ingemar was cool to the notion. He'd already beaten the Italian three times as an amateur, so what was the point? Besides, Pellegrini was a notoriously dirty infighter. Since turning pro he'd won 12 of 15 fights with all three losses via DQ for low blows. Still, Ingemar needed the ring work.

On March 4 at Masshallen, Ingemar was cruising to another apparent win when Pellegrini landed a perfect left hook to the chin. It took several seconds before Ingemar realized he was on the mat. He heard a voice, disembodied, distant—"*five, six, seven....*" In *Seconds Leave the Ring*, Johansson described what it felt like to be rendered senseless by a blow to the head: "There is no pain or fear. A swaying feeling comes in waves, which become shorter and farther apart the farther away one gets from the blow. At first one is powerless for three or four seconds. Then comes a clear period of a couple seconds, then a new wave for a couple seconds."

Ingemar was in real trouble for the first time in his career. He'd been knocked down by Koski in 1951, but that was more fatigue than trauma. Now, against Pellegrini, he managed to pull himself up at the count of eight. Pellegrini charged, eager to finish.

Ingemar circled the ring, putting the ref between him and his opponent. The extra seconds saved him and he survived the round. Two

Ingemar fought only once in 1954, a fifth-round kayo of Weiner Weigand (*Kurt Durewall*).

rounds later, in the fifth, a frustrated Pellegrini was DQ'ed after a third warning for low blows.

Not untypically, the positive-thinking Johansson found the near-calamity enlightening. "I now knew I could be calm and deliberate in such a situation, to bear a blow if it became necessary."

* * *

On April 3, Ingemar was back in the ring, in Stockholm, against his strongest opponent yet: former Italian heavyweight champ Uber Bacilieri, the top-ranked challenger for the European title held by Franco Cavicchi of Italy.

Today, the Johansson-Bacilieri fight can be viewed on YouTube, but viewers expecting to be dazzled by a young man on the cusp of destiny will be sadly disappointed. Awkward and hesitant, Ingemar never connects cleanly with the right, his jab a soft, open-gloved pawing motion reminiscent of Stooge Joe Besser's sissy slap (*"not so fassst!"*). The bout goes the distance, and when the ref raises Johansson's hand, the crowd sits in stony silence. The fight's a stinker. "The public," Ingemar later admitted, "got a bad value."

Ingemar was now ranked fifth on the list of European boxers. Ahlquist's short-term goal was a shot at Cavicchi's title. To that end, he lined up seventh-ranked Gunther Nurnberg, the 6'3", 220-pound German. The fight took place June 12, 1955, at Dortmund, Germany, Ingemar's first fight outside Scandinavia. Nurnburg proved too slow and ponderous, too easy to hit, and in the seventh he was felled by Ingo's lethal left-right combo.

The American sporting press was beginning to notice Sweden's Jab'n'Hammer Kid. Nat Fleischer, publisher of *Ring* magazine and the sport's *éminence grise*, wrote: "I want to congratulate Sweden. Now you have brought forth a heavyweight for whom I prophesy the great chance of reaching the top of the world. Ingemar Johansson is a positive surprise."

Next up for Ingemar was the formidable Hein Ten Hoff. The German giant would be Ingemar's first opponent who was well-known on the world stage—which is to say, recognizable to American fans. In 1949 Ten Hoff met Jersey Joe Walcott in a bout to determine a challenger for Ezzard Charles's title. Ten Hoff lost on points, and one year and two days later Walcott got the shot—and the title. For three months in 1951, Ten Hoff held the European Heavyweight crown. Now, at age 36, he was past his prime but still dangerous. "Tell me which hospital Johansson will be going to," Ten Hoff's manager told reporters before the fight, "so I know where to send the flowers."

On the night of August 28, 1955, 17,000 fans jammed Göteborg's Ullevi Stadium. At the opening bell, Ten Hoff rushed Ingemar with heavy body shots that drove his opponent to the ropes. The two clinched and wrestled for position. Now Ingemar pinned Ten Hoff against the ropes and landed a left hook to the body and, an instant later, a straight right to the jaw. "He sagged slowly," Ingemar recalled, "like air going out of a balloon and he keeled onto the canvas"—a stunning first round kayo. The fight was Ten Hoff's last. After a distinguished ten-year career—32 wins with 28 knockouts against 7 defeats—Hein Ten Hoff was done.

Three years had passed since Ingemar's Olympic humiliation. He was now undefeated in 12 fights and showing promise as a genuine future contender. European boxing fans may not have forgotten Helsinki, but they were at least willing to forgive. As long as Ingemar kept winning, that is.

*   *   *

In the fall of 1955, Ingemar accompanied Edwin on a five-week trip to America. The two arrived in New York City in early October and checked into a hotel near Central Park. Like a proud papa showing off his debutante belle, Edwin wished to present Ingemar to the boxing world at large, or to the part that mattered, anyway. In the 1950s that meant Stillman's Gym, the legendary "University of Eighth Avenue" and so-called center of boxing's universe.

Stillman's opened in 1919 as a place for ex-cons to unbosom their aggression in a constructive environment. The concept proved faulty, as it wasn't long until former Sing Singers had stripped the gym clean of equipment. Within a few years, owner Lou Stillman converted the joint to accommodate professional pugs and wanna-bes, and it quickly established itself as Manhattan's mecca of mayhem. If you were a Somebody, or a Nobody who wanted to be seen by a Somebody, you found your way to Stillman's.

Jack Dempsey had trained there, as had Georges Carpentier, Primo Carnera, Sugar Ray Robinson, and Rocky Marciano. In the 1920s, Damon Runyon hung out at Stillman's just to listen, and molded its wiseguyese into a literary voice. In the '40s and '50s, celebs dropped by to soak up the gym's grimy testosteronic vibe, among them Milton Berle, George Raft, Dean Martin with or without Jerry Lewis, and Frank Sinatra.

*   *   *

Ingemar began his New York mornings with a jog around the Central Park reservoir, then spent afternoons working out at Stillman's. Edwin asked Nick Florio, the trainer of Floyd Patterson, then a 20-year-old ranked heavyweight, to give Ingemar a look-see. After watching the

41

Ingo casts a wary eye toward Floyd Patterson's trainer Dan Florio at Stillman's Gym, 1955 (*Bilder i Syd*).

big Swede spar, Florio suggested Ingemar ditch his signature move, the near-simultaneous left-right, and work on throwing more deliberate punches instead—advice Ingemar wisely ignored.

"He was new but you could see he was going to be all right," Florio told journalist Jimmy Breslin years later. "You showed him something, he learned it. He was on to us to let him [spar] with Hurricane Jackson, who was big then, but Ahlquist didn't want to hurt the kid's confidence. But you could see all along he was a guy who would make it good one day."

In the evenings Ingemar walked Broadway at a leisurely pace, soaking in the experience, amused at the seemingly exaggerated display of respect American men showed to females. On a crowded Manhattan elevator he pushed his way out instead of scooting aside and allowing females to pass, and "people looked as if they wanted to knock me to the ground."

Life in America seemed a bit much to the kid from Göteborg. "In Sweden everyone feels like they mean something," Ingemar wrote in his memoirs, "but in America you felt your lack of importance in a hard, ruthless way." After five weeks he was glad to be home again.

* * *

For his first fight of 1956, Ingemar met Joe Bygraves, an accomplished Jamaican-born, Liverpool-raised fighter who, a year after this fight, would kayo Henry Cooper for the British Empire title. Bygraves brought his 30–7 record into the Masshallen arena on February 24.

The fight began poorly for Ingemar, and after three rounds he'd absorbed more blows than in all his previous bouts combined. As Ingemar sat on his stool awaiting the fourth, his face a bloody mess, Edwin told him he must try something different, as his customary cautious approach wasn't working. Eschewing defense, Ingemar waded into Bygraves, forcing

1958 (*Kurt Durewall*).

43

retreat, never allowing the big Jamaican room to unwind. The tactic worked. Ingemar dominated the rest of the way and won on points.

It was a painful lesson, but Ingemar came to a realization: "I had to change my style, get closer to my opponent, drive him and tire him physically and psychologically every second."

In April of 1956, in his first ten-rounder, the new and improved Johansson met Hans Friedrich, Germany's top-ranked heavyweight, in Stockholm, and knocked him down three times in the ninth and once in the tenth to win on points. Afterwards, Hans's manager told the press: "I envy Edwin Ahlquist. Green and gold forests await him and his boxer."

Ahlquist immediately began campaigning for a shot at Franco Cavicchi's European Heavyweight title. There were several boxers in line ahead of Johansson, so Ahlquist was surprised when he got a call from Cavicchi's promoter offering a shot at the crown in Bologna on September 30, 1956. Ingemar's purse would be his biggest payday to date—$20,000. The bout was a fifteen-rounder, so Edwin brought in middleweight and light-heavyweight sparring partners to build Ingemar's stamina, and hired an amateur wrestler for daily grappling sessions to increase his infighting strength.

The week of the fight, Edwin, Ingemar, and trainer Nils Blomberg boarded the train to Bologna, where they were met upon arrival by hundreds of cheering Swedes. On the morning of the fight, Edwin entered Bologna Stadium to inspect the ring

A Swedish newspaper's pre-fight cartoon proclaims Ingemar is "finally ready to fight Cavicchi for the European title," and predicts that "Ingo's speed will be a problem for the great Italian" (*Kajsa Andersö*).

Leaving Bologna with the spoils of victory: the European title trophy, a bouquet, and a squeeze from Momma Ebba (*Kamerareportage*).

and discovered that it was 14 square feet smaller than standard—"specially designed," Ingemar said, "for Cavicchi's wild rushes."

When Edwin threatened to call off the fight, Cavicchi's seconds exploded. Enraged, they began chanting, *"Ricorda l'Andrea Doria!"*—(Remember the *Andrea Doria*!)—a reference to the Italian luxury liner infamously rammed two months earlier by the Swedish ship MS *Stockholm*, a disaster resulting in 46 fatalities. Things were getting tense (and a bit weird) but Edwin stood firm. Finally, a carpenter was called and the ring was enlarged.

That night 32,000 fans watched as Cavicchi took the fight to Inge-

The newly crowned European heavyweight champion and son Thomas celebrate Christmas in Göteborg, 1956 (*Kamerareportage*).

mar, landing heavy blows and bulling his opponent about the ring. In the ninth, Cavicchi, ahead on points, opened a nasty cut over Ingemar's left eye; sensing victory, the Italian tried desperately to attack the eye. Ingemar fought him off.

In the 10th, as Cavicchi's energy drained, Ingemar began landing shots of his own. In the 13th, two hooks to the body and a right to Cavicchi's heart took the champion's breath and he fell spread-eagle onto the canvas, conscious but unable to move, while the ref counted to ten.

Europe had a new heavyweight king, its first Swede since Tandberg held the crown for six months in 1943. Ingo Fever was about to sweep the continent, but not before a new face was added to Team Johansson, that of a comely, curvaceous cutie named Birgit.

5

Birgit

At the height of Ingo's popularity they were the Scandinavian Liz and Eddie, Bobby Darin and Sandra Dee, Joe D and Marilyn. They were Sweden's First Couple—Ingo and Birgit.

And like Elvis or Beyonce, just one name would do.

Ingo. Birgit.

They met one weekend in 1954. Ingemar, 21, had recently turned pro. Birgit (pronounced with the hard "g") Lundgren, 17, was a striking green-eyed brunette, the only child of a Göteborg garbage truck driver. (In Sweden, that's considered a plum position with a fat salary and comfortable pension. Years later, after traveling abroad, Birgit was surprised to learn that Americans don't consider sanitation a particularly attractive career path.) Like most Swedish girls of the era, Birgit's public education ended after the eighth grade. Weekdays, she worked as a secretary.

This particular day, Birgit was playing handball at a park in Göteborg, in a skimpy outfit that accentuated her athletic frame. "I could feel a pair of eyes watching me," she recalled. Ingemar and a couple of buddies were gawking and leering and making comments.

Birgit took an instant dislike. "I wanted to pull down my pants and moon him and ask, 'Have you seen enough yet?' I was there to play handball, not have these guys drooling over me."

She knew who he was. Everyone in Göteborg knew the Johansson kid: his amateur fistic triumphs, the ignominious Olympic crash-and-burn, the early pro success. She knew something else, too. "I knew he'd been married when he was still in his teens," she recalled, "and that he had children living with his former wife." Birgit, who had never had a serious boyfriend, wasn't interested.

That weekend Birgit met some friends at a local dance hall. Ingemar spotted her and asked her to dance. When he began rattling off his favorite vacation spots, expensive resorts on Sweden's southern shore,

Birgit thought he was trying to act the big shot. "My opinion of him," she said, "got even worse."

At evening's end, Ingemar offered his new acquaintance a ride home, a big deal in Sweden. According to custom, it meant the boy wished to see his fair damsel again. Plus, Birgit lived clear across town, a thirty-minute drive. "If he was willing to do that," she remembered thinking, "he must have liked me a little."

The two began dating and Birgit discovered, to her surprise, that this big lug was "a modest, honest, and ambitious young man with whom I had much in common—movies, music, athletics, and birthdays in September one day apart. My opinion of him changed."

Birgit was impressed by Ingemar's devotion to family. Even though Ingemar's custody arrangement with Abramson (the two were not on speaking terms) allowed him to see his children twice a week, the kids regularly spent three or four days a week at the Johansson abode, a modest two-story, five-room frame house paid for in part by Ingemar's boxing earnings.

Ingemar and Birgit began spending all their free time together: swimming, dancing, skating, skiing, fishing, going to movies. Ingemar taught Birgit to trap shoot and play golf. "By 1955," she said, "I had become part of the family." Birgit recalls:

> I had never met a family with such powerful closeness. No matter how crazy the boys acted, their parents' love was unconditional towards them. Jens worked during the day, came home, took a shower, put on nice clothes, went to work at a restaurant, and came home in the middle of the night. He worked so much that sometimes he would fall asleep trying to eat. Ebba always wanted her children well dressed, so she washed and ironed daily, to keep their appearance up. She was a world champion at ironing shirts.

When Birgit began traveling with Ingemar—London, Copenhagen, Paris—the media began arching its collective brow. (This would be especially true when the two came to America. Once, a reporter for a New York newspaper called Ingemar's Manhattan hotel room and Birgit answered. "Ingemar's in the shower," she told him. "I'll have him call you back." The writer was aghast. Unmarried couples, especially those in the public eye, simply didn't openly cohabit in the Innocent '50s.) When reporters broached the subject, Birgit explained: "In my country we don't make a big mystery of sex. We study it in school and

Ingo and Birgit (*Kamerareportage*).

accept it as a natural fact of life, not something … tempting but forbidden."

Reporters with a nose for news knew that Birgit was *söt parfym*—sweet perfume—and scoring an interview became obligatory. Press reports invariably described Birgit as shapely and stylish, and seldom failed to mention her job as Ingo's "secretary." (She did in fact work for Ingemar, mostly answering his fan mail and warding off overzealous females.) And reporters who described her as Ingemar's fiancée were quick to add, with a cleverly worded wink, that no definite date for the nuptials had been set.

Fact was, Ingemar had never quite gotten around to divorcing his first wife, which didn't seem to bother Birgit in the least. She certainly sounded like the perfect girl for Ingo.

*   *   *

Following his win over Heinz Ten Hoff, Ingemar found his name appearing for the first time on *Ring* magazine's ranking of the world's top heavyweights, debuting at 10. For Ingo it was a particularly fortuitous time to be 23 years old and a ranked heavyweight, not to mention mischievously handsome and possessed of the game's mightiest right. In April of 1956, Rocky Marciano announced his retirement after three years and six fights as champion. With the title vacant and up for grabs, a series of elimination bouts were held to determine a new champ.

That August, Floyd Patterson met Tommy "Hurricane" Jackson in a battle of top contenders. Floyd won a split decision and the right to face light-heavyweight king Archie Moore for Marciano's crown. On the evening of November 30 at Chicago Stadium, Patterson, 20, became the youngest heavyweight champion in history with a fifth round knockout of the 38-year-old Moore.

Edwin and Ingemar must have been secretly delighted. After all, at 185 pounds, Floyd was never more than a glorified light-heavy with peek-a-boo hands and a touch-and-go chin. But if Edwin and Ingo dared to ponder the possibilities, they kept those thoughts to themselves. There was work to be done.

For one, the struggle against Joe Bygraves convinced Ingemar that further progress up the international ladder meant embracing a more offensive approach. Ingemar had asked Edwin to film the Cavicchi fight, the better to analyze his performance.

The film provided a revelation: Ingemar had developed a bad habit of throwing a punch and taking an almost immediate half-step back, a hesitation that gave opponents time to escape. To remedy this flaw he worked long hours in the gym to replace the retreat with a half-step *advance*. "The new style," Ingemar explained, "meant I figuratively hovered over [the opponent] the whole time ... to hamper his attacks, keep him off balance, and punch through his gaps."

* * *

On December 28 Ingemar fought Englishman Peter Bates in Göteborg. In 29 pro fights, Bates had never been knocked down and was

Souvenir program for Johansson-Cooper, May 19, 1957 (*author's collection*).

Whoever said, "The sun never sets on the British empire," forgot to inform Henry Cooper (*Bilder i Syd*).

coming off a fifth-round TKO of highly regarded Henry Cooper. But he proved no match for Ingo. In the second round, two lefts and a right put Bates down, out—and into Sahlgrenska Hospital with a broken jaw.

After several months' rest, during which he was dropped from the rankings for "inactivity," Ingemar was pressured by the European Boxing Association to defend his title against Henry Cooper. The fight took place on May 19, 1957, at an outdoor arena in Stockholm. Over 10,000 fans settled into their seats as the fight began beneath a late-afternoon sky.

"The crafty so-and-sos saw to it that [my] corner faced the setting sun and [I] was blinded much of the fight," Cooper recalled years later. "As I went forward in the fifth round hunting him, he drew me towards the setting sun. I could not see a thing and then ... *boom.*"

'Enery had been struck by the first right Ingemar had thrown all fight. Cooper didn't remember much after that, just hearing the ref count ten and wondering why his legs wouldn't listen.

Peter Wilson of the *London Daily Mirror* wrote: "The Englishman's eyes were staring blindly at the blue sky, his limbs twitching helplessly, trying desperately to pull himself upright. But he was like a man who had touched the live terminal of a high voltage wire and had been shocked out of his senses."

After the Cooper kayo, Ingemar moved to seven in the world rankings. "It was time," Ingemar said, "to see how I would shape up against a top American."

*   *   *

Archie McBride was not exactly a top-tier American boxer, but he was close enough. McBride, 28, was a solid B-lister, consistently bubbling just below *Ring's* top ten. In 1948 McBride had beaten the dangerous Cuban Nino Valdes, who by 1953 had risen to Number One contender status. What's more, McBride was willing to come to Göteborg for the opportunity to burnish his resume.

In the November 1957 issue of *Ring* magazine, Nat Fleischer wrote: "McBride is the best possible opponent for Johansson. The Swede is still an unknown quantity on this side of the Atlantic. But as we know McBride's qualifications well we will get a clearer appreciation after this fight of what Johansson is really good for."

An interesting but slightly irrelevant sidenote: McBride's manager was Budd Schulberg, whose 1947 boxing novel *The Harder They Fall* inspired a film of the same name, and whose 1954 script for *On the*

Waterfront won a Best Screenplay Oscar. On anyone's list of American writers, the man was a ranked heavyweight.

Johansson-McBride was scheduled for December 13, 1957, at the Masshallen Arena. A week before the fight, Ingemar was driving through Göteborg when he spied McBride and an older gentleman out for a walk. Ingemar parked his car and approached. He'd never met McBride but recognized his companion, the legendary Whitey Bimstein, trainer/cutman to boxing's elite.

Whitey had worked more corners than a Bowery hooker: Dempsey, Tunney, Leonard, Braddock, Graziano, Marciano—Bimstein served them all. At one point in the 1930s, the champion in each of the sport's fourteen weight divisions were Whitey's guys.

Ingemar had seen Bimstein in action at Stillman's, had his eye on him, even if Whitey had paid him no mind. Now the great man had come to Göteborg.

"Hallo, Mr. Bimstein," Ingo called.

Whitey stuck out his hand. He knew he'd seen the kid somewhere before. "I can't remember your name," he told Ingemar.

"The name's Johansson. McBride has come here to meet me."

By the time Bimstein left Sweden, Ingemar had left a uniquely indelible impression. "All week before the fight Ingo is around the hotel," Whitey told writer Jimmy Breslin in 1959." 'You get enough food?' he keeps asking. He wasn't worried about the fight. He was worried about us."

Just before the fight, Whitey went to Johansson's dressing room, per the sport's custom, to watch the wrapping of the opponent's hands. "The kid was just sitting there calm as you please. He winds the gauze around, then takes the tape and puts it on. He don't need no second to do it. He holds up his hands. 'Is this all right, Mr. Bimstein?' I say to myself, this kid is all right."

The fight, which took place as scheduled on December 13, was a mismatch from the start. Ingemar won every round with an unyielding, relentless attack.

"Johansson hit Archie one shot," Bimstein told reporter A.J. Liebling, "and I seen if he hit him again he like to kilt him. When Archie came back to the corner he said, 'Man, that guy's murder.' I told McBride to go into his shell and just try to stay the ten rounds. He was lucky, at that." At the final bell, the Associated Press reported, "McBride virtually stumbled to his corner."

Afterwards, Edwin was pleased. "You're better than you think," he told Ingemar. Now they knew for certain: Ingo could hold his own against a tough American.

*   *   *

As Ingemar progressed up the heavyweight ladder, his matches came fewer and farther between. Then again, his per fight earnings were increasing exponentially. Ingemar's first three fights earned him a total of $38,000. His purse for winning the European title from Cavicchi in September 1956 was $80,000. (That's about $250,000 and $550,000 in today's dollars, respectively.)

Ingemar fought only twice in 1957—against Cooper and McBride—

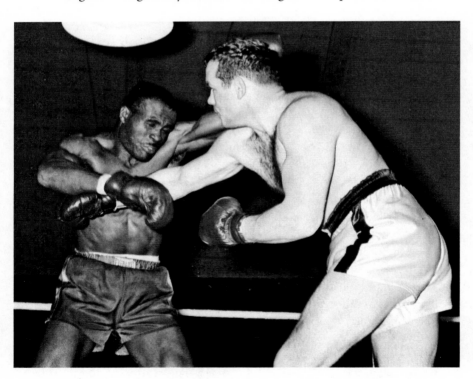

December 13, 1957: Landing the right against Archie McBride (*Kurt Durewall*).

but maintained a vigorous training regimen nonetheless. Yet his life was hardly defined by the confines of rope and canvas.

From the start of his pro career, Ingemar had plunked his winnings into building an excavation business in Göteborg, starting with one bull-dozer which he operated himself (see photograph, page 86). Within five years his operation had grown to include over $2 million in earth-moving equipment and a staff of eight. Most of his employees were longtime friends, guys who needed the paycheck. When Gunner "Silver" Nilsson was down on his luck, Ingemar hired him as a construction foreman.

Ingemar was no mere figurehead trading on his name. A hands-on boss, Ingo proved canny with a krona, earning a reputation as a tough negotiator with a keen eye for cutting expenses—a natural businessman. Still, Ingemar always put family first. He gave his sickly, mentally-challenged older brother Henry a "job" at the company so that Henry would have somewhere to go and a feeling that he, too, was a valued member of Team Johansson. Once, a reporter asked Henry to describe his work. Henry looked blank. An employee whispered, "Tell him, 'electrician.'" Henry proudly repeated, "Electrician."

There were other avenues of income. To Americans, Johansson's blue-eyed mug was unfamiliar and his name known only to boxing fans. But as the European victories mounted, Ingemar became a major Scandinavian celebrity. He was huge, endorsing clothing lines, sports cars, and sporting goods.

Ingemar was also in the fishing business, purchasing an 84-foot, 100-ton steel trawler and hiring his uncle, an old sea salt, to take a crew of seven on month-long expeditions off the coast of Iceland. Then there was "Ingo's," the American-style restaurant-tavern he opened in down-town Göteborg, where patrons munched cheeseburgers while films of the owner's fistic triumphs flickered on an overhead screen.

To keep abreast of his various enterprises, Ingemar took flying lessons and earned a pilot's license. When he asked his pal, fellow boxer Lennart Risberg, to go up with him, Risberg declined, well aware of Ingemar's penchant for fast cars, high speeds, and fearless—some would say reckless—driving. The intrepid Birgit was usually game, however, even if Ingemar's piloting skills hardly inspired confidence. Once, as they approached the Göteborg airport on a flight from Copenhagen, Ingemar began having issues with the plane and decided to circle the airport while he worked things out. "Reach behind you," he told Birgit, "and hand me the pilot's manual." With preternatural cool—one hand on the stick, the other thumbing through the instruction book—Ingemar managed to bring them down in one piece.

When in Göteborg, Ingemar made a point to visit his childhood friends. Didn't matter that they were still stonemasons, or taxi drivers or whatever, and that he was a rising star. Even after he won the world title Ingemar enjoyed hanging out with the old crowd. Ingo may have been cocky; he was a national celebrity and sports star and he knew it. But haughty? Not Ingo.

*   *   *

In Great Britain, fans and press were trumpeting a pugilistic hero of their own: reigning British Empire champion Joe Erskine of Cardiff, Wales.

Erskine was 32–1 with wins over Cooper and Bygraves, his only loss a first-round kayo at the hands of Valdes. Promoter Harry Levene of London had already promised Erskine a world title shot against Patterson in July. All he had to do was get past the big Swede, a fight Erskine felt would be no more than a tuneup. The Erskine-Johansson match was scheduled for February 21, 1958, in Göteborg.

The people of Wales have been boxing-nutty since at least the nineteen-teens when three landsmen dominated the lower weights: Percy Jones and Jimmy Wilde at flyweight, Freddie Welsh at lightweight—world champions all. Now Joe Erskine appeared ready to carry *Y Ddraig Goch* to heavyweight glory.

Days before the Johansson fight, hordes of Welshers arrived by sea and air as full-on Erskine-mania swept into Sweden. They eagerly accepted bets on Joe at three-to-one, despite the fact that official wagering placed Ingo the 2–1 choice. Erskine himself seemed supremely confident, bolstered by the British press, which deemed Erskine's win a foregone conclusion and the fight itself a mere formality. Plus, there were reports from the Johansson camp that Ingo had injured his mighty right. It was true: while training on the heavy bag, Ingemar had scraped the skin off his right knuckles.

"Before the fight," Ingemar said, "the English newspapermen wrote, 'He's going to win easily, Joe Erskine, he's the best fighter in the world.'"

A pre-fight newsreel from early February 1958 shows Ingemar in full hiking gear—heavy boots, loaded backpack, a Floyd R. Turbo cap on his head—trudging through rocks and snow as a voiceover intones: "Ingo hikes the Alps to build his legs and general conditioning," adding, "Everyone in the United States has heard of Johansson's power even though he has never fought outside of Europe. Eighteen wins, ten by knockout, all by his right hand which he calls his 'toonerbolt.'"

Come fight night, Ingemar used his ailing right sparingly, controlling Erskine with hard stinging lefts and pressing forward, allowing no room or rest. A video of the fight can be found on YouTube, and viewers will no doubt be impressed by Johansson's improvement over his 1955 performance against Bacilieri. "I hardly needed my right against Erskine," Ingemar recalled. "I went into him with my new style, put my left

February 21, 1958: Ingemar defends his European title against British Empire champ Joe Erskine (*Bilder i Syd*).

hand in his face and never stop. From the fourth round I could do what I liked—the most easy fight I ever had."

As the bell rang for the 13th, Ingemar suddenly danced across the ring with his arms upraised. Erskine remained on his stool, his face swollen and cut, unable to answer the bell. In the stands, meanwhile, wads of currency changed hands—a crushing blow, one presumes, to the gross national product of Wales.

*   *   *

For Edwin and Ingemar, their goal—a shot at Floyd's title, sports' Holy Grail—must have seemed tantalizingly near. Even so, Johansson was still a work in progress. His new offense, the smothering half-step and stinging left, needed time to ripen. Ingemar admitted as much, telling one reporter: "I have no intention of challenging Patterson until I improve my technique."

For Ingemar's next opponent, Edwin signed former European Heavyweight Champion Heinz Neuhaus for July 13, 1957. The big German's resume included 42 wins against seven defeats with victories over Bygraves and former World Light-Heavyweight Champion Joey Maxim. To test Ingemar's drawing power, Edwin booked Ullevi Stadium, Göteborg's gleaming new soccer facility with 55,000 seats. Eight thousand, Ahlquist figured, would be a splendid turnout.

On fight night 14,000 fans endured a steady rain and screamed their approval as Ingemar drove Neuhaus to the ropes and battered him with both hands. In the fourth round Neuhaus went down under withering blows. He was up at eight, but moments later a left to the body and a right uppercut sent him tumbling again. His handlers tossed a towel while the ref was still mid-count. Ingemar's 19th professional victory, his 14th knockout, earned him a tidy $95,000.

Ingemar had beaten the best boxers Europe had to offer. Ahlquist's next target: a top-ranked American contender.

6

Taking on Machen

In 100-plus years of professional heavyweight boxing there are just a handful of knockouts so utterly brutal that one's spine shivers at the thought. Joe Louis-Max Schmeling was one, Rocky Marciano-Joe Walcott another.

To the list add Ingemar Johansson-Eddie Machen.

Once viewed, the September 14, 1958, fight between Ingemar and boxing's number one-ranked contender can scarcely be forgotten. When it was over, the world had a new number one; the other guy went back to his corner, sat on his stool, and wept.

The Machen-Johansson match nearly didn't come about at all. If it hadn't, one imagines the scenario that might have followed: Machen, the troubled ex-con, gets a shot at Patterson, at redemption, wins, becomes heavyweight champ of a love-smacked world, and the warmth of a thousand suns beams down on him forever. Instead he gets the holy hell kicked out of him and Ingo gets the shot and the crown and the thousand suns.

After his savage beating, it took Machen two years to reenter the ring. A few years later he declared bankruptcy, got rearrested, and was in and out of mental institutions the rest of his life, which ended in August 1972 at the age of 40 after a mysterious fall from a window.

To this day no one knows for certain what happened to Machen that August night. Sleepwalking, the authorities speculated. Or was it suicide? Or careless accident? This much is certain: After two minutes and sixteen seconds in the ring with Johansson, life was never the same for Eddie Machen.

*   *   *

In July 1958, two days after defeating Heinz Neuhaus, Ingemar sat in Edwin Ahlquist's office in Stockholm to plot his future. Johansson was sixth in the world among ranked heavyweights. He'd exhausted the supply of qualified European contenders; had beaten Archie McBride, a tough American; and had proved he could draw fans to an outdoor arena. The question for Ingo now was … whither thou goest from here?

Ahlquist suggested taking on world number three Willie Pastrano, but Ingemar wasn't sure. Pastrano could box but not punch. He'd beaten Cavicchi and Bygraves but was no crowd pleaser. Ahlquist then proposed world number-two Zora Folley, like Pastrano a master boxer without real kayo power, but discovered Folley was already booked that summer to fight Pete Rademacher, the former Olympic champion.

"We didn't want to go down the list," Ingemar said. "It had to be someone near the top."

That left the number-one contender, Eddie Machen, the powerful knockout artist from California. Problem was, Edwin wasn't sure Ingo was ready for Eddie.

"I wasn't going to let Johansson fool with Machen, not at this stage," Ahlquist told reporter Harry Grayson. "I considered Machen to be the hardest hitter of all the heavyweights. I advised him against it." Ingemar himself was uncertain. The two debated into the night. "Let me think about it for a couple of days," Ingemar told him.

Ingemar's trepidation was understandable. Machen was six-feet and 195 pounds of exquisitely bronzed stone, as if chiseled to life by Rodin. Undefeated in 25 fights, Machen had beaten Nino Valdes and Joey Maxim twice each and fought Folley to a draw.

Patterson clearly wanted nothing to do with Machen, who was bigger, stronger, hungrier, and way meaner. So Floyd and his manager Cus D'Amato ducked him, fighting instead unranked white tomatoes like Tom McNeely and the aforementioned Rademacher, who made his professional debut against Floyd for the title. It was a disgrace, most sports fans agreed, that Floyd would fight an amateur while legitimate contenders like Machen and Folley and Sonny Liston were forced to fight each other.

Over the next couple of days, Ingemar wrestled with the proposition: "Eventually, I told myself that I've got nothing to lose. If I lose honorably it isn't a catastrophe. If I win I'm on my way to the top."

When the two met again in Ahlquist's office, Ingemar told him: "We'll box Machen."

"You'll take the fight?" Edwin asked.

"Get him here. If there's a heavyweight who hits quicker and harder than I do it's time we found out."

*　*　*

Ahlquist contacted Machen's manager Sid Flaherty and proposed a match for September at Ullevi Stadium. Flaherty accepted. That afternoon, Ahlquist purchased plane tickets for Machen, Flaherty, and six members of their team, and placed the tickets in the mail along with a signed contract for the fight.

The next day, when the news hit Swedish newspapers, Ahlquist's switchboard lit up. The first week 22,000 tickets were sold.

Ingemar set up camp in a Göteborg soccer stadium. Ahlquist wanted an American sparring partner, someone tough and experienced, and who could "teach Ingemar all the thief-tricks that occur in American rings." He flew in Baltimore heavyweight Bert Whitehurst and his manager George Gainford. Three months earlier, Whitehurst had gone the distance with the fearsome Liston.

Ingemar liked to go easy during sparring sessions, working mainly on stamina and rhythm, rarely flashing his lethal right. "What good is a sparring partner if he's on the floor?" Ingo liked to say. On the first day of sparring, Whitehurst came out flinging heavy hooks and roundhouse rights. Between rounds Ingemar complained to Edwin.

"Then show him who the bouncer is," Edwin told him. "Let him see the right."

Whitehurst came out swinging. "Suddenly—*bam!*" Ahlquist remembered. "Ingemar had flicked a heavy right and the American went down." From ringside, George Gainford jumped to his feet. "What a *punch!* What a *right!* He will kill Eddie Machen!"

In the stands sat Sven Holmberg, Flaherty's Swedish contact and a friend of Machen's. Ahlquist remembers seeing Holmberg slink out of camp with a distressed look on his face. "After that visit," Ingemar recalled, "Flaherty began to talk of a return bout in America."

No one knew it at the time, but the knockdown of Whitehurst, Holmberg's panicked report to Flaherty, and Flaherty's last-minute insistence on a return bout would set off a chain reaction that nearly derailed the Johansson-Machen bout entirely.

* * *

With the fight a week away, Ahlquist began suffering buyer's remorse. He hadn't, after all, been entirely sold on Machen to begin with. Now every time he picked up a newspaper he read Johansson's obituary. "Eddie Machen is currently the world's best heavyweight," wrote one sportswriter, "with knockout power in both fists. Against this American hitter the unknown Swede is nothing more than a big zero." Oddsmakers had made Machen a 2–1 favorite.

Worried, unable to sleep, Ahlquist drove unannounced to the Johanssons' villa just outside Göteborg where Ingemar lived with his parents and siblings. (Jean and Thomas, Ingemar's children with Barbara Abramson, spent considerable time there as well.) It was just before dawn when Ahlquist arrived. He parked out of sight and got out. The land was rugged and steep. At first light, Ingemar stepped onto the porch in a light tracksuit. Ahlquist remained hidden. He watched as Ingo dashed up the mountain road, "with hideous speed [and] terrible force, [then] took a new incline without reducing speed ... before disappearing among the trees."

When Ingemar emerged a half hour later, "sprinting like a madman," Ahlquist's fears subsided. He knew Ingo would be ready, "at any cost, to have the strength and stamina to keep up with Machen." He got back in his car and left unseen.

Ingemar's confidence rose as the fight grew near. Rolf slipped into Machen's camp one afternoon and watched the big Californian spar. "He comes in with his head straight up," he told Ingemar. "I can't believe he's going to box like that. Your right will get in there quick."

Ingemar completed his training on Friday morning, September 12, three days before the fight. The idea was to relax, let the muscles rest. Ullevi was sold out, all 55,000 seats. No fight in Sweden had ever drawn close to that. Fans had begun streaming into Göteborg from all parts of Europe, even abroad.

That afternoon Ahlquist received a telephone call from Flaherty. They needed to talk. Now.

Ahlquist rushed to Göteborg's Park Avenue hotel where a grim-faced Flaherty demanded that a provision be added to the contract, a return-bout clause, calling for a rematch in San Francisco in the event Machen lost.

"Contracts have been signed and approved," Ahlquist told him. "There will be no changes." Flaherty demanded to speak to Ingemar. "Impossible," Ahlquist responded. "He's at a secret location outside the city and has nothing to add to the matter."

Flaherty turned "dark as a thunderstorm in the face," Ahlquist recalled, then summoned a porter and demanded a phone. "I think you should hear this conversation, Eddie."

Flaherty dialed. "Yes…. I'd like to reserve eight seats on the first plane to the United States. It is very urgent. We're going to New York."

Ahlquist was stunned. As the promoter of the event, he stood to lose a fortune if Flaherty and Company bolted. He asked for a few hours to think it over.

Ahlquist immediately contacted his lawyer who advised: "Sign the new contract, but make sure it's printed on the hotel paper with date and time, and that it is legally witnessed. Under Swedish law this is an illegal coup."

Ahlquist returned to Flaherty with the new clause typed on hotel stationery. The fight was back on. (Months later, when Ingemar signed to

Pre-match negotiations turn tense. Left to right: Sid Flaherty, Eddie Machen, Edwin Ahlquist (*Kurt Durewall*).

fight Patterson, Flaherty took the issue to court. By that time Team Johansson had a new argument in their favor: Ahlquist was Ingemar's "advisor," not his manager, and thus not authorized to approve any contract changes.)

* * *

Finally the big night arrived. Outside the stadium, fans stood in long queues for standing-room tickets even as the prelims were under-

Official program for Johansson-Machen, 1958 (*author's collection*).

way. When Ahlquist entered the dressing room deep within Ullevi, he spied Ingemar lying on a wooden bench. Trainer Nils Blomberg put his finger to his lips. "Quiet," he whispered, "he's asleep."

Ingemar awoke and laced his shoes. Edgardo Romero, one of Machen's seconds, arrived to watch Ingemar wrap his fists. Romero poked at the gauze. The wraps are too long, Romero said. They should be removed at once and measured. "I know what you're doing," Ahlquist told him angrily. "You're trying to rush Ingemar right up to the match and get him agitated." He summoned two cops and had Romero escorted from the room.

There was a knock on the door. Time to go. Ingemar slipped on a white full-length terry cloth robe that was actually one of Ebba's beach cover-ups, as if to draw strength from his family's hermetic bond.

The three men made their way to the ring. The arena was dark but Ahlquist could see "human masses as shadow-figures, as glows from thousands of cigarettes gleamed like glow-worms in the gloom."

Ingemar stepped between the ropes and Edwin felt "a fierce cheer like a thunderstorm" sweep through the arena. Ingemar threw combinations into the dense air. Machen was already in the ring, wearing so many layers he looked like a Sherpa guide ready to ascend Everest: track-suit, wool sweater, cotton shirt, long pants, hooded windbreaker, purple satin robe—a California boy completely out of his sunny element. It took him nearly fifteen minutes to disrobe.

Meanwhile, Ingemar shadowboxed and shuffled his feet as Ahlquist spoke into his ear: "Think of the opportunity, Ingemar. Think what this means for you and your family."

Across the ring, Machen glared at his opponent. Ingemar avoided his gaze. Later, he would explain: "I never look at an opponent before a fight. They're apt to think you're nervous."

The referee, Andrew Smyth, called the combatants to ring-center for the traditional instructions. His actions this night would still be the target of opprobrium a half-century hence.

* * *

The bell rang and Machen, standing rod-straight—no bob, no weave, just as Rolf observed—immediately came at Ingemar, firing lefts and driving him to the ropes. Ingemar escaped and circled clockwise, throwing lefts of his own but mostly coming up short. At ringside, Ahlquist noticed how Machen dropped his left ever so slightly after throwing the jab, leaving his chin exposed. He wondered, had Ingo seen it too?

He had.

Sixty-five seconds into the fight, Machen threw a tentative left. What happened next appears as a blur when seen on film in real time. Afterwards, even Ingemar had to watch the film several times to explain exactly what occurred: "I struck out my left partly as a feint and partly to balance myself for the longest right I have ever punched in my life ... up from the shoulders and downward, like a cat striking with its paw. It came by itself. I hadn't had time to think consciously."

The impact on the jaw of Eddie Machen can still be heard today. A sharp audio/video of the fight appears on several boxing-related websites. Listen for the lancinating *phwapp* as Ingo's Bingo hits home. Fist on bone—at once sickening and satisfying, it's boxing's primal appeal condensed into a frozen moment.

Machen fell onto his back, the first knockdown of his career. He arose at the count of five with a sick smile, embarrassed, perhaps, at his own carelessness. Clearly in trouble, Machen grabbed Ingemar in a desperate attempt to buy time. Ingemar pushed him off, then landed a stunning right uppercut. As Machen began to fall, a left hook sent him violently to the canvas, his head snapping on the bottom rope on his way down.

Machen lay still for a few seconds, then rolled to his left and willed himself up at the count of seven. He tried to stand but staggered on gelatinous legs, a dead man's arms at his sides. Utterly defenseless, stripped bare, Eddie Machen became a human heavy bag.

Without question, Smyth should have stopped the bout. Instead he bade the game go on.

Ingemar trapped his prey in a neutral corner and unleashed an unholy reign of lefts and rights. Machen appeared out on his feet—knees buckled, arms limp. Propped up by the ropes, he froze in a seated position as seventeen unanswered blows crashed into his unguarded skull. Finally, mercifully, he slid off the ropes to the floor. The ref began to count.

Machen lay motionless with his head outside the ropes on the ring apron. When Smyth's count reached three, one of Machen's seconds

September 14, 1958: the shocking first-round destruction of Eddie Machen (*Bilder i Syd*).

entered the ring, ran completely around Smyth and Machen, and exited between the ropes.

By all known boxing rules, this should have ended the fight. Somehow, Smyth failed to notice. The scene is almost comical to watch. Clearly, it's one of the most abysmal jobs of officiating in fistic history.

When Smyth reached 10, Ingemar threw up his fists in triumph, hugged Edwin and Nils, and, smiling broadly, waved to his family at ringside. Dozens of photographers surrounded the ring and their bulbs turned night into day. It was a scene of unbridled joy.

Machen's seconds dragged their fallen comrade back to his corner. On film, he appears to be asking them what just happened. At one point he mouths the word, "Really?" As Machen ran his left hand over his face, as if to reassure himself his features were still intact, Ingemar walked over and spoke a few words. This time it was Machen who looked away. As he sat on his stool, an ice pack applied to his neck, Machen must have begun to process the magnitude of his loss. Ingemar noticed he was crying.

* * *

The jubilant in-ring celebration was still in progress when a tall sober-faced gentleman bolted from his ringside seat, made straight for Edwin Ahlquist, and introduced himself as Bill Rosensohn.

Ahlquist knew the name. Rosensohn was the American boxing promoter and an executive with TelePromTer Corporation, which had pio-
neered the new technology of
closed-circuit broadcasting.
Rosensohn, an ally of Cus
D'Amato, had staged the Floyd
Patterson-Roy Harris fight in
August. Now Rosensohn was
imploring Ahlquist to bring
his boy to America, where a
good-looking kid like Ingo, a
big hitter ... well, they could
all make a ton of money.

Ahlquist told him: Come
to our victory celebration at
the Park Avenue Hotel and
we'll talk about it.

Later that evening, Team
Johansson and friends assembled in the hotel's elegant dining room. There were endless
platters of food, an orchestra,
and much toasting, dancing,
back-slapping and general fri-
volity. Birgit recalled one
female guest arrived wearing
"a helmet-type hat with a tiny
prize-ring built on top and
dolls in the ring, and the Ingemar doll had just knocked out
the Patterson doll."

Ingemar remembered the
moment he met Rosensohn.
The orchestra was playing
"Johansson ror pa pakarna"
("Johansson, Get Moving"), a
lively pop tune shooting up

**Post-Machen hugs and kisses, from Ebba
(top), and Birgit (above) (*Kurt Durewall*).**

70

the Swedish charts. Ingemar felt a hand on his shoulder. "How would you like a shot at Floyd Patterson?" Rosensohn asked.

"There's nothing in this world I would rather do," Ingemar told him.

Before the night was over, Rosensohn secured Ingemar's signature on a document giving the promoter 40 days to put together a Patterson-Johansson fight. In return for his signature, Ingemar would receive $10,000.

The next morning Ingemar was at the Göteborg airport to catch a flight to Stockholm for a television appearance. In the waiting area sat a broken Eddie Machen. Ingemar strolled over and tried to make small talk but Machen would have none of it. Machen mumbled a few bitter words and the two men parted, each to his own destiny.

* * *

Ingo's stunning kayo was not just a victory for Sweden. All Europe had cause to celebrate.

"Machen was a probable world champion," a justifiably self-satisfied Ingemar reflected, "and I was an unknown Swede who could be somebody in my own little corner of the world, but a nobody in the hands of an American." The victory, Ingemar proclaimed, "utterly dispelled" the long-held belief that Americans were superior fighters.

In America, news of Machen's demise at the hands of this relative unknown hit with tsunamic force. "I thought Archie Moore's right was the best in the business," Sid Flaherty told *Sport* magazine, "but I was wrong. Johansson has the most powerful right in the world." Jersey Jones, writing for *Ring* mag-

Boxing's new top-ranked contender, 1958 (*Kamerareportage*).

71

azine, added: "It seemed strange to see an 'alien' who has never fought professionally in the United States listed as the No. One challenger. In fact, this is the first time anything of the sort has happened since the *Ring* initiated the custom of rating fighters thirty-three years ago. For the sake of world boxing in general, and the heavyweight division in particular, it is to be fervently hoped that Johansson is as good a fighter as his record would seem to indicate."

America was about to find out.

7

Edwin and Cus

Edwin Ahlquist was Ingemar's mentor, business partner, and father-figure, and there is no doubt that Ingemar's ascent to top contender would never have happened without him.

Ingemar was inherently stubborn, defiant, and distrustful of authority, but Ahlquist's genteel manner and old world code of honor won Ingo's trust. Agreements between them were sealed with a handshake. Both men were proud of that.

The biographical details of Ahlquist's life reflect nothing less than the history of professional boxing in Sweden. The man had a Zelig-like way of connecting himself to the nation's fistic zeitgeist: Harry Persson to Arne Andersson to Olle Tandberg to Ingemar Johansson, Ahlquist was at the center of it all.

The son of a forester, Edwin Ahlquist was born in 1898 in Södermanland, on Sweden's eastern shore, in the same county that would produce tennis champion Bjorn Börg. In 1920 Edwin was working construction in Eskiltuna, an industrial town 250 miles east of Göteborg, and earning a few extra krona writing freelance sports for a local newspaper. Like so many Swedes, Ahlquist pined for America, and in the spring of 1922 he found employment on a Dutch steamer that carried 700 passengers between Göteborg and New York. He was the number four cook for third-class dining—bottom rung, but it paid $150 a month. It took three or four round trips before the seasickness ceased.

Ahlquist made a total of seven round trips. On each journey, it seemed, another shipmate escaped, melting anonymously into Manhattan's immigrant stew. When Edwin's opportunity arose, he slipped off board and found a seedy hotel in New York's notorious Hell's Kitchen. That night he tore the weighted bar from the hem of the drapes and placed it under his pillow for protection.

Back in Manhattan, Ahlquist drifted from job to job, all the while writing freelance articles for the Swedish magazine *All Boxing*. "In America in the 1920s I had two great interests: boxing and journalism," he said. He dreamt of starting a magazine of his own.

In 1927 he opened a small Scandinavian restaurant in Brooklyn and fell in love with a dark-haired Göteborg native who worked as a housemaid at an estate outside Philadelphia. They married the following year and Ahlquist sold the restaurant, pocketing $4,000, a princely sum in those days (about $43,000 in today's money), and returned to Sweden.

Back in Göteborg, Ahlquist fattened his nest egg working construction and by 1932 had saved enough to start his own small bi-weekly magazine, *Fresh Sports*, which proved a rousing success. It also opened doors: Ahlquist began promoting local wrestling and boxing matches, routinely drawing 5,000 to Göteborg arenas.

Edwin's career took a leap forward in 1933 with the opportunity to promote a boxing match involving Harry Persson. The name may not mean much to American sports fans, but in his prime—roughly 1923 to 1926—Persson was the most famous and popular sports star in Sweden, the Great Hope upon whose shoulders lay his nation's dream of a native-born heavyweight champion of the world.

Persson, like Ingo an untutored stonemason as a youth, was the reigning European champion when, in 1926, he came to America in hopes of securing a match with Jack Dempsey for the world title. On September 23, at Philadelphia's Sesquicentennial Stadium and in front of the largest crowd ever to witness a boxing match—including Ahlquist, covering the match for *All Boxing*—Persson kayoed journeyman Jack Adams on the undercard of the first Dempsey-Tunney bout.

Edwin Ahlquist (*Kurt Durewall*).

The victory pushed Persson's record to 24–1–1. But it was his last moment of glory, as he soon fell victim to American underworld corruption and his own naivete. Unwilling to fire his Swedish manager and hire an American, the trusting Persson never stood a chance.

In December 1926 he lost a twelve-round decision to journeyman Pat McCarthy despite winning, by most accounts, ten rounds. In November 1927 against Bud Gorman, the referee disqualified Persson for landing a "low blow," ignoring the fact that Gorman had pulled up his trunks until they were practically under his armpits.

Persson returned to Sweden a broken fighter, no longer a viable contender for the crown. Sadly, it was the shell of Harry Persson who fought for Edwin Ahlquist in October of 1933, at Göteborg's Masshallen arena, against Fred Lundahl. Persson managed a points victory, then fought twice more before retiring with a record of 35–5–4. He spent the rest of his life working odd jobs and died in 1979 at age 81, at a sanitarium outside Stockholm, where not a soul visited him during the last seven years of his life.

* * *

Ahlquist sold *Fresh Sports* in 1935 and concentrated on promoting, always with an eye for a boxer he could take to the top. In the fall of 1937 he was approached by a 19-year-old kid, six-foot-three and strong as rebar. Lately he'd earned quite a reputation as a bar fighter and he'd worked for a time as a strongman for a traveling circus. "My name is Arne Andersson," he told Ahlquist, "and I want to be a professional boxer." Ahlquist agreed to manage the kid and booked him into the same Göteborg arena where, fifteen years later, he would first lay eyes on Ingemar.

Before long Andersson was the talk of Europe and filling arenas, displaying kayo power in both fists and proving impervious to pain. Even *Ring* magazine was trumpeting his talents. Perhaps, Ahlquist thought, Arne was The One.

But after only six fights in Sweden, Andersson yielded to the lure of America, and like Harry Persson it proved his undoing. In February of 1941, in the seventh round of a fight against Lou Thomas at Chicago's Marigold Gardens, Andersson was felled by a right hook. His head slammed into the canvas, hard. Attempts to resuscitate failed, and Arne, 23, died on the ring floor.

In Göteborg in the fall of 1942, Ahlquist put together another magazine, *Rekord*, a combination of lavishly illustrated sports and adventure stories. Ahlquist wrote almost all the articles, using five different aliases to give the appearance of an impressively large staff. One of the magazine's most popular features was serialized installments of the novel *Knockout King*, written by Ahlquist, in which a Swedish boxer knocks out every contender in Europe before coming to America and winning the world heavyweight title.

Readers must have been thinking: "Hmmphh. If only."

* * *

By mid–1942 Hitler's Nazi army was goose-stepping through Europe, invading Denmark, Norway, Holland, and Belgium to the west, and Russia to the east. Aerial bombing of London had commenced, as had the construction of concentration camps.

Even as Sweden remained stubbornly neutral, illustrated tales of heroic Danish and Norwegian freedom fighters began appearing in the pages of *Rekord*, along with anti–Nazi editorials and cartoons.

The Swedish state department pressured Ahlquist to desist. Instead he pushed on. In 1943 he persuaded three train engineers to smuggle *Rekord* into Norway. Copies were placed in the middle of stacks of tightly bundled newspapers and thrown overboard at designated spots. To reach Denmark, copies were smuggled by sea, past German patrol boats, across the Oresund Strait. "We took a stand against Nazism," Edwin liked to boast, "long before it was fashionable."

In 1945, Edwin started a second publication, *ALL SPORT*, a Swedish version of *Sports Illustrated*. It too proved a smashing success, its circulation climbing over 100,000 within a few years.

In 1947, Ahlquist hooked up with Olle Tandberg, the reigning Swedish heavyweight champion and successor to Harry Persson as the nation's next Great Hope. At six-foot-three and 210 pounds, Tandberg was not only a physical specimen but a superlative boxing technician. Tandberg had everything Ahlquist was looking with one exception: he lacked a kayo punch. A childhood accident had left him with a weakened right hand, rendering him bereft of power—a hammerless Thor.

Even so, Tandberg had rung up a record of 16–4 when Ahlquist signed him for a bout against American Joe Baksi, the world's fourth-ranked contender. Three months earlier, Baksi had broken the jaw of European champion Bruce Woodcock en route to a seventh round TKO. As a result, contracts were drawn up for a title shot against Joe Louis. Baksi wanted additional ring work before facing Louis, and the light-hitting Swede seemed an ideal opponent.

The fight, on July 6, 1947, at Stockholm's Råsunda Stadium, drew the largest gate in Swedish sports history, despite the prospective mismatch. Thirty thousand hysterical Swedes watched as Tandberg boxed his way to a shocking majority decision victory that cost the American his title shot. The *New York Times* called it "the biggest upset in eleven years ... since Max Schmeling knocked out Joe Louis in 1936."

The scenario sounds remarkably similar to the events of 1958: an unexpected upset of a top contender at the hands of a relatively unknown Swede. But if Ingo's win over Machen forced a showdown with the champ, then Tandberg was no Ingo. In his dressing room after the fight, the taciturn Tandberg quashed talk of a Tandberg-Louis match. "I think Louis is too big for me," he told reporters, with typical Swedish effacement.

Instead, Tandberg headed to America without Ahlquist, and lost to top contender Joey Maxim at Madison Square Garden. It was Maxim who would get the title shot (against Ezzard Charles, in 1951).

Tandberg fought for Ahlquist one more time, in August of 1949 against number-two contender Jersey Joe Walcott. The fight drew a record 45,000 spectators to Råsunda. But alas, Jersey Joe kayoed Tandberg in the fifth round, and in less than two years Walcott would beat Charles for the title.

The bout against Jersey Joe was Tandberg's last. He retired with a record of 23–6–1, a legend in Sweden, perhaps, but in the end, just another European heavyweight who landed short of the dream.

Meantime, Ahlquist had been keeping an eye on this Johansson kid for several years, but he waited until Ingemar turned eighteen in the fall of 1950 before agreeing to a formal partnership. They took to each other immediately, this undereducated roughneck kid and the middle-aged millionaire unwilling to relinquish his crazy dream of a Swedish world champion. Because Ahlquist was never financially dependent on boxing—his magazine empire saw to that—he was exceedingly generous with his fighters. While most managers routinely took a third of a boxer's purse plus expenses, for example, Ahlquist received an "advisor's" salary, and took not a dime from Ingo's purses. It was the start of one of the most mutually beneficial partnerships in the history of the sport.

*   *   *

Edwin Ahlquist with Ingemar and Birgit, early 1960s (*Bilder i Syd*).

Like it or not, in the fall of 1958 the man with a stranglehold on the heavyweight title was ... no, not the champion, Floyd Patterson. It was his manager, the cantankerous, paranoid, eccentric—and, according to some, the slightly demented—Cus D'Amato.

It was D'Amato, after all, who chose Floyd's opponents. More importantly, he decided who Floyd *wouldn't* fight, namely, anyone with connections to the notorious International Boxing Club (IBC). As manager of the heavyweight champion, Cus had declared all-out war on the IBC.

The IBC was a group controlled by Jim Norris, a wealthy Chicago businessman with extensive ties to organized crime. Using unethical and illegal tactics—fixing fights, forcing boxers to hire its stooges as "managers," controlling arenas and fight cards—the IBC managed to exert near-total control over professional boxing throughout the 1950s.

Managers knew the score: if they wanted their fighters to advance up the ladder, they had to play footsie with the IBC. Norris wielded a virtual monopoly over the sport and managers bent to his will.

All except Cus D'Amato.

It explained why Patterson seemed to fight mostly modestly skilled white guys. All the top black heavyweights were in bed with the IBC. Tough luck for Zora Folley, Cleveland Williams, Eddie Machen, Doug Jones, and Ernie Terrell, but a stroke of good fortune for Ingemar, who, in IBC terms, was pure as the snow atop Sweden's permafrost peaks.

* * *

Shortly after Ingemar's victory party at Göteborg's Park Avenue Hotel, Edwin Ahlquist placed a transatlantic call to D'Amato in an effort to make Patterson-Johansson happen. But Cus wouldn't conduct business by phone. Phones can be bugged. He demanded that Edwin and Ingemar fly to New York, on separate planes, to keep the IBC off their scent.

Within days Edwin and Ingemar checked into a hotel overlooking Central Park. Cus called three hours later with instructions: *Just Edwin, not Ingo, and I'll send a driver.*

Ahlquist recalled the driver's "unnerving, mysterious, meandering" path to D'Amato's secret hideaway on Long Island, a private room in the back of a German-American restaurant. "Finally I sat face to face with Cus D'Amato, a short, white-haired man with narrow peppercorn eyes and hands that fluttered like lark wings as he spoke."

Cus immediately launched into an extended diatribe against the IBC. Ahlquist tried to steer the conversation to Patterson-Johansson but couldn't get a word in. An hour later the two departed with nothing of substance achieved. Not by Ahlquist, anyway. Cus seemed to be laying the groundwork for a return-match clause, to prevent Ingemar, in the event he won, from defending his title against an IBC-controlled boxer.

The next afternoon, Cus summoned Edwin and Ingemar to a private home on Long Island where the two visitors weaved past a pair of giant snarling dogs chained at the entryway. "In this town," Cus told them, "you have to guard against everyone." Once they were inside, Cus discussed the possibility that Floyd's next defense would be against Henry Cooper. Ahlquist had heard enough. Hadn't Ingo knocked 'Enery into next week? If this was D'Amato's ploy to force his terms on Team Johansson, it wasn't working. Ingemar stormed out in a huff and Ahlquist followed.

Despite Cus's cloak-and-daggery, word leaked to the press. On December 1, 1958, the following item appeared in *Sports Illustrated:*

> The most ruggedly handsome face to arrive in the United States last week belonged to the dashing European champion and incontrovertible No. 1 challenger. Johansson's journey was kept an elaborate secret from the press. He spent last weekend closeted with Cus D'Amato. The purpose of their meeting was to hold preliminary talks for a Patterson-Johansson fight, a fight which promises to rouse the heavyweight division from its moribund condition. Johansson is an ideal rouser, handsome to a fare-thee-well ... he whizzes about the Swedish countryside in a racy sports car and has a quiet enthusiasm for modern poetry.

*   *   *

The three met twice more, once at a remote summer cottage along the Hudson River, again at a private hotel suite in Manhattan (where Cus obsessively kept checking under the beds). Each time Cus dominated conversation with his endless ravings against boxing's evil empire. At one point Floyd himself was brought in, the first face-to-face between champ and challenger. When the two gladiators shook hands, Ingemar couldn't help noticing: "It was like shaking a lace curtain. He seemed ... soft."

After five meetings, the parties were no closer to putting the fight together. Edwin and Ingemar returned to Sweden without a contract.

Circa 1960, left to right: Cus D'Amato, Floyd Patterson, Ingemar Johansson, Edwin Ahlquist (*Kamerareportage*).

"Cus was a man of many sides," Ahlquist concluded. "All of them unpleasant." Even so, Ahlquist seemed confident Cus would come around. "There was a lot of money for Floyd and D'Amato in such a match, and Floyd's last championship farces had not been very lucrative," he reasoned.

And then there was Bill Rosensohn. The promoter had paid Ingemar a non-refundable $10,000 for the right to put together a fight with Floyd. The time was ticking on his 40-day option.

The turning point in the negotiations occurred in early January 1959 when D'Amato dispatched Jack Dempsey, former heavyweight king and Cus's newly-appointed "promotions director," to Göteborg. Cus was aware that Ahlquist and the Manassas Mauler were good friends. After dinner, Ahlquist recalled, as they took a "walk through town in the winter gloom, Jack billowing on his thick cigar," the men reached an accord: Edwin and Ingemar would return to New York, where a contract would be drawn up and signed.

* * *

Edwin and Ingemar flew back to New York. On this trip, however, Cus D'Amato made no secret of the Swedes' presence. Ingemar was officially introduced to the press during a special luncheon held in his honor on January 23, 1959, at Mamma Leone's Restaurant on West 48th Street. Johansson was sporting a navy double-breasted blazer that, according to Joe Nichols of the *Times*, "made him look like a yachtsman."

After schmoozing the press—"Johansson made a favorable impression, athletically and socially," Nichols noted—Ingemar spent three hours with Ahlquist, Rosensohn and D'Amato hashing out the contract's fine points. "All basic terms were decided," Nichols wrote. "Johansson intends to remain here until the formal signing. Although he says his father is his manager, he will sign all the articles himself."

The contract, which included a return-match clause, called for Floyd to receive 40 percent of the gross receipts against a $250,000 guarantee. Ingemar would receive 20 percent against a $100,000 guarantee.

The official signing took place at New York's Stockholm Restaurant. In attendance was Whitey Bimstein, who had helped train Archie McBride for his fight against Johansson. When Ingemar spotted boxing's most revered second, he asked him to work his corner. Bimstein accepted. For Edwin and Ingemar, Team Ingo's trinity was now complete: the father, the son, and the holy cutman.

*   *   *

And so all the pieces were in place for Ingemar's shot at the heavyweight crown.

Not quite.

Cus had managed to convince Ingemar that he needed to employ an American manager if he intended to fight for the title in America. Not surprisingly, there was no such regulation. So Ingemar, whose manager of record was his father Jens, signed a contract that not only named Cus crony Harry Davidow as manager, but entitled Davidow to 10 percent of Ingemar's purse, plus promotional rights to one fight a year. It was skullduggery worthy of the IBC.

Fortunately, the dirty dealings came to the attention of the New York State Athletic Commission, and a hearing to investigate the matter was held Friday, May 22, at commission headquarters on West 47th Street. Davidow, a beefy 47-year-old Brooklyn luncheonette operator, took the stand. One of the first questions asked by commission attorney Julius Helfand was: "Aren't you acting only as a stooge for Mr. D'Amato?" Davidow, who hadn't held a manager's license in over a decade, denied the allegation. "I asked Johansson if he was satisfied [with the contract]," Davidow testified. "He said he was."

Next it was Ingemar's turn. "I was told that I would have to have a manager acceptable to Mr. D'Amato," he testified.

Had D'Amato provided a list of available promoters?"

"No," Ingemar said, "only Davidow."

Ingemar told Helfand that D'Amato originally demanded that Davidow receive 33 percent of Ingo's earnings, and when Ahlquist and Ingemar blanched, Cus settled for ten. Further, it was revealed that a contract between Davidow and D'Amato obligated the restaurateur to split the money with Cus, 50–50.

The three commission members huddled for less than a minute before announcing their decision: the contracts were declared void, and Davidow would not be acting as Johansson's manager.

As the hearing adjourned, Helfand articulated the feelings of the New York State Athletic Commission and most of the boxing world in general. "I address myself to you, Mr. D'Amato," he said. "The things you've done in this affair are so rotten they stink to high heaven."

Freed from D'Amato's attempt at indentured servitude, Team Johansson could now turn its attention to the business at hand: winning the most coveted title in sports.

8

Grossinger's

As April turned to May, Ingemar had yet to secure a training site. When Edwin asked D'Amato for suggestions, Cus referred him to Rosensohn, who referred him back to Cus, who stalled and dodged the issue. All very classic Cus.

Meanwhile, with the fight seven weeks away, Floyd had gotten a head start, squirreling himself away in monk-like seclusion at his camp in Summit, New Jersey, thirty miles from Manhattan.

Finally, the New York Police Athletic League offered Johansson their gym on 10th Avenue in central Manhattan, featuring state-of-the-art training facilities and a boxing ring. Ingemar had no sooner settled in than a stifling heat wave hit the city. "It was sultry and difficult to breathe in town," Ingemar said, "[with] thick petrol fumes in my breath intakes when I ran in the mornings in Central Park."

Ahlquist called Rosensohn: "You must do something immediately. Not tomorrow ... *now,* or I go to the Boxing Commission and report you."

Five minutes later, Edwin's phone rang. It was Cus: "Eddie—I've found the place for Ingemar's training. We can go look at the site right now." They took a taxi to Manhattan's west side, to Hell's Kitchen, where petty thieves, big-time mobsters, and teenaged gangs have run amuck since the 1890s. The cab stopped in front of a huge demolition site, where a crew of workmen were clearing rusted husks of wrecked autos to clear space for Ingo.

"There's where you'll have your ring," Cus said. He seemed positively elated. "The location is the best. Here, thousands of people will flock to watch Ingemar train. You can charge three dollars to get in. We just want a third of the money. You can keep the rest."

Ahlquist stared in disbelief. "Cus," he said, trying not to explode, "this takes the prize. You want Ingemar to train in *this* rat hole? Then I

Ingo at the controls, moving the earth one shovelful at a time (*Kurt Durewall*).

have a suggestion. Let Floyd move his training camp here. Then you can keep every dollar you take in."

"Unfortunately," Cus told him, "Floyd's already made arrangements and paid in advance."

Ahlquist gave Cus an ultimatum: find a suitable outdoor facility or Ingo takes his gloves and goes home.

That afternoon Ahlquist received a phone call from Grossinger's, a resort in the Catskill Mountains.

* * *

It was known as the Jewish Alps, a one thousand-acre fantasyland where everyone was *mishpucha*, where the kitchen was strictly kosher, and, most importantly, where a good Jewish boy could meet a nice Jewish girl. *What? Not married yet, such a smart boychik? So this summer you'll go to Grossinger's, you'll meet someone.*

They built it, and they came. The Grossinger family opened their hotel in 1919. By the 1950s, at the height of its popularity, "The G" was probably the most famous resort in the world.

Open year-round, it welcomed visitors who enjoyed golf, tennis, dancing, horseback riding, bingo, cards, boating, skating, skiing (in 1952, the G became the first resort in the world to use artificial snow), and indoor and outdoor pools. In short, enough activities to keep families busy and singles mingling 24/7. Weekends featured big name entertainment in Grossinger's showroom: Milton Berle, Alan King, Henny Youngman and the like. An unknown Eddie Fisher, a former Grossinger boat hand, made his professional singing debut there in 1949.

Barney Ross was the first boxer to train at Grossinger's, in the spring of 1934, in preparation for his bout against World Welterweight Champion Jimmy McLarnin. (Ross would win the fight and the title in front of 60,000 fans at the old Madison Square Garden Bowl.)

Right from the start, boxing and Grossinger's proved a fertile mix. It was win-win. The resort provided the boxer indoor and outdoor training facilities, lodging, and meals. In return, Grossinger's received worldwide publicity.

Lou Goldstein, The G's legendary *tummler*—that's "social director," to the Yiddish-impaired—recalled the summer of 1951, when British challenger Randy Turpin trained at the resort for his fight against middleweight champ Ray Robinson. "We had reporters from all over the world. Headlines would announce, 'Turpin Takes Good Workout Today,' and below that, 'Grossinger's, New York.'" It was advertising no money could buy.

Resort-goers, meanwhile, thrilled to the sight of a world-class boxer, even if he was only skipping rope and hitting the heavy bag. If he was sparring that day, so much the better. Grossinger's roster included names of the Great and Nearly-So: Billy Conn, Lou Jenkins, Gene Fullmer, Max Baer, Joey Maxim, among others.

But by far the fighter most identified with the resort was Rocky Marciano. The Rock came to Grossinger's in the summer of 1952 to train for his fight against reigning heavyweight king Jersey Joe Walcott. Rocky would win that fight, the kayo blow an Ingo-like right for the ages. For the next three years the champ lived part-time in a cottage at the resort's airstrip. Rocky described it as "my second home." For his biggest fights, Marciano entered the ring in a satin robe with "Grossinger's" embroidered across the back.

*   *   *

The Johansson traveling circus added their names to Grossinger's guest list with their arrival on Friday, May 15, 1959. Ingemar, Birgit, Jens, Ebba, Eva, Henry, Rolf, and Rolf's fiancée Annette were lodged in a plush, roomy villa with views of the surrounding mountains. The large supporting cast bunked in cozy cottages nearby and at the main hotel. This included Ahlquist, Bimstein, Blomberg, sparring partner Lennart Risberg, Ingemar's personal physician Gösta Karlsson, and various members of the Swedish press.

"All meals in Ingemar's villa were cooked by Ebba," recalled Ahlquist. "Ingemar wanted things as much like home as possible."

Every morning before breakfast, Ingemar and Risberg, a promising light heavyweight from Stockholm, completed their roadwork, eight miles a day through rustic forest trails.

At 4:30 every afternoon, Ingemar sparred eight rounds in the outdoor ring, mostly with Lennart, and sometimes with Rolf, himself an accomplished amateur middleweight. Then Ingemar would hit the heavy bag, followed by a workout with a weird device that Ingo brought with him from Sweden. "It was called a slung ball," Whitey Bimstein told the inquisitive. "It had a 16-inch strap handle, hung from a bang board, and swung around in all kinds of crazy circles, like a guy bobbing and weaving." It proved perfect for preparing for Patterson.

"After a few weeks," Ahlquist said, "it was noticeably clear that Ingemar was in getting in shape, moving easily and elegantly in the ring."

A shot at the title: Team Johansson leaves for America, 1959. Left to right: Jens, Annette, Dr. Karlsson, Rolf, Ebba, Ingemar, Edwin, Eva, Henry, Birgit, Nils (*Kurt Durewall*).

Even so, American sportswriters were not impressed, and Ingemar himself was partly to blame. In his public workouts, Ingo refused to throw the right. Round after round, Thor's Hammer stayed hidden. Reporters grew frustrated, many of them downright skeptical that this Thor ever had a hammer to begin with. One reporter quoted Edwin Ahlquist thusly: "Dere is toonder in his right. You vill see." The writer then described the reaction among the press. "We all laughed," he said.

"I was called a Palooka," Ingemar complained, "a sham boxer who had cocked himself up to a world championship fight with a lottery win over Machen."

The criticism was getting to him. "The period in America became … so tough and troublesome," he said, shortly after winning the title, "that I don't know to this day whether I would have accepted the fight if I could have foreseen the difficulties."

In particular, *New York Journal-American* columnist Jimmy Cannon took especial delight in skewering Ingemar. A sampling from the Cannon canon:

Prepping for Patterson: Ingemar with his proprietary "slung-ball," 1959 (*Kurt Durewall*).

The United Nations should step in and prevent Ingemar being smashed to a pulp by Patterson....

Ingemar is a nice boy. I wish he could compete with Floyd in the Charleston instead of boxing....

He is so bad that I doubt what my own eyes have seen. I can't understand how someone who felled Eddie Machen can be so wretched....

> I like the boy. He knows how to behave to a man behind a counter in a big store and he boxes like a shop assistant, too.

It wasn't just Ingemar's refusal to throw his vaunted right hand. Boxing insiders didn't cotton to Johansson's seemingly cavalier approach to training. Prize fighters were supposed to train in a Spartan atmosphere of self-denial. "Camp should be for getting in shape, not for being comfortable," complained Whitey Bimstein after joining Team Johansson. "He should get mean and hate everybody, which doesn't happen when a fighter has it too soft."

Take Patterson's camp, for example, in rural Summit, New Jersey, an all-male enclave one reporter called "shabby and dilapidated." Here the champion lived in a barn Floyd described as "only a couple nails above a squatter's shack," where he shared a room, bare save for a record player and TV, with assistant trainer Buster Watson. During the weeks of training, Floyd ate mostly beefsteak and saw neither his wife nor his two daughters. In the ring, Floyd abused his sparring partners, going after them with fury, pulling no punches.

It was how boxers were supposed to train. Not like Ingo, canoodling with a gal pal and noshing on pickled herring and strawberry cheesecake. Every few days a new controversy swirled around the Johansson camp. Ingemar and Birgit were spotted on the Grossinger dance floor and the next day's newspapers screamed "Ingo Dances Away His Chances!"

One evening, Ingemar left camp for New York City, for a scheduled appearance on *The Steve Allen Show*. Afterwards, Ingemar unwound at the Lexington Hotel's swank Hawaiian Room night club, where scantily clad hula dancers shimmied and shook. "I almost went wild when I heard about it," Whitey Bimstein said, "but the next day, back at camp, he was real relaxed and looked good sparring."

Actor William Holden visited The G one afternoon to watch Ingemar train, but instead found himself entranced by the boxer's lovely quasi-fiancée. (Holden and John Wayne were co-starring in United Artists' newly released feature film *The Horse Soldiers*, and the two had signed with ABC radio to provide pre-fight analysis—and to hype their flick.) According to one reporter, Birgit eagerly reciprocated the actor's interest. Holden invited the two to lunch and they accepted. Later, a reporter asked Birgit how she handled the delicate situation. "I looked into Mr. Holden's eyes," she said. "But I held Ingemar's hand."

On another occasion, Edwin and Ingemar lunched at The G's private dining room with the recently widowed Elizabeth Taylor, another of the many stars who were suddenly drawn into Ingo's orbit. Taylor brought along a small black poodle—one of her twenty identical black

Training at the G, 1959: Nils Blomberg, Ingemar, and Whitey Bimstein (*Bilder i Syd*).

poodles, handled by a special nurse—which slept on Edwin's feet the entire meal.

Later, Bimstein bumped into Ingemar and Birgit at the hotel casino. Whitey insisted that Ingo get to bed. "It doesn't look right," he said. "These people will start saying that you're drinking." Ingemar and Birgit left and hit the sack.

During sparring sessions, Whitey pleaded with Ingemar to throw the right, telling reporters afterwards: "Maybe 100 times I told Ingo, 'You won't be able to use it in the fight unless you work out with it.' He would look at me … maybe the dame would be there … and Ingo would say, 'No, Whitey. I am saving the right for Patterson.'"

But Whitey was keeping a secret. Late at night, after reporters had returned to their press rooms and taverns, Whitey would meet Ingemar, Lennart, Rolf, Nils, and Edwin at Grossinger's indoor gym, where a ring had been set up and blackout paper hung over the windows. Doors were locked and entry required a secret knock. Here, under cover of dark, Ingemar would throw the right. "Thor's hammer was at Grossinger's," Edwin admitted years later. "But not for public display."

*   *   *

The contract between Patterson and Johansson prevented the challenger from accepting a match before the title fight. Since there were no such restrictions on the champion, D'Amato decided that Patterson, who had not fought competitively since August of 1958, needed a tune-up before facing Ingemar.

British Empire champion Henry Cooper was a logical choice. He was IBC-free, only modestly talented, and easy to hit. But when 'Enery asked for too much money, Cus settled on the bloke Cooper had beaten for the title: the more modestly talented and easier to hit Brian London, the so-called Blackpool Rock.

Still, it was risky. If Patterson lost or suffered a cut or serious injury—small likelihood against the likes of London—the million-dollar fight against Johansson would disappear.

And so began one of the strangest episodes in the strange odyssey of boxing in the Age of Cus.

The fight was originally set for April 21 in Las Vegas. The promoter was D'Amato associate Cecil Rhodes, Jr., who had never promoted a fight but talked a good game, claiming to hold three degrees from Harvard, which turned out to be a lie. He was, in fact, another shady mountebank from D'Amato's bottomless barrel of shady mountebanks. Rhodes was, literally, a horse thief. It came to light that Rhodes was being sued by a breeder of trotters for $48,000. That was how much Rhodes agreed to pay for Lady Ann Reed, a world champion 3-year-old trotter. Rhodes got the horse but the trainer never saw a cent, and the mess wound up in court. In short order, Rhodes was replaced as promoter and Rosensohn was brought in to save the match.

Fight night was pushed back to May 1 (Rhodes had neglected to have tickets printed) and the site moved to Indianapolis, "to steer clear of gambling interests," according to the *New York Times*. NBC bought the home television rights for a bargain-basement $175,000.

On April 11, 1959, Brian London arrived in New York with wife Veronica; mother Agnes; father Jack, himself a former British Empire champ; and brother Jack, Jr. The party was met at Idlewild airport by D'Amato's lawyer Edwin Schweig, which in itself should have set off warning bells.

The press was out in force to cover the arrival, but the normally comically loquacious London—he once told a reporter he was "merely a prawn in their game"—responded to queries with a terse "No comment." Schweig whisked London away to parts unknown. All very mysterious, and for good reason: D'Amato was up to his old tricks.

First, he arranged for London to secretly train at his Gramercy Gym, then assigned him a trainer and sparring partners from the D'Amato stable. No one outside Cus's inner circle was allowed upstairs while London was working, lest the press catch wind, and apparently Brian wasn't astute enough to object.

Ingemar flew into Indianapolis on April 27 to hype his own upcoming title shot and to get a first-hand look at Floyd. Asked what he thought of London's chances, Ingemar's response—"My kid sister could lick Brian London"—quickly lit up wire services around the globe, the 1950s equivalent of going viral. The betting experts agreed with Ingo, making Brian a 10–1 dog. Even London's family expected the worst. A reporter asked Jack, Sr., "What will you do if your boy wins?" According to the *New York Times*, the old man "looked surprised, as if the idea never had even entered his mind. He thought long before he answered. 'Get drunk, I guess,' he said."

The bout, the first in Indiana history for a title in any weight division, was held at the Fairgrounds Coliseum and drew a mere 10,088 paying customers. Ingemar, introduced before the fight, was cheered lustily as he climbed through the ropes and shook each fighter's hand. Then he took a seat ringside, where he recorded his observations for a promised post-fight article for *Life* magazine.

The fight was an absolute dud, as both men stunk out the jernt. For eleven tortuous rounds the pride of Blackpool cowered and covered, barely landing a blow, while a ring-rusty Patterson let London hang on. Finally, with a minute gone in the 11th, Floyd landed a left hook that rendered the challenger 10-and-out. As the ref announced the result, "jeers, boos, and catcalls rent the air," reported *Ring* magazine, "while Patterson stood in the ring somewhat bewildered at the unfriendly display from the crowd." Afterwards, a contrite Patterson told a reporter, "I was terribly embarrassed by that fight."

* * *

Ingemar shared his post-fight observations in *Life's* May 10 issue: "I don't know after this how good Patterson really is because he was not pressed. If somebody push him harder we know more, [but] if Patterson does not fight any better against me than he did against London I do not worry."

Then Ingo waxed rhapsodic about one of the wonders of the natural world: "There is something strange about my right hand, something very hard to explain. It is almost as if it was not a part of me at all. I never know when it is coming. The arm works by itself ... faster than the eye.... Without my telling it to, the right hand goes and when it hits, there is a good feeling all down my arm and down through my body. It is a wonderful feeling. Something just right has been done.... It is something almost mystic."

The press had a field day with those remarks. Whoever heard of such? Talking about his right in the third person, as if it had a mind of its own! *Crazy talk!*

Soon enough, the Hammer of Thor would make believers of them all.

9

No Longer a Dream

Fight Day: March 25, 1959, a Thursday—*Thor's* Day. The weigh-in was scheduled for 10 a.m. at the hoity-toity Century Room at the Commodore Hotel on East 42nd across from Grand Central Station. The joint was hopping with boxing's usual mix of gamblers, press, and crumb bums. But this crowd also included a gaggle of young women, unheard of at a weigh-in, eager for a look at the young Norseman.

At 9:50 a.m. Ingemar arrived in casual slacks and checked sport shirt, accompanied as always by Jens, Ebba, Birgit, Rolf and Anette. Ingemar waved and winked at the crowd.

Fifteen minutes later, Floyd arrived in a white terry cloth robe, a dour frown on his mug and his eyes, as ever, cast down. Sportswriter Oscar Fraley thought Johansson looked cool as "a guy collecting butterflies high on a windy hill." The grim Patterson, by contrast, "looked like he'd be a bad risk wielding a broken beer bottle." The two fighters posed for pictures. Not a word passed between them.

When it came time for the boxers to strip to the skivvies, a fight official asked all women to leave the premises. The doctor examined both men and found them fit, the challenger at 196 pounds, Floyd at 182—his lightest weight since claiming the title.

It was announced that both parties had agreed to six-ounce gloves rather than the eight-ouncers Floyd had worn against Brian London. Advantage Johansson, as the lighter gloves figured to favor the harder puncher. (Today's heavyweights, by comparison, wear 10-ounce gloves.)

*   *   *

Ingemar returned to his suite at the Commodore. He hadn't eaten since supper Wednesday in order to appear as light as possible for the weigh-in, and he was starving.

Floyd, on the other hand, had another ceremony to attend. He changed into street clothes and rushed to P.S. 614. It was graduation day at his old school, located just blocks from Cus's Gramercy Park Gym where he learned to box. Patterson arrived just in time to present a silver loving cup to the winner of the school's Floyd Patterson Award for sportsmanship, then went through the lunch line with students and drank an extra carton of milk. Floyd hadn't missed a graduation ceremony in years.

By the time Floyd returned to his suite at the Hotel Edison he learned what Ingemar already knew: the decision had been made to postpone the fight until Friday night. The Yankee Stadium infield, where the $100-a-seat high-rollers perched, sat ankle-deep in muck, with more rain predicted.

"There was nothing to be done," Ingemar said, "except pick up the papers or look at the TV."

Shorn of a fight, sportswriters seized on the angle *du jour:* which fighter figured to be helped by a day of forced inaction? Most felt the agreeable Swede was constitutionally better equipped to roll with the tide. He hadn't fought in nine months, so what was an extra day? Besides, the rain gave Ingemar's traveling guru, Dr. Gosta Karlsson, additional time, as the good doc put it, "to supercharge Ingo's brain," and put him in a "killing mood."

Reporters had another 24 hours to dissect the fighters' opposing styles: Johansson the straight-up, one-punch headhunter short on finesse; Floyd the crouching, leaping combo-throwing peek-a-boo'er. The contrast provided no end of speculation.

Writers in search of copy found no shortage of aging pugs and ring denizens eager to opine. There was surprising support for Ingo.

Former light heavyweight champ Billy Conn told reporters, "When a guy has a right hand like [Johansson's], you've always got to give him a chance." Conn knew what of he spoke, having famously walked into a Joe Louis right in 1941, a punch that ended his title hopes while he was ahead on points in the 13th round.

Former champ Max Schmeling, the last European to wear the crown: "Ingo's right is the best in the ring today. He's smart and knows what he wants to do." It was Schmeling who advised Johansson to keep his right under wraps, unseen, until fight time.

George Gainford, manager of Sugar Ray Robinson: "Johansson will be the next world champion. He's like an engineer who has detailed blueprints and carries out his plans with precision."

* * *

Beleaguered promoter Bill Rosensohn, meanwhile, was fretting over his decision to postpone. Thousands of out-of-towners had come to New York for the fight, including hundreds of Swedes, many of whom had already booked transportation home. Ticket sales had reached $450,000—Rosensohn's break-even point. With his profit hanging in the balance, Rosensohn announced there would be no refunds. The response, predictably, was not positive.

TelePromTer Corporation, which was handling the closed-circuit broadcast, had lined up 170 theaters and arenas in 135 cities and was poised to rake in another million dollars. Postponement meant going toe-to-toe with NBC-TV's popular *Friday Night Fights* from nearby Madison Square Garden. The coast-to-coast broadcast—a live 10 round middleweight bout between Tiger Jones, an aggressive crowd-pleaser with a Ray Robinson win on his resume, against highly-regarded challenger Victor Zalazar—figured to siphon off potential viewers.

Rosensohn must have felt he was born under a bad sign, as Thursday evening the skies cleared and cool temps prevailed. A nice night for a title fight. Then, on Friday afternoon, Rosensohn watched in horror as thunderstorms rolled in from upstate and settled over the city.

* * *

Ingemar slept well Thursday night and awoke Friday morning like a man with nothing more pressing on his mind than yardwork. As the day progressed he began to tense. Later, he would recall singing softly to himself in an effort to "shut out everything which isn't concerned with the fight, everything which steals strength and concentration."

Outside, the unremitting rain doused the town and the evening air was clingy and still, raising the prospect of another cancellation. But Ingemar was ready for his moment, ready to fight. "The rain cascaded onto the asphalt but I didn't take any notice. The whole time I thought how wonderful it would be to get up in the ring and get it done. I longed to be home for the summer in Sweden."

About 9 p.m. the Johansson entourage left the Commodore for the short drive to Yankee Stadium. The rain stopped as they arrived. New York's finest led Ingemar to his dressing room, a canvas-enclosed cubicle in the stadium's catacombs, where he donned ring attire and shadow-boxed to loosen up. The fight was scheduled for 10:30 p.m. At 10:15, Dan Florio, one of Patterson's seconds, came in to inspect the wrappings on Ingemar's hands. "He had to say something, I suppose," Ingemar said. "Whitey quieted him with a few words."

The fight doctor arrived, took Ingemar's pulse, and check his eyes with a flashlight. "He was looking for possible doping. Of course I was loaded." Ingo was referring to the endorphin high that shot through his body—"as if I had armor around me."

At 10:25 a ring official gave Ingemar the word: it was go time. Just before leaving, he slipped a plastic bootie over each shoe, as the path to the ring was still slop. It looked as if this hulking, fearless Viking was wearing a pair of Momma Ebba's daintiest slippers.

Ingemar and Whitey stood in the gangway of the historic stadium. Open to the heavens, the cavernous ball yard provided balm to, in Ingemar's words, "the dead unmoving air beneath the stage." At exactly 10:30, Ingo and Whitey, accompanied by Blomberg, Ahlquist, and Karlsson, began their long walk into history.

* * *

The instant Ingemar climbed through the ropes and into the ring, a flash of heat lightning ignited the night sky. At ringside, Red Smith made a note of it for his next day's *Herald-Tribune* column.

Ingemar shadow-boxed and shuffled his feet to test the canvas as Floyd entered the ring with Cus and trainers Dan and Nick Florio and second Bubba Watson.

Ring announcer Sam Traub: "Zero hour has arrived.... One of the greatest international championship matches held in years. To my left, the undefeated European heavyweight champion, from Göteborg, Sweden, wearing black trunks, weighing 196 pounds, here he is— Ingemar Johansson." Full-throated cheers greeted Ingo's introduction. Then: "To my right, the great heavyweight champion of the world, from Rockville Centre, New York, wearing white trunks, weighing 182 pounds, our own Floyd Patterson." A tepid response from the crowd—

are they pro–Ingo? Or just fed up with Cus and his mollycoddled champ?

Referee Ruby Goldstein called the fighters to ring center and reminded the combatants that, as this was a championship match, there would be no standing eight-counts, nor would three knockdowns end the fight. "Will you shake hands now, not when you come out," he told them. "And good luck to both of you."

An instant before the bell Ingemar locked eyes with Birgit at ringside. *"Det år inte lângre en dröm,"* she thought to herself.

It is no longer a dream.

10

Patterson-Johansson I

Today, anyone with a computer can visit YouTube and watch grainy black and white footage of Patterson-Johansson, but I don't recommend it. At least not until you've had a chance to listen to the live ABC Radio broadcast. Hearing it today evokes a great lost golden age when, perhaps for the last time in our collective past, families still gathered around a radio to listen to a signal event in American life: a fight for the heavyweight championship of the world.

Behind the scenes at ABC Radio in the summer of 1959, a neophyte producer was tasked with lining up a color commentator for the fight, someone to complement the blow-by-blow account of veteran announcer Les Keiter. The producer was an ambitious, opinionated, nasal-voiced ex-lawyer whose areas of expertise were baseball, basketball, and football. He knew next to nothing about boxing and had never even attended a match in person until 1957. But the producer, itching to break into big-time sportscasting, hired himself as Keiter's color man. The producer was Howard Cosell, and Patterson-Johansson marked his first exposure to a nationwide audience. Improbably, within a few years (and after attaching himself to Muhammad Ali), Cosell would become America's most prominent sportscaster and the voice, if not the conscience, of boxing.

* * *

Yankee Stadium, Friday night, June 26, 1959. On film, announcer Les Keiter can be seen at ringside, right hand on the mic and left cupped to his ear, old-school style, as he sets the scene: "The menacing mystery man from the land of the midnight sun … the first Scandinavian to challenge for the big crown, the handsome, personable contender with the fabled right hand of mystery, the thunderbolt few have seen. And now the night's hour of destiny is at hand. An aura of suspense, spine-tingling anticipation, dominates the scene at ringside."

The bell rings for round one. Ingemar, circling clockwise, throws 13 jabs before Floyd gets off his first punch. Keiter: "Patterson bobs, weaves, to the left, to the right in that peek-a-boo style.... Ingemar just pawing away with that left. He couldn't hurt you with it, the way he's pecking away at the moment. A left and a right by Johansson to the chin of Patterson, crowd roars, no damage however."

This is a feeling-out round. Ingemar launches 96 jabs, many of them in retreat, most of them peck-and-paw, but they keep Patterson at bay and measure him for the right. Floyd, meanwhile, twice attempts to land his proprietary leaping left hook—the "kangaroo punch"—but fails to connect. At ringside, reporter Martin Kane notes that the champ is facing "something new—an opponent who could nullify his famous punching speed with speed of foot."

At round's end, Ingo sits and takes a cascade of water to the face from Blomberg's sponge. Whitey grabs a handful of Everlast waistband and pulls, the better for Ingo to breathe. "It's all shaping up," Ingemar tells them. In Floyd's corner, Cus tells Floyd: "Keep that right up!"

On the air, Howard Cosell takes over between rounds: "Caution the word to describe the first round. No material damage done to either fighter. Johansson slightly red in the nose and upper right lip."

*   *   *

Round two. Keiter: "Johansson pecks away, backs away ... a great retreating style shown to good advantage thus far by Ingemar. Patterson bobbing and weaving, never in the same place for more than a second or two. The champion in a crouch, the challenger in his upright style. Johansson takes a hard left to the head that bounces him off the ropes."

Patterson throws some quick combinations and lands a stiff left that reddens Ingo's mouth. Ingemar continues to move and jab, jab, jab—107 in this round, most of them picked off by Floyd's gloves. Halfway through the round Ingo throws a wild, powerful right that whistles harmlessly, ominously, past Floyd's head. Floyd lands a stinging left to the ribs, another to the chest, and in the closing seconds the fighters clinch for the first time in the fight.

At the bell, Floyd, perhaps out of frustration, does something totally out of character: he gives his opponent the Sonny Liston hate-stare—"the bad eye," Ingo calls it.

Ingemar returns to his stool. "How do I look?" he asks Edwin.

"Fantastic! How do you feel?"

"Beautiful."

* * *

Cosell, between rounds: "The first round ... could have gone either way. But there was no question about the second. It was Floyd Patterson. [But] tonight he's facing a strange kind of retreating style.... Patterson is calm, detached, almost indifferent as ever. Johansson looking a little more determined now than when he first came into the ring."

Round three. Keiter: "Patterson gave Johansson a long look at the end of the second round. Johansson with a left hook that lands high on the cheek of the champion. JOHANSSON KNOCKS PATTERSON DOWN! FLAT ON HIS BACK WITH HIS RIGHT HAND! PATTERSON'S HURT!"

"The blow landed around the bottom of his nose," Ingo said later. "If it had landed on his jaw the match would have ended at that moment."

Keiter: "...5, 6, 7, 8, he gets up! His knees are rubbery."

Patterson is "wobbling like a 3 a.m. drunk," wrote one reporter, like "a hypnotist's stooge," wrote another.

Keiter: "Johansson goes after him. Patterson's hurt. He turns away."

Floyd casually ambles toward a corner, as if he thinks the round is over. Trouble is, he's headed for Johansson's corner and there's an eternity left in the third. Belted stupid, Floyd turns his back on his opponent. "I couldn't let the chance go," Ingemar said. "This was a world champion, not a sparring partner." Ingo attacks.

Keiter: "PATTERSON IS KNOCKED DOWN! HE'S FLAT ON HIS FACE! The count is 4, he's up on one knee—5, 6, 7."

At ringside, Floyd's wife Sandra runs to the ring, screaming at Goldstein. "Stop the fight! Please stop it!"

Keiter: "Patterson gets up. He's looking away from Johansson at the crowd. Johansson gets him in a corner. Patterson takes a right to the chin! PATTERSON DOWN ON HANDS AND KNEES! THE COUNT IS 3, 4, 5."

Toonder! Yankee Stadium, June 27, 1959 (*Bettman/CORBIS*).

Jack Dempsey has seen enough. He gets up from his ringside seat and leaves. He wants to beat the traffic.

Keiter: "Patterson doesn't know where he is! He stands up. His knees are rubbery. TAKES A LEFT, RIGHT TO THE CHIN! PATTERSON DOWN RIGHT OVER OUR MICROPHONES! Falling over to his back! The count is 4. Patterson pawing at the ropes, 5, 6, 7..."

At this point, Floyd remembers thinking: "My goodness, that's John Wayne. Why am I looking up at him at this angle? That's when I realized I was on the canvas." Wayne was ringside, next to Cosell, to promote a movie between rounds.

Keiter: "He's up at seven. Johansson on top of him … shoots a left and a right, a left, and Patterson tries to tie him up. Johansson with a left … a right, a left and a right. Patterson is defenseless … what's holding him up? A RIGHT BY JOHANSSON … KNOCKS HIM DOWN, FLAT ON HIS BACK! The champion on one knee—4, 5, Johansson waiting for him to get up, 6, 7—Johansson waiting."

New Yorker reporter A. J. Liebling notices Johansson's chest hairs are matted with blood from Floyd's nose and eyes.

Keiter: "Now Patterson's standing up. He's wobbling, his legs rubbery. Takes a right and a left, a right—AND DOWN GOES PATTERSON! HE DOESN'T KNOW WHERE HE IS! His nose is bleeding—4, 5, Patterson kneeling, holding onto the middle strand—7, 8, 9. He barely gets up at 9! Johansson right on top of him, ducks away from a wild left … hits Patterson, KNOCKS HIM DOWN WITH A RIGHT TO THE CHIN! Patterson gets up, staggering…. WAIT A MINUTE! THE FIGHT IS OVER! THE FIGHT IS OVER!"

The stadium explodes. Knockdown timekeeper Arthur Mercante called it "the loudest, most sustained sound I ever heard—a thundering, reverberating cacophonous din."

As Goldstein raises the new champion's arm, ring announcer Traub addresses the crowd: "Ladies and gentlemen, referee Ruby Goldstein stops the fight at two minutes, three seconds of the third round. The winner, and new heavyweight champion of the world, Ingemar Johansson."

*   *   *

Cosell was in the ring while Traub's words still hung in the air. "Ingo," he asked, "did you think it would be this easy?"

"Well, in the first round I saw my right hand was going in, even my left hook," the new champ said.

"Were you surprised at how vulnerable he was to the right hand?"

"No, I knew my right hand was coming."

Cosell turned to Bimstein. "How about you, Whitey, did you think the boy was gonna do this well?"

"Never for a *moment* did I doubt it," Bimstein said, his voice crackling with elation. "I always *knew* he'd knock him out."

This must have been difficult for Cosell, who had grown close to Floyd over the past five years, developing, as he wrote in his autobiography, "an almost fatherly affection." Cosell and Cus had developed mutual admiration as well. Perhaps they felt a kindred connection: both were outliers, apart from the mainstream and distrustful of it. Howard was firmly anti–IBC and the one journalist Cus allowed into his tight inner circle.

Now, at center ring in Yankee Stadium, Cosell wanted a word from his fallen friend. "Floyd…. Floyd…. Floyd," he called. In Patterson's corner, Ingemar was thanking Floyd for the opportunity to fight for the title. Cosell, crossing the ring, intoned: "A gallant champion, ladies and gentlemen, down seven times…." Ever the reporter, Howard had kept count amid the tumult.

"Floyd," Cosell asked, "what happened?"

"Well, he hit me with a right hand."

"Didn't you see it coming?"

"Yes, but it was too late."

Howard, as was his wont, pressed on. "You went down seven times, probably a heavyweight championship record, certainly exceeding the Firpo-Dempsey bout. What kept you getting up?"

Before Floyd could answer, Cus leaned into the ABC microphone: *"A CHAMPEEN'S FIGHTING HEART!"*

As the broadcast wound to a close, in the background, one could hear Cus tell Ingo, "You are a good champeen." Then D'Amato turned back to Howard for the final word. "I think that Floyd Patterson will be the first heavyweight champeen in history to regain his title."

And then Cosell signed off for the night: "That's it from ringside. Bedlam as you can hear…."

*   *   *

The moment was too much for the hundreds of Swedes who had crossed the Atlantic in hopes of witnessing just such a moment. Between rounds, their organized cheers echoed as one: *Hej Sverige! Hej Ingemar!*—Come on, Sweden! Come on, Ingemar!—as if this were a World Cup soccer final. Now, with their hero holding his arms aloft, victorious at last, they lost all sense of Swedish reserve and stormed the ring, exploding through police lines, trampling press tables, upending Smith-Coronas. One Swedish reporter, his notes strewn asunder, merely laughed and left his post to join the joyous horde.

At ringside, a pale and shaking Rolf hugged everyone in sight. Eva sobbed like an infant. Jens and Ebba shouted for their son, who was now far beyond their call. The impassive Birgit was coolest of all. She may have wiped away a tear, but if it was more than one no one saw it.

At the center of it all stood Ingo, right fist raised to the sky. Climbing over the top ropes he shouted *Yahh!* at the heavens, brought his fist to his mouth, and planted a kiss on the gnarly knuckles of Thor.

* * *

A wild scene was beginning to unfold outside Johansson's dressing room, deep within Yankee Stadium. Police had been instructed to keep everyone out until the champ had showered and collected himself. Even Ingo's family waited in the airless, sweaty corridor along with the largest assembly of reporters ever to cover a heavyweight fight—a writhing, sweaty mass of American letters.

Oscar Fraley, the dean of UPI sportswriters and author of the 1957 best-selling FBI memoir *The Untouchables*, was first to gain entry. While the other reporters jousted and jostled, Fraley, who happened to be among the few who picked Ingo to win, approached cops guarding the door. *"Gut dag I ban iz vadder,"* he told them. The nonsense syllables sounded vaguely Swedish enough to fool New York's finest. He entered just in time to see actor Errol Flynn—drunk to the gills, fully dressed, and dripping wet—hugging a still-showering Ingo. How Flynn breached security is anyone's guess.

The new champ spied Fraley and threw a beefy arm around his neck. "You picked me and we look good, smart fellows, yes?" Fraley had to agree.

Outside, the pushing and shoving was getting dangerous. Finally the cops relented, and, in the words of one reporter, "like cattle going into a death chute we funneled into the steamy room." Ingo's family remained outside. A reporter spied Birgit and asked how she felt.

"Vunderful," she said.

Was she surprised he won?

"No. I saw him as he left for the fight and his eyes, they were confident."

What were his final words to you? The scribe's pen was poised to record the star-blessed lovers' dreamy sentiments for posterity.

"'You can go in the other car,'" answered Birgit.

* * *

In victory, Ingo was the Anti-Ali. Moments after winning the title by upsetting Sonny Liston in 1964, Cassius Clay bellowed to reporters, *"I shook up the world! I shook up the world! I MUST be the greatest!"*

In his own hour of greatness, the phlegmatic Swede sang a more restrained refrain. "I fooled you," he told reporters in the dressing room. His tone was one of bland, if joyous, assurance: "You thought my right hand was a fantasy. I show you. And I also show Patterson. We train to make Patterson back off from my left then catch him with my right as he come back. When I throw my right hand, it moves so fast no one can see it. When I hit him that first time in the third round I knew I had him.... I saw the opening and—BOOM!—there it was. He kept getting up. But I knew he could never come back."

What about that look, the bad eye, at the end of the second? "I gave it to him right back. It's not nice to do that ... so I try to punch harder."

Ingo's idol Rocky Marciano pushed through the crush to extend his hand. "It was fantastic," he told Ingemar. "I never saw anything like it ... so quick and so deadly."

Ingemar made his way to Floyd's dressing room. The conversation between combatants was brief.

"Are you hurt, Floyd?"

"No."

With that, boxing's new king excused himself. He had a victory coronation to attend, a blowout at the Stockholm restaurant for family and friends. As he arrived, an impromptu song broke out, a serenade to Ingo:

> *Ja kan han leva länge*
> *Ja kan han leva länge*
> *Ja kan han leva länge*
> *För hundra år.*
>
> Yes may he live long
> Yes may he live long
> Yes may he live long
> For a hundred years.

* * *

Floyd Patterson was standing in front of Mickey Mantle's cubicle in the Yankee locker room. The fallen champion's face was unmarked, but one of Johansson's blows had punctured an eardrum. D'Amato had barred reporters for 40 minutes until the fog had lifted and Floyd had showered and dressed. Now reporters began firing questions at Floyd, who whispered his answers to Cus, who repeated them to the crowd.

"I was waiting for him to do something with that right hand," Floyd explained. "I kept thinking, maybe he doesn't have a right, maybe that's why he didn't use it in training. He's a thinking fighter. He outfoxed me."

In the ring immediately after the kayo, Patterson told Cosell he had seen the right that felled him. Now, with his head clear, he admitted he never saw it coming.

Floyd had been heavyweight champion five days short of two years and seven months.

11

Delirium

An estimated three million Swedes, nearly half the nation's population, stayed awake all night listening to Radio Luxembourg's live blow-by-blow from Yankee Stadium. (Sweden's state-controlled radio, which frowned on the manly art of head-bashing, refused to carry the fight.)

By the time Patterson hit the canvas for the last time, it was nearly 4 a.m. in Sweden. No matter. In cities across the nation folks spilled into the streets. There were horns and noisemakers and shouts of *"Skoal! Skoal to Ingemar."* Bakers on their early morning runs handed out free buns and cakes and pastries. Total strangers hugged and kissed. It recalled the scene in Harlem the night of June 22, 1934, when Joe Louis kayoed James Braddock for the heavyweight crown.

In Stockholm and Göteborg, restaurants and bars stayed open all night, fortifying the masses with untold quantities of Aquavit, the 100-proof kick-ass Norwegian whisky that Swedes like to boast makes Russian vodka seem like *modersmjölk*—mother's milk.

In Göteborg, orchestras mounted on flatbed trucks paraded the streets playing a delirious mix of Dixieland and rock and roll. Fireworks lit up the dusky sky from the islands off Göteborg that comprise the country's western archipelago.

Amid the din, the voice of Thor himself boomed over loudspeakers; it was Ingo, in a live post-fight interview broadcast over Radio Luxembourg. His master's voice set off a new wave of celebration: more shouts of *Skoal!*, more Aquavit.

At the offices of the Göteborg newspaper, over a thousand fans stormed the doors as the new day's paper clacked off the press, as if the idea of a Swedish heavyweight boxing champion was so unfathomable one had to see it in print before it could be believed. "Those self-styled boxing experts in America have been stripped bare by devastating proof of their own incompetence," read an account from a Göteborg daily, which proclaimed Ingemar "the greatest athlete ever born in this country."

The frenzy was still in high gear 24 hours later when Göteborg's Liseberg Amusement Park, one of Europe's largest, threw open its gates and invited everyone to celebrate, no charge. This was no time to sleep.

As the celebration wound down, a bleary-eyed reveler waving a bottle of ale told a United Press reporter: "Not a bad blowout, but we're only practicing for the day Ingo comes home." He wouldn't have long to wait.

* * *

The day after the fight, Ingemar settled into a comfy chair in his Commodore Hotel suite and looked through a pile of metropolitan newspapers: The *Times*, *Daily News*, *Post*, *Mirror*, *Journal-American*, *Herald-Tribune*, *World-Telegram*. In all of them, vast photo spreads: Ingo crashing a right upside Floyd's noggin; Ingo towering over a fallen Floyd; Referee Goldstein, arms in the air, calling a halt to the slaughter; Ingo post-fight, hair matted, flashing the "OK" sign; Birgit planting a kiss on her warrior's unmarked cheek.

Hundreds of telegrams poured in from fellow Swedes, most notably from Secretary-General of the United Nations Dag Hammerskjöld, from Prime Minister Tage Erlander, and from Prince Bertil, the sports-crazed son of King Gustaf VI Adolf. Later, a friend from Göteborg dropped by and told Ingemar, "There aren't many sportsmen who get a telegram from the King." The King? Johansson had no idea. Turns out Ingemar had seen the wire and brushed it aside. "A lack of schooling in Latin meant that I didn't know 'R' meant Rex—King," Ingo admitted later.

* * *

Over the next few days the aftershock of the title change exploded onto pages of publications around the globe. Writers who had given Johansson no chance were suddenly thumbing through thesauri to find appropriate superlatives.

The *New Yorker*'s Liebling called Ingemar's third-round punch, the one that knocked down Patterson the first time, "as good, in its way, as the right with which Rocky Marciano knocked out Jersey Joe Walcott in their fight for the championship in Philadelphia in 1952." High commendation indeed, considering that a 2006 ESPN poll voted Marciano's bone-crusher the "greatest knockout ever."

Nat Fleischer, who watched his first professional bout in 1899, founded *Ring* magazine in 1922, and was on a first-name basis with every heavyweight champ since James J. Corbett—on the subject of boxing, he was America's *vox Dei*—was forced to eat crow, admitting: "We all misjudged his true ability. The Swede's victory was as clear cut as any ever fought for the world's most lucrative crown.... There was power in that right not even Joe Louis, Jack Dempsey, or Rocky Marciano could have bettered."

Covering the fight for the *Herald-Tribune* was Jesse Abramson. He'd joined the *Herald* in 1922 and was one of the few men retained when it merged with the *Trib* in 1924. Fellow sportswriters called him The Brain for his encyclopedic recall of sports facts, stats, and stories. Abramson called the third round "one of the greatest rounds in fistic history," adding: "There's been nothing like this since Dempsey worked over Firpo." He was referring to the legendary first round of the furious war between champion Jack Dempsey and Argentina's Luis Firpo on September 24, 1923, at the Polo Grounds, in which Dempsey knocked down Firpo seven times and Firpo returned the favor twice.

Sports Illustrated's man on the scene was Martin Kane. His postfight account reads: "The sports world has a new look today, a fine, delirious look, thanks to the virile right hand of a handsome Viking who scored one of the most stunning upsets boxing's heavyweight division has known.... The right hand, scorned by many a skeptic as a preposterous Nordic myth ... must go down in boxing's history texts as one of the best the sport has ever seen."

*   *   *

On Monday, June 29, seventy-two hours after the deposing of Patterson, Ingemar and Birgit boarded a plane to Florida for a brief vacation. At Miami International Airport, 500 fans swarmed the tarmac to greet boxing's royal couple. The champ, nattily attired in blue blazer and grey flannels, shook hands and signed autographs.

Ingemar and Birgit were accorded a siren-shrieking police motorcade to Ft. Lauderdale, where Mayor John Russell presented the champ with a key to the city. The couple then headed 11 miles north to Pompano

Beach, where they spent the next several days at the plush ocean-front home of another fortunate son of Göteborg, millionaire paper mill industrialist Gustav Von Reis.

Ingemar and Birgit were spotted in downtown Pompano—the champ sporting a spiffy red cap and plaid shirt, Birgit in a tasteful two-piece swimsuit (in plaid that matched Ingo's shirt, naturally) and cover-up—strolling among the shops like a couple of workaday tourists, where they bought typical Florida tchotchkes for friends back home.

One day they went deep-sea fishing. Ingo played a round of golf the next. Mostly, though, the couple dodged publicity and spent the rest of their time lolling among the sea oats and sand dunes, a brief respite from a crazy world where sudden fame and the dangerously addicting adulation of strangers would change their world forever—in retrospect, in ways they could never, in a thousand years, predict.

*   *   *

Ingemar's return to Göteborg, this time as world champion, was scheduled for Saturday, July 4, 1959. The city went all-out. Downtown merchants festooned store windows with flowers, photos, and boxing gloves dangling like precious baubles. Peddlers hit the streets hawking Ingo hand-puppets and miniature boxing gloves inscribed with the champ's faux signature.

At the local airport, a crowd of 6,000 delirious fans awaited their hero's arrival, their din nearly drowning the jet engines as the big plane touched down. Team Johansson stepped off the plane and descended the rolling stairway. At its foot, an awaiting dignitary shoved a bouquet of flowers into Ingemar's calloused paws. Conspicuously absent from the welcoming committee were representatives of Sweden's Social Democratic government, which frowned upon boxing as a brutish, uncivilized pursuit. Göteborg bigwigs even refused a request to declare Ingemar Johansson Day. It bothered Ingo not a bit.

On the tarmac an impromptu press conference broke out. Reporters peppered the champ: "How does it feel?" "What was it like?" When asked about the punch that sent Patterson to Palookaville, Ingemar said it was "the fastest I ever threw. My right hand worked as I had hoped."

Ingemar approached the crowd. Police held back the surging masses while the champ worked the 215-foot rail, shaking hands and accepting well-wishes. *Life* magazine, on hand to document the occasion, described Johansson as "the most famous Swede conqueror since Charles XII, the 18th Century king who licked the Russians, the Saxons, and the Poles."

If this were Hollywood, we'd throw in a scene where our Viking hero spies a wheelchair-bound man in the crowd. We'd have Ingo walk over, genuflect modestly, and hand the man the floral bouquet. Sure enough, that's *exactly* what happened.

Ingemar and Birgit then boarded a Swedish Navy helicopter for the short flight to Göteborg's Ullevi Stadium, where 26,000 crazed fans were stomping, clapping, and listening expectantly for the *whrrrr* of chopper blades. As the helicopter approached, fans leapt to their feet and pointed as one.

The copter circled the stadium several times, whipping the crowd into near hysteria before finally landing on the soccer field. A red carpet, normally reserved for visiting heads of state, led to a boxing ring mid-field.

Birgit was first out to wild applause. Then Ingemar stepped out. Those who were there had never heard such noise. It anticipated the Beatles arriving in Shea Stadium five years hence, except this was no shaggy moptop. Ingemar entered the ring wearing a finely tailored suit, looking for all the world like a preppie Ivy League Wall Street stockbroker. The comely Birgit remained at ringside, telling reporters, "The glory should be all Ingemar's."

In the ring, Swedish sports officials stepped to the microphone to extol the champ. The head of the Göteborg Sports Association told the crowd: "Now the world knows who Ingemar is. They know he's strong and not scared." Another speaker told Ingemar, "You won the world title and at the same time won a victory over yourself."

In a moment that must have seemed especially poignant to the once-shamed Johansson, the president of the Swedish Amateur Boxing Federation presented a championship trophy. At long last all was forgiven. Could anyone have foreseen such a turn after the infamous Olympic debacle?

As Ingemar waved to the crowd, loudspeakers replayed the radio broadcast of the fight and fans cheered as if the knockout were unfolding before them live. The event drew to a close and the sun began to disap-

Hail to the champ: The conquering hero returns to Göteborg (*Kurt Durewall*).

pear over the western horizon. But this was midsummer in the land of eternal sun and there was no darkness, only a sky of deepening blue.

*   *   *

The Göteborg love-fest was just the beginning of a joyous "royal tour" that figured to add another 250,000 krona—that's $50,000 U.S., nearly $400,000 today—to Ingo's burgeoning bank account. According to an Associated Press report: "People from the southernmost ferry points to the remotest Laplanders' villages under the midnight sun want a chance to see their idol in person. Being a businessman, Ingemar doesn't miss any opportunity. During the next two weeks Johansson will visit 20 places, shake hands, accept bouquets, and tell again and again what happened in the third round in Yankee Stadium."

Ingo's itinerary for Sunday, July 5, included a scheduled appearance at Stockholm's Grona Lund Amusement Park, where a capacity crowd of 20,000 had gathered for the event. Outside the gates hundreds more clamored for a peek at the champ. Over loudspeakers the crowd was treated to the latest addition to the Swedish hit parade, the "Ingo Cha-Cha-Cha."

The champ arrived and was hustled onto a makeshift stage on the amusement park grounds. On hand to greet him were the reigning Miss Sweden, Marie Ekström, and American blues singer Dinah Washington, who was touring Europe.

In the 1940s Washington had scored big on Billboard's Harlem Hit Parade, which charted America's top-selling "race music." Washington was enjoying her first mainstream top-ten record, as "What a Diff'rence a Day Makes" had hit #4 on the U.S. pop charts, making Dinah one of the first African-American crossover stars. She had befriended Ingemar and Birgit, and the three traveled Sweden together, Ingemar serving as her unofficial translator. (Dinah's saga would come to a sad end on the morning of December 14, 1963, when her seventh husband found her dead of a barbiturate overdose at age 39.)

*   *   *

Ingemar's next stop was nearly his last. He was scheduled to make a cameo appearance at a big auto race in the Swedish west coast town of Falkenberg, where promoters wanted Ingemar and Birgit to drive a souped-up 240 hp Ferrari on a slow-speed spin around the track so fans could gawk at boxing's newly crowned king and queen.

Ingemar had other ideas.

As soon as the couple were snugly belted in, Ingo dropped another Hammer of Thor—the right foot this time—on the accelerator. Tires screeched and spun and the Ferrari took off like a Mercury rocket, reaching speeds exceeding 100 mph. As they approached the final hairpin curve, a spot where even experienced race drivers knew to decelerate, Ingo kept the hammer down. The Ferrari went into a hair-raising skid before Ingemar instinctively hit the brakes.

"The crowd gasped and tensed for an impending crash," reported the AP. Somehow, the car slid through the turn and around the curve before straightening out and braking to a stop. Birgit emerged white faced and ashen. "Ingo himself," the AP noted, "who does not easily lose his composure, was pale and shaken for a brief spell." The next day, newspapers around the globe headlined "Ingo's Brush with Death."

The next weeks must have seemed a blur. In the town of Uppsala, 45 miles north of Stockholm and site of the largest educational institution in Scandinavia, Uppsala University, Ingemar's appearance attracted 7,000 admirers. Three thousand showed up at the small east coast fishing port of Osthammer.

At each stop Johansson would pocket a cool $1,000, then he and Rolf would spar a few rounds, the champ mostly flicking out the left and keeping the right silent. Afterwards, Ingemar would answer the inevitable questions about that mystic right, the hand that made skies rumble. "No one in the world can stand up to it, it is impossible," he would say. "I do not know myself when it fires. The right feels an opening even before I see it myself. It goes by itself and afterwards I thank God for it and head for my corner."

The obligatory tour of his homeland over, the new champ would soon be making international headlines by challenging the sport's most pernicious opponent: the organized crime elements that had controlled boxing for decades.

12

Fighting the Fight Mob

If there's not a hall of Fame for bad predictions, there should be. There would be a wing for British Prime Minister Neville Chamberlain's 1938 declaration of "peace in our time" (Nazi troops stormed into Sudetenland the next day), and another for the Decca Records exec who in 1962 turned down four British moptops with this dismissive sniff: "Groups with guitars are out."

Honorable Mention would go to *Ring* mogul Nat Fleischer, who, immediately following Ingo's ascension to the throne, wrote the following: "The victory of Johansson brings boxing into a new era…. Henceforth we are certain there will be no more shenanigans, monkeyshines, machinations, with greed, jealousy, and double deals to thwart the progress of the sport."

Nat—seriously?

(To put Fleischer's prediction into perspective, consider: in 1959, Don King was just another Cleveland numbers runner, with only *one* murder under his belt.)

Still, you can't fault Fleischer's optimism. In August 1959, *Life* magazine suggested that Johansson might go down "in sporting history not just as champ, but as a crusader who helped clean up the boxing game." There was reason to believe it might be so.

Ever since Joe Louis retired in 1949, boxing had been dominated by Jim Norris's IBC, which had paid Louis $150,000 to retire, then signed the top contenders to exclusive contracts. Like any entrepreneur, Norris had other business ventures to oversee, so he left the management of the IBC to Frankie Carbo, former hit man for Murder Incorporated and still a mobster of no small repute, as his five arrests for murder will attest.

By the time Rocky Marciano (whose manager, Al Weill, was an IBC operative) retired in 1956, Norris's empire exerted near complete control over every fighter, manager, and venue in the game. Their web extended to the new frontier of television as well, where all three networks broadcast a prime-time Fight of the Week; the IBC decided who fought whom.

It was a clear monopoly, but Norris was too powerful to challenge.

* * *

Enter Cus D'Amato, the seventh son of a Bronx peddler who sold ice from a horse-drawn cart. In 1939, Cus and a partner opened the Gramercy Gym on 14th Street and attracted some of the city's top fistic talent. At first, Cus played footsie with the IBC. Gradually, however, he came to detest their dictatorial ways. Still, what was a guy to do?

Enter Floyd Patterson, who first met Cus in 1949 when Floyd was fourteen and recently released from a special school for troubled children. The kid wanted to box, so Cus taught him the D'Amato Way: hands up around the face, elbows tucked to protect the midsection—the "peek-a-boo." In 1952, the two traveled to Helsinki for the Olympics and brought home gold in the middleweight class.

Under D'Amato's tutelage, Patterson fought his first professional bout in the fall of 1952. The kid had championship potential; Cus could see that. But the old man saw something else. Floyd could be the means by which Cus might demolish the IBC monopoly.

Sure enough, Patterson stepped into the void following Marciano's retirement and won the world heavyweight championship by stopping Archie Moore. With title in hand, Cus could now choose to *avoid* boxers and promoters aligned with the IBC. But where to find an independent promoter?

Enter Bill Rosensohn, the Ivy League son of a physician, fresh out of the Navy by way of Yale Law School. Rosensohn combined a visionary entrepreneurial bent with a love of sports and created a company that beamed Notre Dame football games into movie theaters via the newest technological breakthrough: closed-circuit broadcasting. Soon he was working for TelePrompTer Corporation, the leading player in closed-circuit technology.

In August 1958, Patterson defended his title against "Cut-and-Shoot" Roy Harris at Wrigley Field in Los Angeles. (Floyd won via TKO in 12.) When the original promoter ran into difficulties, Rosensohn stepped in at the last minute and turned a tidy profit. When Bill asked if he could promote another fight, Cus told him yes, provided he could find another IBC-free opponent.

A month later Rosensohn flew to Göteborg for the Johansson-Machen fight. "My ambition was to get a hold of a guy who would take us both to the championship of the world," Rosensohn told reporters. "After seeing Johansson in action, I felt I had found him."

Now, in the immediate aftermath of Johansson's stunning victory, the Boy Promoter was riding high. The press heralded Rosensohn as the sport's "white knight" and lauded him for eschewing the shady Cauliflower Alley regulars, and for bringing in new blood like West Point executive Joe Cahill, hired to handle publicity. "I'm out to give boxing a much needed clean new look," Rosensohn proclaimed, "[and] ... to bring honesty back into boxing."

After a decade of IBC totalitarianism, after five years of D'Amato dodging top contenders, Rosensohn seemed like the savior the sport needed. At his side strode the mighty Johansson, the one fighter beholden to no man or organization.

*   *   *

It was a short new era.

Mere weeks into Johansson's reign, sordid details began to emerge. It seemed that while Ingemar had been merrily sparring and dancing and reducing Grossinger's inventory of pickled herrings, another drama was unfolding, with the action, as in ancient Greek theater, occurring off stage. Not surprisingly, it involved Cus D'Amato.

Bill Rosensohn flew to Göteborg as sole owner of Rosensohn Enterprises. His contract with Johansson gave him 40 days to put the Patterson fight together or lose money already invested. All he needed was D'Amato's signature, but the clock was ticking and Cus, master manipulator, was holding out.

A week before the scheduled fight, a desperate Rosensohn caved to D'Amato's demands and secretly signed two documents. The first relinquished all revenue from television, radio, and closed-circuit broadcasts from this or any future fights involving Floyd Patterson, to TelePromTer boss Irving Kahn. The second document surrendered two-thirds of his stock in Rosensohn Enterprises to a pair of D'Amato cronies: Tony Salerno and Charlie Black.

Göteborg, 1959: Promoter Bill Rosensohn, left, meets with Ingemar and Edwin Ahlquist (*Kamerareportage*).

Salerno, also called Fat Tony (but not to his face), was the infamous consigliere of the Genovese crime family and boss of a $50 million numbers racket. Charlie Black was the alias of connected ex-con and bookie Charles Antonucci.

"Rosensohn had no choice," according to Peter Heller, author of *Bad Intentions*, the definitive discourse on D'Amato's devious dealings. "It was either sign over two-thirds of the promotion or lose the fight completely."

The Boy Promoter was in over his head, which was about to get lopped off entirely. Six weeks after the fight, Rosensohn received a telegram from Salerno's attorney Vincent Velella, informing him that Black and Salerno had appointed Kahn as chairman of the board of Rosensohn Enterprises. Rosensohn, squeezed out of his own company, promptly resigned and sold his remaining stock.

"He was a nice young boy trying to do a man's job," Velella told reporters, "[but] he could not take orders."

Cus, it appeared, had replaced the notorious IBC with an equally pernicious syndicate of his own. When Rosensohn went public with his protestations, the District Attorney's office assigned him a team of detectives to act as around-the-clock bodyguards. You crossed guys like Carbo and Salerno at your peril.

* * *

Back home in Sweden, Ingemar fumed. He and Edwin Ahlquist had trusted Rosensohn to steer them clear of racketeers, gamblers, and thieves. Now, Johansson was having second thoughts about honoring D'Amato's contract for a return match.

With Ingemar ready to spill his guts, *Life* magazine dispatched correspondent John Mulliken to Sweden. When the August 24, 1959, issue hit the stands, there on the cover was the ethereal visage of Jackie Kennedy in pink chiffon and double-strand pearls, with her husband Jack, the presumptive Democratic presidential nominee, in soft focus behind her. But the dominating all-caps headline, above Jackie's Kenneth-coiffed head, screamed: "I FIGHT THE FIGHT MOB BY INGEMAR JOHANSSON."

Inside, Ingemar let it fly. "We have heard a lot of very crooked things in American boxing, but we never realized [it] could be so bad," he told Mulliken. Ingo spelled out step-by-step the hostile takeover of Rosensohn Enterprises by Cus and his henchmen: "I'm disgusted and mad ... at a group of people in American boxing who are making deals behind my back.... I feel that I am being robbed. I understand why I have not yet received one cent for the Patterson fight—the contract calls for delayed payment. But.... I can't even get an accurate accounting of what I might receive.... I have a feeling that if I should lose a second Patterson fight, with the same people running it, I would not receive a cent for that fight either."

Ingo revealed to Mulliken that he had received lucrative offers to break his return bout clause with Patterson: a cool million to fight Archie Moore, a half-mill to take on Roy Harris. In the end, however, "the man I am going to fight is Floyd Patterson. I have given my word to fight him and I keep my word." In return, the new champion voiced demands of his own. "I must have my money in a bank in my name before I come to America," he said, "[and] a good explanation of who is promoting the next fight. I can't fight Patterson and the fight mob, too."

Ingo's outrage produced results. In September 1959, the New York State Athletic Commission launched a month-long investigation into the machinations surrounding the fight. Hearings were held, 800 pages of testimony taken, and penalties meted out. In the end, D'Amato's manager's license was revoked, and Charles Antonucci, aka Charlie Black, was barred from promoting, or even *attending*, another fight in the state of New York.

* * *

Ingemar Johansson vs. Rocky Marciano: it's one of the more intriguing what-if's in boxing history. How close it came to actually happening is speculation, but one thing is certain: within days of Johansson's victory over Patterson, the Brockton Blockbuster was thinking comeback.

"There is no sense fooling around with you, I've been thinking of a comeback," Marciano told journalist Jimmy Breslin in July 1959. "If there's one thing I love, it's a fight. But the first thing I have to do is lose some weight. Sure the money is important. But there's more to it … it's the glory, making it back. I could be the only one."

Rocky had already arranged for a boxing ring to be set up at the Cape Cod resort he planned to use as a training site. He began daily roadwork to shed thirty-plus pounds of easy living, and even enlisted trainer Lou Duva to work his corner come fight night.

Johansson-Marciano, in Breslin's opinion, "would probably set an all-time financial record for boxing." According to Duva, Rocky had been offered $1.4 million to fight Ingo. And despite Rocky's claim that it was glory, not bucks that drove him, he'd recently taken a blow to his bottom line. A sketchy mook from the old neighborhood, known as Jimmy Potatoes, had convinced Rocky to invest a substantial sum in a potato farm in Florida, and an early, unexpected frost wiped them out.

"Marciano has completely sold himself on a comeback," Breslin concluded, "[but] wants to keep the story quiet until the weight comes off and his family, particularly his wife Barbara, is ready to go along with it." Rocky must have figured the surest way to keep a plan under wraps was to share it with the self-promoting, hard-drinking, bombastic Breslin.

Next day, the story was all over the news.

Boxing Illustrated made it their month's cover story, devoting five pages to it, including five artfully rendered illustrations showing Rocky pummeling Ingo to a pulp. The article, titled "My Plan to Beat Johansson" and purportedly written by Marciano, told readers how he wanted to be "the guy who brings the title back to America, where it belongs," and how he'd watched Ingemar spar at Grossingers, thoroughly unimpressed.

"Ingo is not tough," he wrote. "I can name a dozen guys nobody ever heard of around Brockton who would kill Johansson in a street brawl." Rocky laid out the strategy he'd use, which boiled down to bull-rushing Ingo and throwing rocks till he dropped. Rocky was never much of a strategist.

Contemplating a comeback: Rocky Marciano, with Nils, Ingemar, and Whitey at Grossinger's in 1959 (*Bilder i Syd*).

Reporters cornered Rocky's mother Lena. "I do not want my son to fight again," she said. "Yes, Rocky talked to us about a comeback when he was here last week and he knows how we feel about it. I never wanted him to be a fighter, so when he retired he made me happy. Of course it's my son's life. If he wants to fight again I don't know what I can do to stop him." Lena was famously boxing-averse. Not once did she watch Rocky box live, nor would she listen on radio.

Ultimately, Rocky trained halfheartedly for two months before abandoning the project. Even in his salad days, Rocky never enjoyed the rigors of training; at age 35, shedding the weight of four sedentary years had proven tortuous. Then there was Cus D'Amato's rematch clause, which bound Ingemar to Floyd like blood brothers and pushing Johansson-Maricano ever further into the future. And there was this: "I don't want to be remembered," Marciano said after putting the issue to rest, "as a beaten champion."

*   *   *

Until the late 1950s the craft of sportswriting bordered on hero worship. In major cities across America, columnists and beat writers tapped out glowing hagiographies on ballplayers and prize fighters. It was a symbiotic, if unholy, relationship: writers were granted access (and their expenses covered by team owners and promoters), while athletes received positive press, their peccadillos, if any, studiously ignored.

Arthur Daley of the *New York Times*, who wrote the city's marquee column, "Sports of the *Times*," was no exception. Daley was strictly old-school—he'd been with the *Times* since Gene Tunney was champ—and was still delivering party-line palaver. To read Daley was to believe that Babe Ruth had a tummy ache when he was benched in '23, and that The Mick was a clean-living country boy. In truth, Babe had a touch of syphilis and Mantle was an alcoholic womanizer. To Daley, who indulged a penchant for alliterative nicknames that reduced athletes to easily digestible turns of phrase, Ingemar Johansson was the "Smorgasbord Smasher," the "Valiant Viking," and the "Dimpled-Cheeked Swede." (And Cus was the "Machiavelli of Maul," while the introspective champ was "Freud Patterson.")

But even as Daley was pounding his Royal Corona into submission, the profession of sportswriting was changing, morphing into something that resembled actual *reporting*. By the early 1960s the movement had a name: New Journalism, coined to describe the immersive, hyper-real, gnat-on-the-locker-room-wall style of reporting.

The movement spread to other media. On WABC radio, the *sui generis* voice of Brooklyn attorney Howard Cosell made its nationwide debut in 1959 at the first Johansson-Patterson fight. No ball club lackey, in the pocket of no promoter, Cosell vowed to "tell it like it is." Hell, it was radio—the man didn't even need his toupee, for God's sake.

Even the *Times*, known as the Gray Lady for its staid, text-heavy appearance, joined the burgeoning vanguard, hiring University of Alabama grad Gay Talese, who began writing offbeat, insightful profiles. Talese developed a fixation on Floyd Patterson and devoted 38 columns to the enigmatic fighter.

In 1959 the *Times* added another New Journalist to its staff: Robert Daley, 28, a Fordham University grad like his ol' man—who just happened to be the aforementioned *Arthur* Daley. Robert bore a striking physical resemblance to his dad, but the similarity ended there. When the *Times* assigned Daley the Younger to profile the new champ, he approached his subject in proper New Journalism fashion.

* * *

Sportswriters who'd previously interviewed Johansson mostly stuck to the script, depicting Ingemar as a debonaire, witty, educated sophisticate—Hugh Hefner with a straight right cross over the jab.

Daley cut through the crap, the first writer to pierce the preciously crafted Johansson mythology. His in-depth profile, "Non-Ringside View of I. Johansson," appeared on Sunday, May 23, 1960. In true New Journalism style, Daley had flown to Switzerland to hang with Ingemar—and to write it like it is. When the two met for the first time over lunch at a crowded self-service cafeteria in mid-town Geneva, the reporter made note of every variance from the champ's media-created persona, starting with Ingemar's surprisingly soft handshake.

"According to his image," Daley noted, "Ingemar is a dapper dresser who trains in night clubs while wearing a dinner jacket ... amusing, subtle, highly intelligent, his refined face almost handsome. Little of this is accurate."

Readers who bought into the notion that Ingemar floated through life swathed in silk by day and velour by night were sorely disappointed by Daley's encounter. The champ showed up for lunch in an unpressed shirt, dirty leather jacket, unshined shoes, and—*egad!*—filthy fingernails. Ingemar must have caught Daley sizing up his cuticles. "There is something in the gloves," he took pains to point out, "which gets under the nails and I can't get it out."

To Daley, Johansson appeared athletic yet not especially graceful, with thick arms and shoulders that seemed ready to burst the seams of their vestments. Every time Ingemar moved about, Daley expected a table or chair to be upended.

"In photos," Daley observed, "his face appears unmarked, his features very refined. In fact his face is broad and heavy ... a boxer's face." The real Ingemar Johansson, Daley decided, was "a young roughneck" closer to his high school dropout, street-paver roots than the mainstream press let on.

Daley punctured the notion that Ingemar took training lightly. Before the Patterson fight, American sportswriters had perpetrated the image of Ingo as a nightlife gadabout. "Johansson's idea of roadwork is the samba," wrote *Los Angeles Times* columnist Jim Murray. Daley begged to differ.

"Every morning at eight he ran five miles and every evening at five he went fifteen hard, fast rounds," he reported. After that, Ingemar hit the heavy bag for three rounds—"clubbing it with his right until the noise could be heard across the lake." Then he skipped rope "at top speed for twenty minutes without stopping."

Unlike most successful prize fighters, Ingemar knew how to hold onto a dollar. Which is to say: the man was, if not cheap, then notoriously frugal. Johansson's Swiss abode was a nondescript furnished four-room flat in a working class apartment building. "Ingemar hated the place," Daley noted. Yet here the champ lived alone save for sporadic visits from Birgit or family members, so that he might avoid Sweden's avaricious tax code. And although Ingemar owned a sleek new Corvette Stingray, it rarely left his garage. Instead this International Man of Mayhem escorted Daley around Geneva in a clunky Plymouth Valiant because the Chrysler Corporation furnished him one gratis. Writer and boxer met several more times over meals, and each time, whenever the check arrived, Ingemar's meaty fists remained tightly clenched.

(Ingemar's penuriousness was already well known among Swedish reporters; it was an image Ingo himself liked to spoof. Once, Ingemar

127

met a group of Swedish sportswriters for lunch, after which the writers plumbed their pockets to pool enough coins to cover the tab. Ingemar reached into his jacket and pulled out a huge wad of bills and slammed it on the table, proclaiming: "*I'm* the guy with the jack!" The writers looked relieved. That is, until Ingemar stuffed the wad back into his pocket and exited, laughing.)

*   *   *

Daley found one aspect of Ingemar's public persona spot on: he did indeed have an eye for the ladies. While at lunch at the cafeteria, Ingemar rarely made extended eye contact with the writer, as he was too busy visually sweeping the room for Scandinavian tarts. "When he found one, he would try to get her attention ... and follow her with his eyes until she was out of sight."

On another occasion, Daley brought his wife to meet the champ. "My wife was quite a good-looking girl," Daley told me, "and Ingemar couldn't keep his eyes off her. I was asking him questions but I don't think he looked at me once. He directed all his conversation to her. It was quite amusing."

Ingemar was a wolf at the wheel as well. When the Valiant would stop in traffic, Ingemar would scan pedestrians in search of a hot little number. "He is likely to honk the horn at her," Daley wrote. "If she turns he gives a smile and a little bow."

Even while picking apart the Ingo Myth, Daley was hardly immune to the champ's considerable charisma. "His eyes are baby blue," the writer noted, "and his smile has a charming innocence. He smiles a lot and is easily amused by life." Daley was also impressed by the fighter's consideration for others, as when a Swedish photographer drove 250 miles to Göteborg for a photo shoot, only to discover a forgetful Ingemar had already departed for Geneva. To make amends, Ingemar arranged for Volvo to hire the photographer for a particularly lucrative shoot.

Daley asked Ingemar if he realized that, with a few more wins as spectacular as his last, he could go down in history as one of the great heavyweight champions of all time. Ingemar was far too pragmatic, too grounded, to consider the possibility. "I was much more worried about my fight with Patterson," he said, "than with [future fights]. My whole future was at stake then. This time my future is already made."

13

Pop Culture Ingo

Ingemar enjoyed a near-ubiquitous media presence during his year as world heavyweight champion. Below, a look at some of his more memorable appearances.

The TV Shows

WHAT'S MY LINE?

To Greatest Generation parents and their boomer offspring, the program *What's My Line?* was a staple of Sunday night television viewing. TV's longest-running game show aired from 1950 to 1967, and starred John Charles Daly as host.

Each program featured contestants with an unusual occupations—birdbath salesman, chimney sweep or the like—which the *WML* panel tried to guess by asking questions that could elicit yes or no answers. And each show featured a celebrity "mystery guest," usually an entertainer but frequently an athlete, for which the panel was blindfolded.

Right from the start producer Gil Fates recognized the attraction of sports stars. When *WML* premiered in February 1950, Yankee shortstop Phil Rizzuto was the show's first mystery guest. Over the years the list would include Ty Cobb, Satchel Paige, Jesse Owens, Arnold Palmer, Ted Williams, Mickey Mantle, Joe DiMaggio, Archie Moore, and Sugar Ray Robinson, among others.

From today's perspective, it is easy to overlook the fascination *WML* held for viewers of its time. Today we know all too much about our celebrities. But in the 1950s and early '60s the show provided one of the few windows through which viewers could observe movie stars and professional athletes in the simple act of being themselves.

Five heavyweight champions would appear on *WML*: Joe Louis (in 1952), Floyd Patterson (1956), Jack Dempsey (1965), Ingemar Johansson (1959 and 1960), and Muhammad Ali (1965).

* * *

Ingemar's first *WML* appearance occurred on February 1, 1959, four months after knocking out Eddie Machen. The panel is blindfolded and Ingemar's occupation, "Heavyweight Boxing Champion of Europe," flashes across the screen.

Panelist Martin Gabel, the first inquisitor (and the show's resident sports nut) takes less than a minute to elicit the fact that the night's Mystery Guest is a boxer, and then asks: "Did you knock out an American in one round not so long ago? Are you about to fight next June for the heavyweight championship? Are you Ingemar Johansson?"

Less than ninety seconds and Ingo is outed, an indication not only of boxing's prominent place in the public consciousness, but of the sensational impact of Ingemar's destruction of Machen.

* * *

Birgit Lundgren appeared on *WML* two weeks before Ingemar's title victory, on June 14, 1959, all twinkly-eyed and demure in a skin-tight spaghetti-strap dress and diamond earrings, looking for all the world like Raquel Welch's younger, prettier sister. Her occupation was listed as "Correspondent for Swedish Newspaper." (Birgit was writing a column about her American adventures for the Swedish publication *Woman's World*).

The panel is clearly dazzled by the young woman's beauty, and there's an awkward moment when Gable asks the contestant if she's engaged. Birgit gives an uncertain, hesitant "No." That's all Gabel would need to figure out that this Swedish babe was the squeeze of boxing's top contender, as their photos, along with stories of their quasi-engagement, had been all over the news for months.

Curious viewers will find the clip on YouTube. (Watch for the comical exchange between Gable, clearly taken by Birgit's charms, and his wife, fellow panelist Arlene Francis.)

* * *

Ingemar's second stint on *WML* took place on June 19, 1960, the night before his rematch at the Polo Grounds with Floyd Patterson.

Ingemar takes his seat to wild applause. He's sweating profusely, forcing him to constantly dab his face with a handkerchief. (Rolf believes his brother may have been experiencing side effects from pain medication prescribed by Dr. Karlsson, to disastrous effect the following night.)

It takes the blindfolded panel slightly less than one minute to guess Ingo's identity.

Panelist Eamon Andrews: "Have you anything to do with sport?"

Ingemar: "Oui, Monsieur."

Arlene Francis: "Are you involved in the big fight tomorrow night?"

Ingemar (sheepishly): "Yes."

Francis: "Well, we all know who this is."

Several panelists, in unison: *"Ingo!"*

Francis: "Why aren't you home in bed?"

Fair question, as it's nearly 11 p.m. and Ingo's Monday To-Do List is rather full. Before Ingemar can answer, Daly informs the viewers that Gene Tunney, the night before his first fight with Jack Dempsey, flew from Stroudsburg to Philadelphia. "It was said that this proved he was the coolest man that had ever been in the ring, that he had ice water in his veins," Daly said. "I would submit that Ingo is about as cool as they come, with the championship fight tomorrow night, and here he is on *What's My Line?*"

Ingemar exits stage right and shakes hands with the panel, as per the show's custom. He bows courteously to Arlene and Dorothy Kilgallen.

One can't help but notice the ever-randy Dorothy oogling Ingo, up and down, on his way out.

* * *

I'VE GOT A SECRET

I've Got a Secret was a popular prime time program that ran on CBS from 1952 to 1967. Among game shows, only *What's My Line?* had a longer run.

While post–1960 episodes have aired in recent years on Game Show Network, the 1952–1960 shows have been permanently shelved, probably because each contestant was awarded a carton of Winston cigarettes, courtesy of the show's sponsor, as a parting gift. It's a shame, and not because Winstons taste good like a cigarette should. It's because a lot of compelling television remains unseen. Like the evening of Wednesday, May 13, 1959, for example.

As the show opens, host Gary Moore (toking a Winston) introduces the panel: Bess Myerson, Henry Morgan, Betsy Palmer, and Bill Cullen. Their task is to ferret out, via questioning, a contestant's "secret," usually something unusual or impressive about that person. Contestants receive twenty dollars every time the questioning passes to the next panelist, so the top prize is eighty dollars—and a carton of Winstons.

Moore calls out the first contestant and two men walk out. The first man, the older of the two, doesn't speak English, so he has brought along an interpreter who is a bit taller and thicker through the chest and shoulders and sports black-framed Clark Kent glasses. He's wearing a trim blazer with an embroidered crest.

The older gentleman whispers his secret to Gary Moore, and the following words are superimposed on the screen for viewers at home: "My son will fight Floyd Patterson next month for the heavyweight championship of the world."

The panelists don't know it, but the older gentleman is Jens Johansson, and the interpreter is his son Ingemar.

Moore tells the panel the secret concerns "something that is going to happen." Bess Myerson, a former Miss America, gets first crack. Two of her queries—"Will it happen in the near future?" and "In the city of New York?"—receive a yes.

Comedian Henry Morgan is next. "Mr. Interpreter," he asks, "what language are you speaking?"

Gary Moore: "Say something aloud in your native tongue, like 'Good evening, it is nice to be here.'"

"God kvall," Ingemar replies, *"det är trevligt att vara hår."*

Morgan guesses the language correctly and appears to be on the right track when he asks if there is a prize at stake. Father and son confer and agree, yes, there is a prize at stake.

"Since you're Swedish," Morgan asks, "does it have anything to do with the Nobel Prize?"

Don't these people read the sports pages?

Finally, actress Betsy Palmer elicits a yes with, "Does it have anything to do with sports?" We hear Morgan, off-camera, tell Palmer, "Ingemar Johansson."

Undaunted, Palmer presses forth: "Does it have anything to do with water?"

Good thinking, Betsy.

Moore: "That's $60 down and $20 to go. We come to Bill Cullen, who for the last five minutes had been sitting there like the cat that ate the canary."

Now the viewer is certain the secret is out. There is a reason why Cullen, whose occupation could best be described as Professional Game Show Personality, is always the last inquisitor. He's clearly the cleverest of the bunch. Put him first and the entire show would be over in six minutes.

Cullen: "I noticed the golf jacket on the interpreter. Does it have anything to do with golf?"

Jeesh, Bill.

Cullen: "Does it have anything to do with the heavyweight championship fight?"

Finally.

Cullen: "It has something to do with Ingemar *Johnson*. You are going to second Ingemar Johnson in the fight?"

Cullen is clearly not a fight fan.

Mercifully, the buzzer sounds, and Moore unveils the secret: Jens's son will fight for the title, and, oh by the way, his interpreter is the fighter himself. The big reveal leaves the panel slack-jawed in wonder.

Moore concludes the segment by wishing Ingemar luck, and then hands Jens his booty for stumping the panel: $80 cash and two cartons of Winstons.

* * *

THE *DINAH SHORE CHEVY SHOW*

The public has always been a sucker for a beefy, bruising pug with a hidden sensitive side, which may explain why Ingemar's singing skills were much in demand during his brief title reign.

Ingemar made his American singing debut on the *Dinah Shore*

133

Chevy Show on October 4, 1959, an appearance that marked most viewers' first up-close-and-personal encounter with the new champ. By all accounts it was a winning performance.

On a stool, center stage, in front of a live studio audience and millions of home viewers, Ingemar sang a melancholy Swedish folk tune to Dinah and carried it off like a pro. To the surprise of many, the boxer could not only sing, but knew how to sell a song, as well—a Tony Bennett in Everlasts.

"That was beautiful," Shore told him. "How about doing something together?

With Dinah Shore, 1960 (*Bilder i Syd*).

134

"Good," Ingemar answered. "Your singing always knock me down."
He blew the line. He should have said "knocks me *out.*" But it was funny
anyway, coming from Ingo. Then he and Dinah sang an up-tempo duet
in Swedish.

New York Times TV critic Jack Gould described the champ as "an
engaging stage personality with an attractively shy and diffident manner,"
and added, "thanks to the sincerity and simplicity of his approach he
projected a high degree of boyish charm."

*   *   *

THE KILLERS

Three months after winning the world heavyweight championship,
Ingemar signed to appear as the washed-up boxer Ole Anderson in a
television adaptation of Ernest Hemingway's short story "The Killers."
The drama, which aired Thursday, November 19, 1959, and starred Dean
Stockwell as Nick Adams, marked the premiere of CBS's 90-minute
prime-time *Buick-Electra Playhouse.*

Hemingway crony A.E. Hotchner penned the teleplay, in which two
hit men arrive in a small town intent upon rubbing out Anderson, aka
the Big Swede, for failing to take a dive in the ring.

"Ingo is a natural for us," Hotchner told reporters prior to filming.
"We needed a Swede, so we got the biggest Swede in the fight game."
Director Tom Donovan added: "He's perfect for the part. All he has to
do is lie down on a bed and be a Swede."

There was a bit more to it than that. This was, after all, Ingemar's
first foray into television as a dramatic actor. In Hemingway's story,
Anderson simply lies in bed and awaits his fate, despite a warning from
Adams. But CBS had 90 minutes to fill, so Hotchner added boxing scenes
where Ole double-crosses the mob. (Messin' with the mob... no wonder
the part appealed to Ingo.)

Fight scenes were shot at Stillman's, where peeling plaster and
tobacco-stained floors provided a touch of authenticity. Playing the part
of Ole's opponent was real-life boxer Henry Willitsch, better known as
the only fighter ever to have kayoed himself. It happened September 12,
1959, in a bout against Dominican heavyweight Bartolo Soni. In the
third round Willitsch threw a haymaker that missed, but with such feroc-

ity that he went flying through the ropes, striking his head on the ring apron and knocking himself out.

On Friday, November 20, the TV critics had their say. It wasn't pretty. Fred Danzig of the UPI called the program "incredibly bad." There was plenty of blame to go around, Danzig wrote. He didn't care for Stockwell's performance, Donovan's direction, Hotchner's word-smithery—he didn't even like the musical background. "I'd say the only one who benefited from the show was Johansson," Danzig opined. "Having displayed considerable charm as a singer on a Dinah Shore show, he now seems to have some ability as an actor."

Danzig continued: "Ingo handled his lines with proper feeling, but his movements were unnatural and indicated that director Donovan had over-coached him." That was an assessment Ingemar could relate to. In boxing, it's never the fighter's fault. The problem was his trainer, his manager, he was doped, the sun was in his eyes, he was over-coached by the director.

Red Smith, cheeky columnist for the *New York Herald Tribune*, called Ingemar "the Swedish Brando," and praised him for doing "a first rate job in a dreadful parody." Smith added: "Even before his histrionic talent was revealed, Johansson was recognized as a man of many gifts. A business and industrial tycoon, an agile and tireless operative on the ballroom floor, and a peerless knight ever at the beck of damsels in distress. Now on top of everything else we learn that this Viking demigod is an artist of sensitivity and taste, a Scandinavian Booth with sex appeal. When was there ever a heavyweight champion like this?"

*   *   *

Movies and Song

48 HOURS TO LIVE

Ingemar was quick to parlay his sudden celebrity into a bit part in a feature film, *48 Hours to Live*, released in the fall of 1959.

The movie, written and directed by Swedish-born actor Peter Bourne, starred Anthony Steel, who had been a leading British movie star in the early 1950s. Of late he'd fallen on fallow times, having just divorced Swedish sexpot Anita Ekberg after three years of marriage, during which she claimed Steel was a physically abusive drunk. Steel's career needed a boost, and who better to inject a bit of cool-by-proxy than the reigning heavyweight champ?

The plot involves a reporter named Mike Gibson (Steel) who travels to Sweden via steam ship to interview a physicist about certain nuclear secrets. But alas, an espionage ring kidnaps the scientist and his beautiful daughter. In the end—*spoiler alert!*—Gibson saves them both. Yawn.

The film was still in production when Ingemar won the title, so Bourne wrote a cameo for the new champ. Ingemar, playing himself, is on screen for exactly two minutes, but it's an engaging turn nonetheless.

As the scene begins, Gibson is strolling the deck and bumps into a familiar face. "You're Ingemar Johansson," Gibson says, in a burst of illogical exposition. "I'm Mike Gibson of the *Globe-News*. Are you going on vacation?"

Ingemar brandishes his fist. "Yes," he says, "I'm going to rest my right."

The two men talk boxing as a diminutive Swedish deck hand walks by and asks, "You guys talking about the Patterson-Johansson return match?" When Gibson replies in the affirmative, the swabbie has a tale to tell. "I'm a *personal friend* of Ingemar Johansson," he boasts.

Ingo (sounding impressed): "You *are?*"

Deckhand: "Sure! Ingemar *himself* told me all about the third round." Addressing Johansson: "You be Patterson, OK?" The deckhand pantomimes lefts and rights as Ingemar feigns alarm. "Look," the deckhand tells him, "I'm not going to *hurt* you."

Ingo: "Are you *sure?*"

Deckhand: "So then he saw an opening and—*phlump!* Patterson was down!"

Ingo: "I wish I had seen that fight. Well, so long."

As Ingemar exits, Gibson asks the swabbie: "Do you know who you've been talking to?"

"No, should I?"

"Ingemar Johansson!"

The deckhand's knees buckle as if struck by Thor's Hammer. "*Ohhhh...*" he groans, "I don't feel so good."

* * *

ALL THE YOUNG MEN

Ingo had proven adept at playing Ingo. But could he handle a more challenging role?

Shortly after filming *48 Hours to Live*, Columbia Pictures signed Ingemar to appear in its upcoming Korean War flick *All the Young Men*, starring Alan Ladd and Sidney Poitier. Ingemar plays the part of Torgil, a Swedish soldier who accompanies nine U.S. Marines as they defend a small parcel of land from a North Korean attack.

The film, written and directed by Hall Bartlett, was shot in Montana's Glacier National Park in October of 1959 and was immediately beset by problems. "We needed snow on the ground but no snowing coming down," remembers Joe Gallison, 78, the veteran actor who played one of the marines. "It didn't snow for weeks and we just sat around." The delay cost Columbia $25,000 a day.

Ingemar managed to keep busy, working out every day at St. Mary's Lodge. Gallison: "He set up a ring and had a heavy bag and a speed bag. He had a reputation for not training seriously. But let me tell you, he worked hard every day." Fortunately, Al Silvani, former trainer for Jake LaMotta, Carmen Basilio, and Rocky Graziano, had signed on as a stunt man and technical advisor. (Sivani would train not only LaMotta, but Robert DeNiro *as* LaMotta, for *Raging Bull*.)

Ingemar filled the rest of his time indulging his obsession with American westerns. He bought a pair of six-shooters, holsters, cowboy boots, and western clothes, and convinced Alan Ladd to teach him to fast draw. Ladd, who had shot to stardom in 1953's classic shoot-'em-up *Shane*, bonded instantly with the champ.

By 1959, however, Ladd's career was in free-fall. Dropped by Warner Brothers after a series of box office flops, Ladd had sunk into deep depression. His drinking and insomnia worsened and he'd put on weight. Now a jowly, old-looking 46, Ladd was no longer an attractive Hollywood commodity.

Beverly Linet, in her 1979 biography *Ladd: A Hollywood Tragedy*, credits Ingemar with bringing Ladd out of his funk, temporarily, at least. (Ladd died in 1964 at age 50 from an overdose of alcohol and sleeping pills, a death ruled accidental despite an apparent suicide attempt two years earlier.) "Having the young athlete around seemed to give Alan a new zest for living," Linet wrote. "The two became close companions." Ladd was so convinced the champ's life would make a compelling story that he offered to buy the film rights. Ingemar declined.

The role of Torgil allowed Ingemar to play against type. In one scene, Torgil sings a lilting Swedish folk song as another soldier strums

All The Young Men, 1960 (*Kamerareportage*).

a guitar. Another scene calls for Torgil to cry over the loss of a fallen comrade, and Ingemar turns into a pile of mush with believable ease.

Director Bartlett told reporters, "Ingo has a real future in the movies." Gallison thought so too. "He had talent, very natural and easy-going. Remember, the soundstage was our workplace, not his. But he was accepted very quickly as a member of the group, respected by the other actors."

When the cast wrapped in Montana and returned to California, Ingemar stayed for two months at the Ladds' ranch in Hidden Valley, just outside Hollywood, where he gave twelve-year-old David Ladd daily sparring lessons and boxing pointers. "My son," the actor said, "considers him the world's greatest man."

With shooting complete, Ingemar returned to Europe to resume training for the rematch with Patterson. "Johansson's departure," Linet wrote, "... brought Alan down to another depression." Despondent, Ladd offered to transform his ranch into a training camp for the upcoming fight, a plan vetoed by Edwin Ahlquist. Instead, Ingemar sent Ladd ringside tickets, and Alan and his wife were on hand at the Polo Grounds for the 1960 bout.

All the Young Men opened in August 1960 to generally poor reviews. Most critics cited the plot as cliché-ridden and panned Ladd's performance as wooden. At least Ingemar was spared. One prominent critic wrote: "Johansson's two basic expressions (faintly amused and faintly serious) beat Alan Ladd's range by one."

Of course, by the time *All the Young Men* premiered, Johansson was no longer champion, and advertising and publicity had to be revamped. Bartlett even scrapped plans to feature Ingemar in another film. "I wasn't aware of the fact that Ingo might lose," Bartlett said, apparently clueless to the vagaries of sport.

* * *

INGO ON RECORD

Johansson's dramatic and unexpected ascension to the heavyweight throne provided divine inspiration to Brill Building songwriters Russell Moody and Bert Carroll, the duo responsible for Elvis Presley's 1958 hit "Wear My Ring Around Your Neck." Within days of Ingo's victory the two had cranked out the ditty "Ingemar Johansson."

Recorded by Dutch pop star Johnny Lion and released on the Co-Ed label in July 1959 as a 45 rpm single, the record sold mostly in Europe and South America, where Lion was a popular touring artist.

The record begins, naturally enough, with an opening bell, while the enthusiastic din of a fight crowd is audible in the background throughout. And on vinyl as in life, Moody and Carroll's Ingo is both lover and fighter. After describing the winning knockout, Lion sings, "He kept his promise to his very best girl," and croons of the day when "he marries Birgit in Göteborg."

Over the course of the ensuing decades, most of Co-Ed's master recordings, including "Ingemar Johansson," vanished and were presumed lost forever. The tapes were rediscovered in 2011 in the attic of a retired recording engineer and subsequently purchased and digitized by Beach Road Music.

Today the song "Ingemar Johansson" can be downloaded on Amazon for a mere 99 cents. But consider yourself warned: the song's hand-clapping chorus (Ingemar Johansson's a mighty big Swede / He kept sayin', he kept sayin' / This right hand's all I need") is so indelibly infectious that you will be unable to get the melody out of your head for days, months, years.

Or maybe, *ever.*

14

Back to Work

Edwin Ahlquist wanted Ingemar back in serious training by mid–August. But there were *so* many distractions.

In September, Ingemar celebrated his 27th birthday with a trip to Detroit, where he and Rolf were met by their friend, the millionaire industrialist Jacob von Reis, who accompanied the brothers to Peoria to buy a tractor for the Johansson's construction firm.

Then Ingemar and Rolf flew to Hollywood, where the champ had received so many offers he engaged the William Morris Agency to handle them. Huge chunks of Ingemar's time were spent fulfilling his afore-mentioned movie and TV commitments.

Back in Europe, Ingemar engaged in a series of banquets and boxing exhibitions. In London he posed for a wax effigy which made its debut at Madame Tussaud's Wax Museum.

That fall Ingemar filed for permanent residence in Switzerland, "high above the tax line," in columnist John Lardner's immortal phrase. Not surprisingly, most Swedes felt outraged and betrayed. "Ingemar is seriously ill," the *Göteborg Post* charged. "He suffers from gold fever. Whoever is infected with this disease sees money in everything."

And those were the *least* of his distractions.

In mid–November Ingemar was sitting front and center, at Eliza-beth Taylor's table, on opening night of Eddie Fisher's four-week engage-ment at the Empire Room in Manhattan's Waldorf-Astoria Hotel. Fisher performed two shows a night, at 9:30 p.m. and 12:15 a.m. While Fisher relaxed backstage between shows, Liz and Ingo snuck upstairs to a pri-vate suite. "I was the guardian waiting in the living room while all the action took place in the bedroom," Richard Hanley, Liz's traveling sec-retary, told author Darwin Porter in 2012. Porter, a veteran Hollywood chronicleer and notorious celebrity blab-all, describes the Johansson-Taylor assignation as "one of Elizabeth's least-known affairs." And it was no brief fling, either. The two enjoyed frequent surreptitious trysts in Montgomery Clift's airy East 61st Street apartment, where "they couldn't get enough of each other," Porter said. Liz reportedly told Hanley: "No wonder they call him the Hammer."

The intensity of the relationship was corroborated by celebrity biographer Kitty Kelley. In her book *Elizabeth Taylor: The Last Star*, Kelley lists the men that she believed Taylor, one of Hollywood's most prolific seducers, actually *loved*. Her list included husbands Nicky Hilton, Michael Wilding, Richard Burton, and Eddie Fisher, plus writer Max Lerner ... and Ingemar Johansson.

The champ proved adroit at juggling lovers. During his year at the top, Ingemar was frequently spotted at trendy Manhattan nightspots with actress and Playboy playmate Stella Stevens on his arm. Then there was Italian supermodel Maria Benna, who loved showing off the dazzling six-carat "friendship ring" on her finger, a gift from her heavyweight beau.

One afternoon in the spring of 1960, Ingemar cut short an interview with reporter Roger Kahn in order to rendezvous in a hotel suite with an unnamed "regal blonde movie star." The champ, Kahn noted, "had quickly come to accept civilized assaults on him by beautiful women as routine."

You needn't be a glamour queen to catch Ingo's eye. Any gal was fair game. In 1959, Elaine Sloane was an attractive twenty-something brunette working as a secretary for *Sport* magazine in New York. Ingemar was in town for the week and Sloane was dispatched to his hotel with a message from an editor. She quickly found herself under the champ's spell. "He looks like a little boy," she gushed to a reporter, "and he's got the biggest dimple on his chin. Some girl ought to have that dimple. He took me out three times that weekend. He can really dance up a storm."

For the press, it was then standard operating procedure to ignore the romantic indiscretions of celebrities and public figures. (Kahn didn't write about Ingo's midday encounter until 1999.) The closest Ingemar came to being outed was a cryptic passage in a *Sport* magazine profile that ran in the December 1960 issue: "As far as playboying goes ... the only female that interests him now is Birgit. As a hangover from his Navy days, though, Ingo still has a girl in every port."

Birgit remained tight-lipped on the subject of Ingemar's womanizing. Certainly, she had to have known. But in the manner of the wives of athletes, movie stars, and politicians of the era, she chose to look the other way. Today she will only say: "It was not in my nature to be jealous."

* * *

On the evening of Monday, January 25, 1960, Ingemar donned black tie and tails as guest of honor at the Rochester Press and Radio Club's annual charity dinner, where he was presented the prestigious Hickok Belt as the top professional athlete of 1959. The belt itself was a magnificent sight, featuring a 4.3-carat diamond surrounded by 26 half-carat gem chips and an 18-carat gold buckle, valued at the time at $10,000—nearly $100,000 in today's dollars.

The nation's sportswriters had elected Ingo the first non–American Hickok winner, his vote total swamping second place finisher Johnny Unitas. After all, Unitas merely led the NFL quarterbacks in virtually every category and led the Baltimore Colts to their second straight championship.

(Later, after returning to Sweden, Ingemar had the gems replaced with *fugazis*, then had the diamond placed into a championship pinky ring for himself and turned the gem chips into a necklace for Birgit.)

On Monday night, March 14, 1960, Ingemar received yet another accolade, this time at the annual New York Boxing Writers Association dinner. The black-tie affair was held at Ruppert's Brewery , founded by Jacob Ruppert, owner of the Ruth-era Yankees, on Manhattan's Upper East Side. Ingemar was guest of honor, recipient of the group's "Fighter of the Year" Award.

The association, known today as the Boxing Writers Association of America, was formed in 1926 as the Boxing Writers Association of New York, with an eye toward improving the working conditions for local and visiting boxing scribes. The names of five of its charter newspapers evoke a lost epoch: the *New York Sun, Evening World, American, Evening Graphic* (where Ed Sullivan, later of TV fame, wrote a boxing column), and the *Bronx Home News*—all long defunct.

In 1938 the organization initiated its "Fighter of the Year" award, known as the Edward J. Neil Trophy, in honor of one of its founding members, an Associated Press reporter killed while covering the Spanish Civil War.

Called to the dais, Ingemar spoke of the impending rematch: "I hope it will be a clean promotion and a simple contract which everybody can read. For my part, I prefer the way we used to do in Europe: shake hands and get the money the day after the fight." The remarks were greeted with a mix of applause and uneasy laughter. The fight game in America was a mess, and Johansson, who'd yet to be paid for beating Patterson, wasn't going to let them forget it, even on a night like this.

After eighty-plus amateur fights, after his shameful Olympic disgrace, after turning pro only to endure cynical

Receiving the Associated Press Athlete of the Year Award for 1959 (*author's collection*).

sniping by so-called pugilistic pundits (most of whom were in attendance that night), Ingemar had finally and irrevocably shown them all. His name was now etched on a trophy—*the* trophy—where it would remain forever.

Once a champ, always a champ.

* * *

The demise of Rosensohn Enterprises opened the door for Feature Sports, an organization created by partners Roy Cohn, 33, and Jack Fugazy, 73, for the express purpose of staging Johansson-Patterson II.

Cohn had been a commie-busting boy wonder as chief counsel to Senator Joe McCarthy during the infamous Red Scare investigations of 1953. Fugazy was an old-school sports impresario with impressive street cred: in the 1920s he owned the Brooklyn Horsemen of the original NFL and, as a boxing promoter, set attendance records that still stand.

Feature Sports' contract called for each fighter to receive 25 percent of the gate and to split 75 percent of ancillary monies. Most importantly, Ingemar had insisted upon, and grudgingly received, a rematch clause in the event he lost.

The fight would be held at the Polo Grounds, a crumbling ballpark in a deteriorating Harlem neighborhood deserted by the baseball Giants in 1957. Still, it held more people than Yankee Stadium and boasted a rich fistic history. Two of the most talked-about bouts in boxing history were held there: Dempsey-Firpo, which drew 82,000 fans in 1923; and the 1941 Louis-Conn fight, which attracted 60,000.

* * *

Ingemar arrived at Idlewild Airport on Wednesday, May 6, 1960, where he was greeted by Jens and Ebba, who had preceded their son to New York. The champ stepped off the plane carrying two dozen American Beauty roses. He handed them to Ebba and kissed her on the cheek. It was, after all, Mother's Day.

Grossinger's had once again offered its services to the Johansson clan, and by Thursday the retinue of regulars—Jens, Ebba, Birgit, Rolf, Annete, Eva, Nils, and Edwin—settled into resort life while Ingemar began training in earnest.

The champ typically began his day at 7:30 a.m. with a jog over the rugged country trails, followed by a 9 a.m. breakfast of soft-boiled eggs and tea. After a bit of relaxation, which might include a quick nine holes of golf, the big lug liked to take a nap, usually while listening to Frank Sinatra records, or perhaps an aria by renowned Swedish opera tenor (and friend) Jussi Björling. By then it was 1 p.m., lunchtime: steak or chops, dessert, tea. Then maybe a swim, or, if he was feeling adventurous, a horseback ride, which drove his camp crazy, as Ingemar was no great shakes on a horse. Columnist Arthur Daley called Ingo "the relaxingest fighter in history."

Finally, at 5:45 p.m., it was time to get serious, and for the next hour Ingemar would pound the heavy bag, work out with his proprietary "slung-ball," and spar four or five rounds. But unlike 1959, Ingemar threw his right often and with a resounding *thwack*. During sparring sessions,

Nils or Whitey Bimstein (back in Ingo's corner) would yell instructions: "head down," "protect your chin." Most days, Ingemar's workouts attracted up to 300 ringsiders—resort-goers, press folks, celebrities, hangers-on, and the like.

At 6:45 p.m., Ingemar would shower and retire to his cottage for a cup of black coffee and call it a night. Unless, of course, Birgit had other plans, and then the couple might be spotted on the G's dance floor or at a happening New York nightspot.

It wasn't all fun and games. One evening, Ingemar discovered a secret love affair had developed between sister Eva and a married musi-

The "relaxingest fighter in history" at the Johansson compound at Grossinger's. Left to right: Jens, Rolf, Birgit, Ebba, and Ingo (*Bilder i Syd*).

cian in the Grossinger's dance band. Ingemar was ready to belt the poor sap when Tania Grossinger, 22, who'd grown up at the resort, intervened. "Ingemar asked if I'd talk to [the musician], adding that it would be far better for me to talk to him than for Ingemar to meet him outside," Tania recalled. After a brief chat, the musician agreed to end the affair. In appreciation, Ingemar gave Tania two tickets to the fight.

There were signs that the distractions were taking their toll. On Tuesday, May 12, 1960, sparring partner Cortez Stewart knocked the champ back on his heels with a jarring right to the jaw. Embarrassed, Ingemar stormed out of the ring and remained in his quarters for the rest of the day. When he emerged on Wednesday he had harsh words for the newsreel photographers, whose bright lights, he claimed, had blinded him to Stewart's punch.

* * *

A week later, Floyd Patterson—training for the first time in his career without Cus D'Amato, whose manager's license had been revoked—revealed that Joe Louis, the 46-year-old former champ, had joined his camp. The Brown Bomber was helping Floyd develop a more upright stance and improved footwork, the better to slip and block Ingo's punches. Joe predicted the newly mobile Patterson would win by kayo, "somewhere between the seventh and tenth rounds." Ingemar shrugged it off. "Patterson will have to be in the ring by himself," he said. "Louis won't be in there."

Louis had joked that since American spy planes were taking secret photographs over Russia, he might be able to sneak into Johansson's camp on the sly. Louis was referring to the May 1, 1960, incident in which American pilot Francis Gary Powers had been shot down over Soviet airspace. "I have always been an admirer of Joe Louis," Johansson said with typical graciousness. "He does not have to come here as a spy. He is welcome anytime as a friend."

Sure enough, a week later Louis showed up at Grossinger's, and, after watching Johansson spar four rounds, was duly impressed. "He is very clever at keeping his foe off balance with his jab," he told the press, "[and] his right hand is fast enough to catch anyone. I'll have to change my prediction...." At this point, reporters leaned in close, pens at the ready. "I now say it may take Floyd *eleven* rounds."

Three champs, 1960: Joe Louis, Ingemar, and Jack Dempsey (*Bilder i Syd*).

As was his custom, Ingemar called a halt to rigorous training five days before the fight. That's when *Milwaukee Sentinel* reporter Ray Grody found him poolside in plaid swim trunks and white sweatshirt. "I believe in relaxing at this stage of the game," Ingemar told him. "I sit around, walk, do a little shadow boxing. I go over the fight many times in my mind. I guess I have knocked Patterson out 100 times. I want to be in a winning frame of mind, you know?"

Grody saw another side of the heavyweight champ when Rolf walked by holding his infant daughter. "Uncle Ingemar wanted to hold the baby," Grody noted. "He cuddled the little one in his arms as if it were his own and the gleam in his eye told everything. He's a warm and gentle individual, devoid of the brusqueness and roughness usually associated with a fighter."

Ingemar turned to Grody. "There's no finer smell than that of a baby," the champ told him, "so clean, so fresh and fine."

To which Grody responded: *"This* is a *fighter?"*

15

Patterson-Johansson II

Floyd and Ingemar can be accurately described as the last heavyweight champions of the radio era and the first of the cable TV era.

Patterson-Johansson I marked the first heavyweight title fight in history to be simulcast live to theaters via closed circuit. For Patterson-Johansson II, Irving Kahn of TelePromTer was conducting a test run of his latest innovation: a cable-TV feed directly into viewers' homes. An estimated 25,000 cable subscribers in 13 cities around the country were asked to pay $2 for the privilege of watching the rematch in the comfort of their own homes. Kahn still had a few bugs to work out, however: subscribers were asked to mail in their $2 on the honor system, as Kahn had yet to figure out how to isolate the signal to particular homes.

Even so, Johansson-Patterson II would prove to be the richest fight in ring history, eventually raking in over $3 million from radio, closed-circuit, and movie rights.

* * *

June 20, 1960: the most eagerly awaited rematch in years had arrived. Now it was the new promoters' turn to proclaim themselves boxing's "breath of fresh air," with a vow to give the game "a clean new look."

On fight night, ringside ticket-holders found packets of moist towelettes on their seats, while leggy models handed orchids and perfume to the first thousand women. Some ushers wore pressed white shirts, red jackets, and ties. Others wore tuxedos.

Scratch the surface, however, and it was still boxing, and the rusty ringside bell was still rung with an old wrench at the end of a frayed rope. (And 18 months later, Cohn and Fugazy would be squaring off as adversaries in court, each accusing the other of all manner of double-dealings.)

Fans continued to stream into the stadium during the preliminary bouts, not all of them paying customers. Outside the Eighth Avenue entrance to the Polo Grounds, an unruly mob assembled in hopes of purchasing $5 bleacher seats. When an announcement was made over the loudspeaker that all 10,000 outfield seats had been sold, thousands of fans pushed past police, stormed the gates, and poured into the ancient ballpark. Afterwards, Fugazy claimed as many as 20,000 gate-crashers had swelled attendance, announced at 32,000 paid, well past 50,000.

The largest radio audience ever for a sports or entertainment program—51 million listeners—tuned to the ABC Radio broadcast, a total exceeded by only a handful of Franklin Roosevelt's speeches during World War II. Once again, ABC relied on the excitable Les Keiter for blow-by-blow and Howard Cosell for between-rounds analysis. With the opening bell moments away, Cosell set the scene as only he could: "It is exactly 416 feet from the Polo Grounds dressing rooms to the ring set up at second base. That can seem like five miles depending on a man's mental attitude. How long it seemed to Floyd Patterson is perhaps the biggest question before this fight. He has led a monastic life in the hills of Newtown, Connecticut, and at the same time Ingemar has had the most exciting, fun-filled year of his life. For Patterson it's about vengeance and staying away from the toonder in the right. For Ingemar, it is supreme confidence and statements like 'Patterson is really a light heavyweight.'"

With the fighters in the ring, Eddie Fisher stepped to the microphone and belted out the national anthem. When he was done, Alf Alfred sang the Swedish anthem accompanied by a flimsy portable keyboard set up in a neutral corner. When Alf came in on the wrong note and had to restart, it should have been an omen.

* * *

From the opening bell, Patterson launched an aggressive attack that pushed Johansson onto his heels. A minute into the fight and already Floyd had opened a cut above Ingemar's left eye. Clearly, this was not the same fighter Ingemar had faced a year ago. Patterson was out-jabbed in

151

1959 but not tonight. Now he kept his left in Ingo's face, and was working inside, too, pelting the midsection, which he failed to do last time as well. Floyd's strategy was clear: a relentless attack forcing Ingemar to use his right defensively—elbow in to protect the ribs, glove up to protect the jaw.

Forty-five seconds of the second round passed before Ingemar, his face red and his left eye swollen, threw his first combination. Seconds later he delivered his best blow of the night, a right that caught Patterson high on the head and forced a dazed challenger to retreat. Apparently unaware Floyd was hurt, Ingemar failed to follow up. Floyd danced away and the moment passed. As the round ended, the two exchanged jabs at long range.

Floyd continued his left-hooking assault in the third while Ingemar fired several rights that failed to connect. Floyd spent the last thirty seconds headhunting, forcing Ingemar to cover up.

By the fourth round Ingemar's left eye was nearly shut. Floyd continued to score with hooks to the body. Halfway through the round, Ingemar threw his trusty left-right combo, the toonder that had felled Machen, Patterson, and so many others. It landed on the side of Floyd's head, but Ingemar's weight was moving backwards, away from his target, dissipating its effect. When Floyd responded with an immediate right of his own, a telling look crossed Ingemar's face—annoyance? frustration?—as if he'd half-expected Floyd to reflexively hit the canvas.

*   *   *

Six rows back at ringside, almost unnoticed, a derby-hatted Cus D'Amato pulled back his chin to avoid Ingo's jab and jerked his left shoulder to block Ingo's right. Under his seat the old man's legs were dancing. And no wonder: he may not have been Floyd's manager any longer, but he still got a cut of the purse.

Fifteen seconds into the fifth, Floyd landed a short, crisp, inside right to the head and followed with a leaping left to the body. Then, from a deep crouch, his left fist below his waist but already cocked, Floyd unleashed a hook aimed at his opponent's charmingly cleft chin. Ingemar never saw it coming. His head snapped back upon impact and he went down hard, legs to the sky, like Ali in 1971 minus the red tassels. Ingemar spilled out of the ring and onto the apron, then groped his way back and waited on one knee, eyes fixed on Floyd.

Polo Grounds, March 21, 1960, second round: Ingo lands his best punch of the night (*Bettman/CORBIS*).

Up at nine but pinned against the ropes, Ingemar endured a fusillade of clubbing blows. Dazed and on marshmallow legs, he turned away from his opponent, but Floyd spun him around and dug a hard left into his ribs. The final moments of the Ingo Era were at hand.

For the first time in the life of this good and humble man, the sensitive soul of Floyd Patterson summoned pure bloodlust, a desire to kill, and threw all 190 pounds into a left hook for the ages. The punch was still 18 inches away when Ingemar closed his eyes and braced for impact. The leather missile exploded, causing Ingemar's head to whip violently back and to the right, and he dropped straight down as if he'd vanished into a suddenly open sinkhole. Which in fact he had.

Arms out, feet together—if this had been Hollywood, the director would have been lampooned for heavy-handed Christian symbolism— the former champion lay inert save for his right foot, which quivered convulsively. Blood oozed from his mouth and nose, and even his from his eyes, where the force of Floyd's blow had burst his capillaries.

Arthur Mercante counted to ten but there was no need; Ingo was utterly and truly out—waltzing in a meadow of posies. The once and present king threw up his arms in exultation and immediately rushed to Ingemar's side.

Floyd bent down and cradled Ingemar's head as Bloomberg, Bimstein and Karlsson scrambled through the ropes. They tried smelling salts and dousing him with water. Nothing. Cosell entered the ring and asked: "For God's sake, Whitey, is he dead?"

"The sunuvabitch should be," Bimstein answered. "I told him to watch out for the left hook."

∗   ∗   ∗

Ingemar was still out as the ring filled with photographers and police. The ring announcer stepped to the mic: "The time, one minute fifty-one seconds of the fifth round, the winner and the first man ever to regain the heavyweight championship, Floyd Patterson."

Several more minutes passed before Ingemar returned to this world. Then, at the instant Floyd was being hoisted atop the shoulders of his seconds, arms raised in triumph, Karlsson and Ahlquist each hooked an armpit and, gently, pieta-like, lifted Ingemar's remains and dragged the dead weight to a stool in his corner.

It was a sight that would haunt Mercante the rest of his days. "It was such a terrifying feeling to almost lose a fighter," Mercante recalled not long before his death in 2010 at age 90, "that the date and the exact time are forever seared in my memory, along with the image of the fallen Johansson."

∗   ∗   ∗

Edwin Ahlquist barred the press from entering the inner dressing room where Ingemar sat on the trainer's table, a doctor peering into his eyes. "Where are you, Ingemar?" he asked, "What building is this?"

No reply.

June 20, 1960: Waltzing in a meadow of posies (*Bilder i Syd*).

Louder this time: "Ingemar, tell me where you are right now."

Still, no response. The doctor asked again.

"Polo Grounds," Ingemar answered at last.

Ingemar held out his hands and opened and closed his fists while the doctor banged the fighter's knees with a mallet and scraped the soles of his feet.

"Month?"

A blank stare. The doctor persisted: "August? September?"

Finally, Ingo answered: "June."

Rolf massaged his brother's neck and, *sotto voce*, informed his brother of the evening's awful outcome. Jens stood silently nearby.

Just outside the inner sanctum, Ebba was sitting on a bench, crying. Elizabeth Taylor sat down beside her and took Ebba's hands into her own. It had been a rough night for Taylor, too. Between rounds an overzealous fan had grabbed her breast, yanked it from her dress, and bellowed, "Ladies and gentleman, I ask you: is this a beautiful sight?" Taylor brushed the man aside and coolly replaced her bosom. Then, at fight's end, Liz and Eddie were heckled and jeered as they fought through the maelstrom at ringside. In response, the delicate, purple-eyed orchid of the American screen shoved her arm and grabbed her bicep in the time-honored gesture that meant, "Up yours."

Ringside at the Polo Grounds, 1960: Liz Taylor and Eddie Fisher react in horror as Ingemar hits the canvas (*Paul Slade/Getty Images*).

* * *

The doctor told Ingemar he would examine him in the morning. He opened the door to leave and Ebba rushed in and ran to her son's side, embraced him and spoke softly into his ear. A moment later Birgit arrived, calm and composed. Throwing her arms around Ingo, she, too, spoke words only the two could hear. To himself, Ingemar began humming a soft tune as Fisher and Taylor entered. ("Hey-y!" yelled one indignant reporter, eyeing Taylor's generous cleavage as she pushed by, "what paper does *she* write for?") Fisher shook hands with his friend and spoke a few words of consolation, to which Ingemar responded, "Yas, yas."

Former champ Jersey Joe Walcott arrived. "You'll get another chance," he said. Ingemar nodded.

A NYSAC commissioner asked Rolf if his brother was ready to meet the press. Rolf turned to Ingemar, who shook his head.

"No," Rolf said, "no press conferences right now."

Rolf and Nils began to dress Ingemar—T-shirt, blue and white sport shirt, shoes, blue sport jacket. It was like dressing a limp mannequin. The former champion, now blank-faced and unsteady, entered a waiting car and vanished into the night.

An hour after the fight, Ahlquist addressed the nearly 150 reporters who were still camped outside the fallen champ's dressing room. "Ingemar cannot talk to anyone right now," he told them. "If you will be patient we will hold a press conference tomorrow and talk to all of you."

It was well after midnight when Ingemar arrived back at the Stanhope Hotel. He slept heavily through the night as Birgit and Karlsson kept vigil in the next room. The next morning Ingemar awoke with a slight headache and blood on his pillow.

16

After the Fall

Ingemar showed up at Tuesday's post-fight press conference in a sharply tailored blue serge suit, and this time, if he looked every inch the Ivy League scion, it was one with a swollen cheek, a cut ear, and a bruised left eye. He told the three hundred newsmen, photographers, and newsreel guys *(newsreel guys!)* that he couldn't recall anything that happened between the first knockdown and being led back to his dressing room.

His biggest mistakes? Keeping his hands too low, he said, and failing to capitalize on the hard right he'd delivered in the second round. Ingemar boasted he'd be ready for a rematch in 120 days and denied speculation that he'd suffered a concussion. "The boxing commission wanted me to come down and have a physical examination," Ingemar told them, "but I'm leaving for Florida."

Reporters buzzed around Team Johansson, fishing for quotes. "I did not see the knockout," Birgit told them. "There were too many people in front of me, [but] Ingemar is so strong I knew he wasn't hurt."

Edwin Ahlquist heaped praise upon the victor. "Floyd was simply much better this time, in every way. But many fighters have been knocked out and then come back. Joe Louis, for instance...."

"And Floyd Patterson," Birgit interjected, helpfully.

"Yes," Ahlquist said. "There was Patterson."

Ingemar was on his way out the door when reporter Roger Kahn caught his eye. "Was that the hardest you've ever been hit?" Kahn asked.

"I *tell* you!" Ingemar shot back and the room dissolved into laughter.

Patterson's triumph and Ingo's inglorious fall stirred passions around the globe. The day after the fight, President Dwight Eisenhower, in Hawaii after a diplomatic trip to the Far East, requested the film be flown to him via military transport so that he might watch it on his flight back to the mainland.

One kid in particular, a teenager in Louisville, had listened to the radio broadcast with keen interest. Cassius Clay, 18, had already won two national amateur titles and, in May, had qualified to represent the U.S. as a light heavyweight in that fall's 1960 Rome Olympics. So stirred was Clay by Floyd's kayo that he wrote a poem about it. It is believed to be The Greatest's first-ever verse for public consumption. Not surprisingly, Clay's doggerel lobbed a jab at Floyd ("*A lot of people say that Floyd can't fight / But you should have seen him on that comeback night...*"), before grudgingly giving Floyd his due ("*He cut up his eyes and messed up his face / And that last left hook knocked his head out of place...*"), then mercifully concluding with a couplet regarding Ingo ("*If he would have stayed in Sweden he wouldn't have took that beatin'*").

* * *

As in 1959, Ingemar and Birgit planned a post-fight retreat at the palatial Florida digs of Swedish tycoon Gustav von Reis. Reporter Jack Cuddy accompanied the pair as they arrived at Idlewild Airport via a side entrance. "Ingemar was not in a friendly mood as he awaited take-off," said Cuddy, who asked him to respond to proposal from Joe Louis to coach Ingemar for the third fight in exchange for $50,000 if he won, nothing if he lost. "I don't need Louis," a miffed Johansson sniffed. "He's got nothing to do with us."

In Florida, Ingemar seemed uncharacteristically subdued and intro-spective. It didn't help when he received word from the Schick Safety Razor Company that he was being dumped as their spokesman. As champion, Ingemar had been hawking Schick's new blade of "golden Swedish steel," tempered at a plant near Göteborg. But no one loves a loser, not even a clean-shaven one, and Ingo was replaced with a golfer.

Back in Geneva, Ingemar put on nearly 20 pounds before he began training again. There were disturbing reports that a couple of his spar-ring partners had put him on the canvas.

Ingemar made one trip to Göteborg, to spend the Christmas holi-days with his family, and used the time to liquidate his excavation firm. Doing business in Sweden, he discovered, was injurious to his claim of Swiss citizenship.

* * *

In the weeks and months following Ingemar's knockout, Birgit began to brood over that awful night's events. Something didn't *feel* right. Then she remembered an incident that happened about four hours before the bout.

She and Ingemar met a Swedish friend at the hotel's posh restaurant for a pre-match meal. They ordered steaks, which were brought out under separate silver platters. Ingemar reached for one. "No, not *that* one," the waiter told him. "We have made *this* one especially for you."

Birgit thought no more about it. But as Ingemar climbed through the ropes that night, he seemed, well—*different*. Normally, Ingo was all business in the moments before the bell. Now he was peering into the crowd, smiling, his normal razor-focus diffused. And during the fight itself, didn't Ingemar seemed curiously passive?

Birgit became convinced, and remains so to this day, that Ingemar had been slipped a New York Strip mickey. She even managed to briefly convince Ingemar it was so. After all, it appeared *something* fishy was afoot in the hours before the fight. Ingemar claims he lost six pounds, "under mysterious circumstances," the night before the bout.

"I was remarkably slow throughout the bout," he told reporters in December of 1960. "I was practically standing still." Even Whitey Bimstein entertained the possibility, telling the press, "He looked goofy that night."

When asked to comment, Floyd Patterson would have none of it. "My left hook," he said, "was the only dope I can think of."

Today, Rolf has a different explanation. In a 2013 interview with the author, Rolf revealed that Ingemar strained his back in the days before the fight and that Dr. Karlsson gave him some pain pills. Rolf believes his brother had an adverse reaction to the medication, which would explain both the weight loss and the sluggish performance, not to mention Ingemar's excessive sweating during his previous night's appearance on *What's My Line?*

Was Ingemar intentionally poisoned? Impossible to say, but it is certainly not beyond the realm of possibility. Boxing historian Paul Gallender, in his book *Sonny Liston: The Real Story Behind the Ali-Liston Fights*, quotes mob-connected Las Vegas casino mogul Morris Shenker, talking about the second Ali-Liston fight, in which Liston was felled by a so-called phantom punch. Shenker, former chief counsel to Jimmy

Hoffa, told Gallender: "Nobody really believed that it was a fair knock-out. I always suspected that [the mob] doped him up ahead of time."

Then there is George Foreman, who published an autobiography in 1995 titled *By George*. In it, he raises the possibility that he was drugged before entering the ring against Ali in Zaire in 1974. (Foreman was kayoed in the eighth round.) "I can't say for certain," Foreman wrote, "[but] I believed my water had been mickeyed." Foreman's suspicions add a new layer of meaning to the term "rope-a-dope."

In any case, Ingemar's story about the poisoned steak caused quite a stir in the fall of '59. Sports columnists jumped on the story, and to a man dismissed it as hooey, a sorry excuse for a dismal performance.

A few weeks later, Ingemar was eager to drop the subject. "I don't believe I was doped," he said, after being asked for the umpteenth time. "I have no reason to believe that." Ingemar must have known it was an unprovable allegation and that, in the end, whatever was done was done. For the rest of his life, however—according to a source close to Ingemar—the boxer privately harbored lingering suspicions about that venomous steak.

*   *   *

A mere five years after the Patterson-Johansson fights, Muhammad Ali began turning his bouts into epic racial sagas, transforming the relationship between boxing and race radically and forever. In pre–Ali white America, it seemed as if the world of pugilism existed apart from matters of race. Sure, there had been Louis-Schmeling in 1938, but that was more about nations and ideologies.

Of course, the race issue had been there all along, lurking, hidden between lines of hype and linotype. But in the late 1950s and early 1960s—before America's first sit-in, before the Freedom Riders, the March on Selma, and I Have a Dream—race simply wasn't part of the national sports conversation. Still, Patterson-Johansson forced Americans to decide: do I cheer for Floyd, the flavorless black American? Or am I rooting for the dashing white Viking to snatch the title from our shores?

American and black? Or foreign and white?

Even in hindsight, we can say with certainty only this about the racial dynamics of Patterson-Johansson: It's complicated. One can peruse the archives of countless newspapers and magazines in the days leading up to the first Patterson-Johansson encounter and not once come across the words "Great White Hope" to describe Ingemar. That odious, emotionally-freighted phrase dated back to the early 1900s, to the days of the unforgivably black Jack Johnson, and it was still being bandied about in the press as late as 1982 when the mantle was thrust upon white contender Gerry Cooney in his bout against Larry Holmes.

On the surface, at least, the term didn't seem applicable to Ingemar; surely Americans didn't "hope" to see the title pass to a foreigner. Or did they? Not surprisingly, the issue of race managed to bubble to the surface in unexpected ways. For example: at Yankee Stadium on fight night, June 26, 1959, spectators purchasing the official program might have reasonably expected to see photos of the evening's participants on the booklet's cover. Instead, the cover featured a full page painting of white Britisher Tom Cribb squaring off against Tom Molineaux, a black former slave from Virginia, in a bareknuckle fight that occurred December 3, 1810, in Thistleton, England, a fight won by Cribb after 35 brutal rounds. It happens that the Cribb-Molineaux bout was the sport's first-ever interracial boxing championship. The cover served as a reminder, as if one were needed, of the night's inescapable subtext: a white man and a black man were engaged in a war for symbolic racial supremacy.

* * *

The late John Oliver Killens, a black activist, novelist, and twice a Pulitzer nominee, was 43 in 1959. "I shall never forget an evening I spent in a movie house in Hollywood watching a closed circuit broadcast of the first Patterson-Johansson fight," he wrote in a 1964 essay, "and the great shame I felt for my white countrymen as they began to smell a possible victory for the white foreigner over the black American. Forgotten entirely was the fact that soft-hearted Patterson was a fellow countryman. Color superseded patriotism. As I sat there hearing shouted exhortations like, 'Kill the n***r,' I felt that Patterson and I were aliens in a strange and hostile country, and Ingemar was home among his peers."

One can only imagine how Floyd felt. The month before the first fight, staring out at him on newsstands across America, the cover of

Boxing Illustrated declared: "A Johansson Victory: Best Thing for Boxing." Inside, the magazine predicted a Johansson win would give the sport a "shot in the arm."

The day after Patterson dropped the crown, AP columnist Murray Rose wrote: "Johansson is as welcome as a cool breeze on a hot summer

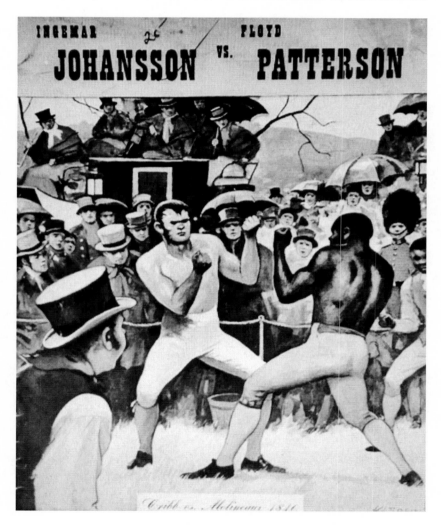

July 27, 1959, Yankee Stadium: Fight program for Patterson-Johansson I (*author's collection*).

night. For the first time in years the champion is a man who calls his own shots [and] knows his own mind." Jack Dempsey, heavyweight king from 1919 to 1926, was quoted thusly: "Johansson is an exciting, inspirational type. He should start a boxing bump. Patterson's loss ... is what the game needs to snap it out of a deadly decline."

In the days following Patterson-Johansson I, the black-and-white fight film was a popular attraction in American theaters, especially below Mason-Dixon. *Texas Monthly* journalist Jan Reid recalled passing a theater in the Deep South; outside the theater, a poster featured an artist's rendition of Johansson standing triumphantly over a fallen Patterson, who was depicted in cartoonish, large-lipped, racially stereotyped caricature.

No doubt Floyd sensed that the vast majority of Americans had eagerly embraced this relative unknown, this personable white knight who took the title and got the girl. It was the handsome Swede, after all, who got the endorsements, the movie and TV roles, the *Life* magazine cover, the adulation of millions. At joint appearances with his rival, the press never failed to describe the fine cut of Ingo's suits. No one seemed to care what Floyd was wearing.

When Floyd regained the title in 1960, *Ebony* magazine trumpeted its coverage with the headline: "IT WAS A VICTORY FOR US!" In the article Floyd made clear that he "preferred to think of his victory as a victory for all Americans," but he must have known it was not a sentiment shared by many.

"Floyd made clear his resentment," the *New York Times* reported in September 1960, "that promoters were still 'running after' Ingemar ... even though the Swede was now only the challenger." Patterson mentioned how reporters called him *Floyd*—"and all year long Johansson was taking bows," he told the *Times*, "and sportswriters were calling him Mr. Johansson."

But what must have cut Floyd to the quick was the relentless sniping from America's black press. Three weeks before the second fight, Major Robinson, influential reporter for the daily *Baltimore Afro-American*, wrote: "Seldom has any white boxer been more popular in Harlem than heavyweight champion Ingemar Johansson. Even though the fight is 'pick-'em' around the nation, Johansson is a three to one favorite among Harlem bettors. Unlike Patterson, who could walk the streets of Harlem unrecognized, Johansson, while never having visited the community but once, is mentioned often in the weekly press as being a friend of Dinah Washington. He is also reported to have struck up a warm friendship with Sidney Poitier while both were making a film."

Contemporaries like middleweight champion Sugar Ray Robinson, Major Robinson noted, are "always favored because of racial pride." Indeed, Sugar Ray was not only a fixture of Harlem nightlife, but a social activist as well. As early as 1960, Ray was organizing Harlem voters and calling out New York Mayor Robert Wagner for his failure to visit the area. "Patterson has never been closely linked in this manner," Major Robinson wrote. "He has always been regarded as an outsider."

Another influential black voice, Wendell Smith of the *Pittsburgh Courier*, referred to Floyd as Cus D'Amato's "slave," and questioned whether Cus was a racist for failing to give black fighters a shot at Patterson's crown.

He may not have liked to show it, but Floyd felt every blow. During contract talks for the second fight, promoter Roy Cohn made mention to Floyd's attorney of Ingemar's negotiating savvy. The attorney then asked if Patterson could review the contract. Cohn responded: "Floyd? Can he read?"

Small wonder Floyd spent his titleless year seething with animus.

* * *

After dropping the title, a deeply depressed Patterson rarely ventured from his home on Long Island and assiduously avoided viewing films of the fight. But every time he turned on the TV, it seemed, there was Ingo, crooning, joking, taking a bow. Ingemar had gotten more mileage out of the title in three months than Floyd had in three years.

In his autobio, *Victory Over Myself*, Floyd describes a Sunday evening in 1959, sitting on the couch with his wife Sandra. The *Ed Sullivan Show* was on, and Ingo was showing Sullivan the punch that had rocked the world. Sandra jumped up to change the channel.

"No," Floyd said. "Leave it on."

It was a transformative moment. "I sat there watching the face of the man who had humiliated me ... laughing and joking with Sullivan....

I sat there and hated him." For the next 356 days Floyd would nurture that hate, cultivate it, embrace it. Then, in the rematch, Floyd threw all that bitterness and resentment into the most perfectly brutal revenge left hook of all time.

Afterwards, sickened by his own emotions, Patterson vowed: "I never want to hate like that again."

17

Dancin' with Johansson

The Boeing 707 from Paris touched down at Idlewild International at 8:50 p.m. on Monday, January 16, 1961. Ingemar Johansson, Edwin Ahlquist, and Nils Blomberg stepped off and were greeted by Whitey Bimstein. Team Johansson had reassembled for a final shot at the title.

One member of the entourage was conspicuously absent.

Dr. Gösta Karlsson had been Ingemar's personal physician for ten years and worked his corner for every fight. But after that nightmare at the Polo Grounds, Karlsson implored Ingemar to retire, or, at the very least, undergo a complete neurological exam before returning to the ring. Rebuffed, Karlsson quit with an ominous, unequivocal warning: Ingemar risked serious brain trauma should he suffer another, similar blow.

Ingemar responded by replacing Karlsson with a young Göteborg anesthesiologist, Dr. Francis Benson, who declared that he was "satisfied that Ingemar has normal reactions and shows no sign of damage," and pronounced Ingo "healthy in all respects and fit for the fight."

* * *

Johansson had been in America less than 24 hours and already he was face-to-face with Floyd Patterson. Not in the ring, but on the dais at the Waldorf-Astoria ballroom, in black tie and tux. The occasion was the 35th annual New York Boxing Writers Association dinner, where Patterson was to receive the Edward J. Neil trophy as Fighter of the Year for 1960.

When Ingemar was called upon to say a few words, he managed to find humor in his current tax troubles. "During and after each round," Ingemar said, referring to the second fight, "all the Swedes were yelling, '*Skoal!*' Then came the fifth round, when I lay unconscious for many minutes. Suddenly I was 'that damned Swissman!'"

Two days later, on a stage in the Commodore Hotel banquet hall, co-promoters Roy Cohn and Jack Fugazy sat at the far ends of a long table with their two principal players sandwiched between them. It was contract signing day. Floyd signed first, then Ingemar, their pen flourishes, like a conductor's baton, triggering the *pip-pip-pip* of flash bulbs—the music of another era.

The contract for the rubber match, scheduled for Monday night, March 13, 1961, at the Miami Beach Convention Center, was similar to the 1960 bout with two notable exceptions.

For one, there was no return match clause. "There are other contenders who have been waiting a long time," Patterson told reporters. "I believe the loser should step aside and give others a chance." In fact, Ingemar had just dropped three spots in the world rankings, behind Liston, Folley, and Machen, and the public, too, seemed eager for fresh blood.

Another new wrinkle: Patterson, who had never fought below the Mason-Dixon Line, insisted on a clause prohibiting segregated seating at the Convention Center. It was a big step for Floyd, who had never been perceived as a "race man."

After the signing, Ingemar and Birgit flew to Miami, then drove to Ft. Lauderdale, where they were met by Gustav Von Reis. Their first order of business: selecting a suitable training site.

* * *

To any other fighter, a "suitable" facility would include a ring and gym and a place to sleep, the more Spartan and spare the better. Team Johansson, on the other hand, headed for Palm Beach, the tony enclave of the moneyed elite; Joe Kennedy owned a compound there, where his son the president played touch football on their majestic oceanfront lawn.

Ebba, Jens, Rolf and company checked in at the Sea Breeze Hotel on South Ocean Boulevard, while several hundred yards away Ingemar occupied a penthouse at the Holiday Inn, with a terrace overlooking the Atlantic—the deposed king in exile. Birgit was registered at the Sea Breeze, but most nights her bed went unmussed.

Ingemar settled into a routine: five or six miles of roadwork followed by six or seven rounds of sparring. Two rings had been set up at the Sea Breeze, one indoors and one outside shaded by a row of palms.

In the evenings Ingemar sparred inside, in private, where the sessions were filmed, to be analyzed by Ingemar and Whitey the next day.

Ingemar still found plenty of time to relax. He swam every day and napped to Sinatra and the classics. One day Whitey walked in and asked Ingemar what he was listening to.

"Beethoven," Ingo told him.

"Beethoven?" Whitey said. "Who'd *he* ever lick?"

Once again, Ebba handled the cooking, mostly traditional Swedish dishes. Whitey suspected his fighter was sneaking food at night, so he began taping the refrigerator shut before retiring for the evening. It took about a week before Whitey realized that, in the wee hours, Ingemar was unwrapping the fridge, grabbing a snack, then carefully taping it shut again.

* * *

In an effort to sell the fight, Feature Sports required Johansson to spar once a week at Miami Beach Convention Center, where a local trainer had agreed to provide sparring partners. Ingemar made the 70-mile trip south for his first contractual obligation on Monday afternoon, February 6, 1961. Two thousand spectators and a gaggle of reporters turned out for the event.

The trainer, Angelo Dundee, had lined up three boxers to spar two rounds apiece with Ingo. One of them no-showed.

"Hey Cass," Dundee called out. "You wanna work out with the Swede?"

Cassius Clay, 19, with three professional bouts under his belt, didn't miss a beat: "I'll go dancin' with Johansson!"

Precisely what occurred in the ring that day, beyond the fact that a former and future champ sparred for six minutes, has been the subject of debate for years in magazine articles, book chapters, and Internet boxing forums.

Like the JFK assassination, the event was witnessed by thousands and a brief film survives, yet no one can say for certain what *really* happened that day, leaving legend, hearsay, and misinformation to masquerade as history. A 30-second clip of the encounter appears on YouTube; over the years its grainy footage has been scrutinized frame-by-frame as if shot by Zapruder himself.

Ali and his supporters—and they are legion, loyal, and vocal—have their version. Ingemar and his admirers, an admittedly smaller troupe, stick to theirs.

The most widely accepted account, that Cassius danced rings around Ingemar and made him look clumsy and amateurish, has been told and retold so many times it's accepted as fact. It appears in books like David Remnick's *King of the World*, Angelo Dundee's *View from My Corner*, and Ferdie Pacheco's *Tales from the 5th Street Gym*, among others. Ali insider Harold Conrad peddled the same story to *Rolling Stone* magazine in 1982.

Conrad's account was typical: Clay "danced like Fred Astaire" and scored at will, while an increasingly frustrated Johansson was missing by a mile. In the second round, Clay began trash-talking: "You ain't nuthin'," and, "I should be fightin' Patterson 'stead of you."

"Ingemar went berserk," Conrad wrote, and at the end of the second round Bimstein "called a halt to the session" to spare his guy further humiliation.

Ali himself stuck to the script, telling author Alex Haley in 1964: "By the end of the first round I had him pinned against the ropes, all shook up and very mad. And he hadn't put a glove on me." To columnist Arthur Daley, Ali added this dramatic embellishment: "Two fellers came over to me afterward with hats pulled down over their eyes like movie gangsters. 'Cass,' says one, 'you better watch yourself. You're gonna mess up a four million dollar gate.'"

* * *

It's a helluva tale: a young kid destined for greatness schooling the guy who's training for the title. Problem is, there are some holes in the "official" story.

For one, Whitey didn't "call a halt" to the session, a claim that appears in Remnick's, Dundee's, and Conrad's accounts. In fact, Cassius was scheduled to spar only those two rounds. (Pacheco managed to misplace the event completely, claiming it happened at the 5th Street Gym.)

Another problem with the story: throughout his career, Ingemar was known to go easy on sparring partners, using them not as punching bags but as a means to hone his in-ring instincts. Sparring for the first

Patterson fight, you'll recall, Ingo went zero for 1959 when it came to throwing the right in public.

Also, the third Patterson fight was still five weeks away, and it is likely that Ingemar, not yet in shape, viewed the session as a mere workout. To the teenage Clay, however, it was an opportunity to shine, and to milk the event for every last ounce of publicity. Indeed, Cassius had a fight scheduled the very next night, against Jimmy Robinson, at the Convention Center.

By the time Ingemar told his side of the story to Swedish journalist Sigurd Glans in 1982, 20 years had passed and it was still a sore subject. "He didn't do a damn thing," Ingemar told Glans, his voice and temper rising. "Just ran and jumped around, and as soon as I got close to him, Dundee shouted from the ring corner: 'DON'T THROW THE RIGHT! DON'T THROW THE RIGHT!' So I said, 'There is no point.'"

Given Ali's nonpareil talent for grandiose embellishment, Ingo's version seems closer to the truth. And seriously, would Dundee have risked his golden boy (the day before his fourth pro fight) in a semi-serious "fight," against one of the hardest punchers in ring history? Not bloody likely.

Contemporary news accounts provide additional enlightenment.

A UPI reporter was present that afternoon and filed this report, which appeared nationwide the following day: "*Ingo appeared to pull his punches* [emphasis added] when he threw his right and concentrated on left jabs.... The workout pleased Ingo so well he asked Clay to join other sparring mates at the Palm Beach fight camp. 'I like a fellow who moves around fast,' Johansson said. 'That's the best workout I've had.'"

After the session, Ingemar and Cassius spoke cordially and posed for photos. The AP described the scene as a "mutual admiration society," quoting Ingemar thusly: "I hope I can get him for more sparring as he sharpens me up. He's good, this fellow."

The two men would be linked again in the fall of 1961, following Clay's ninth straight victory, a sixth round TKO over Alex Miteff. A promoter offered Ingemar $100,000 to shut the Louisville Lip, igniting a war of words between the two. "That guy wouldn't even draw a non-paying crowd, much less any real money," Ingemar said. "It would just be a waste of my time."

Asked to respond, Cassius told a reporter, "Well, if he knows he is going to win, then why don't he come over here and collect that hundred thousand? That's what I don't understand."

Years later, after both men had retired and grown paunchy, Ingemar and Muhammad would often see each other at big fights and sports functions, and a warm friendship developed between the two.

* * *

On Friday, March 10, 1961, three days before the fight, a surprise visitor showed up at Camp Johansson in the person of top-ranked contender Sonny Liston.

Two days earlier, Liston had scored a third round kayo over journeyman Howard King at the Convention Center. Now he was at the Sea Breeze, glaring balefully—did Sonny even *have* another expression?—at Ingemar, who was "affable and smiling," according to the *New York*

The night before Patterson-Johansson III, the fighters appear on *The Jackie Gleason Show*. Ingemar, who seldom missed an opportunity to make a buck, wears a blazer sporting a patch advertising both the Holiday Inn and Sea Breeze motels. Floyd's expression is typical: solemn, eyes to the floor (*Bilder i Syd*).

Times. The two posed for photos, each man brandishing his right under the other guy's chin, like gunslingers in a town not big enough for both of them.

During his pop-in visit, Liston spoke a sum total of five words: "I'll fight Johansson for free," he told reporters. For the Baleful One, that qualified as a torrent of conversation.

* * *

That evening, Ingemar and Floyd appeared together on CBS's *Jackie Gleason Show.* The two combatants sat opposite each other with the hard-drinking, famously obese Gleason in between, but what should have been a compelling segment was hijacked by the Great One. The boxers could barely squeeze in a word.

"You might not realize this," Gleason began, "but at one time I was a heavyweight.... You've heard of the famous Dempsey-Tunney Long Count? I was the only fighter where they had a Wide Count. I've always been athletically inclined. I was one of the greatest shot-putters in my neighborhood. When it came to putting away shots, no one could touch me."

The plan was to show a film clip of Ingo's kayo of Floyd, followed by Floyd's kayo of Ingo. The first clip aired. Gleason: "Well, we just saw Floyd get his. And in just a moment the tables will be turned."

Ingemar to Gleason: "Will *you* get *yours?*"

The unscripted comment broke up the audience, and Gleason, too—by far the best blow of the night. Unfortunately, that's about all either fighter managed to say before Gleason again hogged the spotlight, calling the fighters "real heros, guys with plenty of guts who don't quit when they're beaten but come back to try and win again."

True enough. But Gleason had the two warriors face-to-face three nights before their historic rubber match and he turned it into a monologue. How sweet it is? Well, it coulda been a whole lot sweeter.

Where's Cosell when you need him?

18

Patterson-Johansson III

Monday, March 13, 1961, would be a day of plot twists and controversies.

First, Miami Beach Boxing Commission chairman Al Sherman informed the fighters that Florida regulations required a mandatory eight-count—that is, a fighter knocked to the canvas cannot resume fighting until a count of eight had been reached. Never in history had a heavyweight title match employed such an edict. Right away experts agreed the chief beneficiary of such a rule was Patterson. Ingemar, after all, was the harder hitter and liked to swarm a stunned opponent, and an eight-count would likely rob him of the opportunity.

If the appointment of Billy Regan as referee didn't cause eyebrows to rise, it should have. Regan had established his boxing bona fides as the head coach of the University of Miami's boxing team from 1934 until 1956 (when the school dropped the program), but he'd been working as a Miami fireman ever since. Regan's relative inexperience as a referee—he'd officiated fewer than a dozen bouts—would play a major role in the night's disputed outcome.

There was more drama when the combatants met at Convention Center for the 11 a.m. weigh-in. Patterson scaled 193, the heaviest of his career, but it was all sinew and muscle, his biceps and shoulders bulging like a Pier Six stevedore. The real stunner occurred when Ingemar tipped a whopping 206-and-a-half—*twelve pounds* heavier than the year before, and the weight clung to his thick frame like an extra coat of spackling. Joe Louis took one look and said, "I think Ingemar overdid it at the table."

The fighters posed for photographers, Floyd the picture of relaxation while an unshaven Ingemar looked grim. Trainer Blomberg, asked to describe his man's demeanor, replied: "Edgy and mean, snapping at people." He meant it as a compliment.

* * *

Once again, Howard Cosell and Les Keiter manned the mics for ABC Radio. Just before the fighters entered the ring, Keiter intoned: "All the ingredients of high drama are here—electricity in the atmosphere, the big guessing game among the experts. But one belief is omnipresent: It won't go too long. Someone is going to get clobbered."

Ringside seats were awash with Dior gowns and satin-trimmed dinner jackets, a cross-pollination of showbiz and sports: Marlene Dietrich, Milton Berle, Jimmy Durante, Joe DiMaggio, Charlie Conerly, Walter O'Malley, Joe Louis, Max Schmeling, Rocky Marciano, Debbie Reynolds, Frank Sinatra....

It was a near-sellout of some 16,000 fans, and, thanks to Floyd, the so-called "color ban" for public events had been lifted for the first time in Miami. "Negroes were spotted freely," one reporter wrote, "...in all sections of the well-filled hall ... and no incidents arose from the integrated set-up."

Ingemar was first to make the long walk to the ring, a day-and-a-half stubble on his funereal face. He clambered through the ropes oblivious to the cheers and began shadow-boxing, staring at the canvas. There was no smiling this time, no looking out among the crowd.

It was three minutes before Patterson slipped through the ropes. Referee Billy Regan called the men to ring-center for instructions.

* * *

From the opening bell it was apparent that Patterson was facing a more animated Ingo: on his toes, firing his left, hunting for an opening. Halfway through the round he crossed over a Patterson jab with a right to the temple and Patterson went down. *"THE THUNDER LANDED!"* shrieked Les Keiter at ringside.

Patterson was up at two, dazed, a target waiting to be hit. But this was Florida, home of the mandatory eight, and Ingemar was forced to wait. Just outside the ropes, Whitey Bimstein, who hadn't attended the weigh-in and was unaware of the rule, screamed, *"No... no... no! This'll save Floyd!"*

Even so, moments later Ingemar landed a left hook to the jaw and Patterson crumpled anew.

Ingemar sprinted to the farthest corner as Patterson scrambled to his feet for another octo-count. Then Regan waved the two fighters on and Ingemar was moving in, forcing Floyd to the ropes, when the champ caught him with a swift right to the jaw, then catapulted off the ropes with a leaping left hook that put *Johansson* down.

Now it was Ingo who needed the eight as Floyd locked eyes with Cus and gave the ol' man a wave and a wink. As the round ended Keiter was beside himself—*"One of the great first rounds of all time!"*

In round two both men went headhunting, each seeking to capitalize on the previous round's knockdowns. The men exchanged hard rights. Ingemar kept his left in Floyd's face but took a shot to the ribs in the closing seconds. It was a decent round for Johansson, but on his stool between rounds, looking "pale as a Welsh miner," in the words of one scribe, he began sucking air in huge gulps, practically hyperventilating. Six minutes and already the extra weight was beginning to tell.

In the third, Ingemar began bleeding profusely from a cut over his right eye, possibly from a clash of heads. Ingemar was looping his right now, in great ungainly sweeps bereft of power, as if Thor's Hammer was too heavy to hold. Working inside, Floyd scored with a series of quasi-legal rabbit punches. Ingemar's left eye was starting to swell and in the closing seconds he absorbed a hook that buckled his knees.

Between rounds, Bimstein applied ice to the eye as Keiter intoned: "This fight is bound to go down in history."

In the fourth, Ingemar landed a right that sent Floyd into retreat. Keiter: "As long as he's throwing that right, look out, something could happen." Floyd was cut too, over his left eye and on the bridge of his nose. "They're throwing punches in barrages now," squealed Keiter, "not combinations!"

In the closing seconds, Floyd launched a two-fisted attack that had Ingemar in trouble. Keiter: "They said they couldn't better the first two fights and they've done it already!"

In the fifth round the champ opened with a flurry that forced Ingemar, now bleeding from the nose, to cover up. He pawed with the left, keeping Floyd at bay, measuring his man for a right without success. Keiter: "We're sitting on a honey tonight. Oh baby, what a battle!"

In the sixth, a suddenly rejuvenated challenger landed a series of rights and had Floyd in real trouble for the first time since the opening round. Keiter: "Ingo with a left to the nose, Patterson backing away …

trying to avoid the dynamite. Ingo's eyes look clear as he looks right into our microphone."

It was a big round for Johansson.

Until...

March 13, 1961, sixth round: Down goes Ingo (*Bilder i Syd*).

177

* * *

What happened next would ignite debate in the coming days and weeks, in homes and taverns, around office water coolers, and on playgrounds and schoolyards around the world.

Two and a half minutes into the sixth, Floyd threw a wicked left that caught Johansson high on the forehead, followed immediately by two clubbing rights—one to the neck, another behind the left ear—and down went Johansson, nose first, onto all fours.

Within seconds he was on one knee and in seeming control of his faculties. But when Regan's count hit five, Ingemar lost his balance and keeled over. At nine, Ingemar's knees were lifting off the canvas. He was clearly up, but barely, as Regan tolled ten.

Keiter: "He got up ... wait a minute! According to the referee he did NOT get up in time. Ingo is arguing but Regan is pushing him back into his corner and that means the fight is over! Just when things looked bad for him, Floyd Patterson comes back ... in one of the most scintillating heavyweight fights of all time!"

The announcement "...and still heavyweight champion..." was greeted with a cacophony of boos. As the ring filled with cops and photographers and reporters, Floyd walked to the opposite corner, where his beaten, teary-eyed rival stood. Floyd wrapped both arms around Ingemar's neck and kissed him on the cheek, as if the night had just been one big lovers' quarrel.

Back in the dressing room, Ingemar smiled and asked Birgit how she was doing. "This will take a long time for me to digest," she told him. "You've never fought so well and yet you lose. It is incredible bad luck."

It was about to get worse. When Ingemar stepped out of the shower he couldn't find his underpants. He was still naked when he was served papers by a pair of deputy marshals.

In their hands: a federal "prevention-of-departure" notice, issued by the Internal Revenue Service, in order to ensure Johansson didn't abscond with the million dollars in taxes they claimed he owed from his last two fights.

Ingo must have been thinking: I've had better nights.

An hour later, Ingemar—wearing a dark suit and skinny red tie and no underwear—met the press. There were two pieces of tape over his right eye and a blue shiner under his left. "I thought I was up in time," he said. "I heard the count all the way. When he say ten I was up and ready again. They did not count correctly, I think. I will not retire. I fought my heart out." He looked resigned and weary.

But not so weary as to cancel the evening's plans to catch Sinatra at the fabulous Fontainebleau, in what was supposed to be a victory celebration. No matter. When the battle-scarred warrior and his comely fiancée arrived, Frank introduced them to wild applause and they all partied until 3 a.m.

Partied, you might say, like it was 1959.

* * *

The fight's muddled conclusion left spectators at many of the 207 closed circuit locations throughout the U.S. and Canada in total confusion. There didn't appear to be a knockout. So why did the referee stop the fight?

It was the same question fans around the world asked when the fight film made its debut in theaters a week later.

Fans today can go to YouTube and judge for themselves whether Johansson's knees and gloves were off the canvas in time. The video evidence appears to show knees up at nine, gloves at nine-and-a-titch.

But one wonders why Regan's decision elicited no protests from Ingo's corner. Blomberg, Bimstein, Ahlquist—you'll look in vain for one word or gesture or expression of protest. At the moment Regan stopped the bout, only Ingemar registered dissent, throwing his arms up in disbelief. (Later, Ahlquist did raise an objection to Patterson's kill-shot, calling it an illegal rabbit punch, but Ingemar quashed it: "I hit him like that in the first fight ... and now he hit me. It's all square.")

Viewers can also decide for themselves whether or not the mandatory count cost Johansson the match. Knocked dizzy in the first, Patterson was up at two with Ingemar poised to pounce, just as he had against Machen in '58 and Patterson in '59. Did the extra seconds matter?

Give it a view. Then discuss among yourselves.

* * *

The morning after the fight, one of Sweden's leading newspapers featured a full-page photo of Ingemar on the canvas with the headline:

"Ingo, It's Time to Stop." Another paper called for boxing's abolition under the headline, "Stop this Cruel Sport, It's Murder." A lot had changed in Sweden in the two years since Johansson, now a two-time loser and self-proclaimed Swissophile, had been hailed a hero and the nation fell in love with boxing.

And now he was being held captive in America, a tax prisoner of the IRS, such a danger to society that government agents warned airlines and steamship companies that "any attempt by Johansson to leave the United States was to be prevented." When an immigration official added: "The central office in Washington will notify border patrols to keep on the watch for Johansson," the *New York Times* slyly snarked, "This would be to prevent Johansson from swimming across the Rio Grande."

Meanwhile, the object of this homeland security breach was relaxing in Palm Beach, working on his tan and questioning whether America's cultural exchange program was everything it was cracked up to be.

A week later, Ingemar and his attorneys appeared at the Federal Building in Miami for depositions on the matter. The government claimed Johansson had not paid a cent of tax on his purse for the first Patterson bout. Ingemar contended that this money was not received until April 1960, so his 1959 taxable income was zero. Furthermore, his attorneys argued, a covenant between Switzerland and America exempted the fighter from paying any taxes at all. The deposition dragged on for three hours.

The following day, Ingemar's attorneys petitioned the court to allow their client to leave the country. Back in Göteborg, the health of Ingemar's younger brother Henry had deteriorated precipitously, necessitating risky neurosurgery. As a toddler, Henry had suffered brain damage after striking the back of his head on an iron radiator following a grievous fall in the Johansson home. Now, on the eve of surgery, Henry was asking to see his brother.

Federal Judge Emett Chaote came down hard on the prosecutors. "I'm not going to keep this man in 'prison' because you say he has not paid his taxes," he told the lead government attorney. "You can't do that under the Constitution." A grateful ex-champ, for once impressed by American justice, told the judge: "It is a remarkable thing that a judge employed by the government should represent the people."

Five days later, on March 30, Ingemar was on his way back to Sweden to be with his brother, who, sadly, would never recover; within a year, Henry would be dead at the age of 31.

There were serious questions being raised about Ingemar's health, as well. In June, Gene Tunney was called to testify in front of a U.S. Senate subcommittee investigating corruption in boxing. Tunney insisted that "Ingemar Johansson was a sick man" who stepped into the ring in Miami Beach the victim of "very serious brain trauma suffered when Patterson knocked him out in their second fight." Furthermore, the 64-year-old ex-champ proclaimed, "I believe personally he should not have been permitted to get into the ring for the third match. The brain tissue, once destroyed, can never be rebuilt."

In Göteborg, Johansson called Tunney "an old man who only wants publicity," and added, "I was properly checked and I know better about my own condition than Tunney does."

The passage of time would render a unanimous decision on that fight.

* * *

Most casual sports fans assumed Sweden's ex-champ fell off the face of the earth following the classic Patterson trilogy, or, at the very least, sheathed his hammer and returned to Europe to live off his money, fat and happy for the rest of his days.

He would eventually do all of those things, sure enough. But for the next two years, while a fighter's heart and a boxer's blood still pulsed within, he wanted to fight, needed to fight, and dreamt of one last shot at the title.

First order of business was regaining the European Heavyweight Championship he relinquished in 1959 to fight Patterson. But before challenging reigning champ Dick Richardson, a rugged Welshman with a win over former world champ Ezzard Charles to his credit, Ingemar would need a couple of tune-ups.

First up was Joe Bygraves, the Jamaican-born former British Heavyweight Champ who dropped a decision to Ingemar in 1956. "I want the title back," Ingo, now 29 years old and sixth in the world rankings, told reporters before the fight. "If I do well I'll keep pushing. If I lose I'll hang up my gloves for good."

On February 9, 1962, a sellout crowd of 6,200 filled Göteborg's

Masshallen arena for Johansson's first bout in eleven months. Ingo floored his opponent in the second round with a short right to the chin, but Bygraves arose at the count of four and, retreating, managed to avoid Johansson's awkward attempts to finish. For the remainder of the fight, Ingemar scored at will, and at 2:08 of the seventh round, with Bygraves out on his feet and his hands at his side, referee Andrew Smyth stepped in and awarded Johansson the TKO victory.

Afterwards, the press took Ingemar to task for failing to knock out a clearly overmatched foe. "I didn't want to rush in after that knock-down," Ingemar responded. "I wanted to make sure of winning. So I held off, pushed out those long lefts and softened up Bygraves. My right? It was there if I needed it. But I didn't."

Ingemar earned $20,000 for beating Bygraves, a far cry from his seven-digit paydays but welcome income nonetheless. Funds from his Patterson fights were still tied up in tax litigation, a case that would drag on for the next several years—decision, appeal, decision, appeal. Ingemar not only needed the ring work, he needed the dough.

*　*　*

With a contract to fight Dick Richardson already signed, Edwin saw no harm in scheduling one more warm-up, an April bout against the lightly regarded Dutch heavyweight champ Wim Snoek, a 34-year-old Amsterdam bar owner and journeyman boxer.

The fight, at Stockholm's Tennishallen, produced another sellout crowd. Less than a minute into the fight, Snoek smashed a left hook to Ingo's jaw that sent the former champ crashing to the canvas.

"The Swede went down as if pole-axed," the UPI reported, "and hit his head on the ring floor." Swedish referee Bengt Löwendahl delayed his count until he had escorted Snoek to a neutral corner. A wobbly Johansson took the mandatory eight-count, after which Löwendahl inexplicably held onto his gloves an extra three or four seconds. The delay gave Ingo precious time to recover.

The two men fought on mostly even terms over the next three rounds, but in the fifth, Ingemar landed a long left hook followed, instantly, by Thor's Hammer, a right to the jaw that kayoed the Dutchman.

Afterwards, an angry Snoek unloaded to reporters. The referee, he said, "was slow in counting and even steadied him [Johansson] while he was still dizzy from my blow. Had I been permitted to box on, I'm sure I could have finished him off." The "real winner" of the fight, Wim declared, "was Löwendahl."

*   *   *

Two weeks later, at 9 a.m. on Sunday, April 29, 1962, boxing's star couple—Birgit, radiant in a lime green bridal gown, and Ingemar, stretching the threads of his blue suit near to bursting—were wed in a private ceremony at Rolf's apartment on Rose Street in Göteborg. Rolf and wife Annette were the sole witnesses. It was all very hush-hush. Even the pastor was lined up at the last minute, arriving on a moped from Birgit's church in nearby Härlanda. Immediately following the nuptials the newlyweds left for a week-long honeymoon in Geneva.

Once back in Göteborg, Ingemar began preparing for his upcoming fight against European champion Dick Richardson, and Ingo's Jaguar became a familiar sight in town, snaking its way each day between the Ullevi training site and the Johansson family abode.

Edwin Ahlquist, aware of Richardson's reputation as a rough customer who was not above the occasional head butt if the opportunity arose, flew in Whitey Bimstein to work their corner. As it turned out, Ingemar would need him.

The fight took place on the evening of June 17, 1962, in sold-out Ullevi Stadium. "Before 55,000 virtually hysterical fans, the Swede was in command from the start," the AP reported, "landing sharp left jabs and sudden, savage rights." But in the sixth, a Richardson head butt opened a nasty gash over Ingemar's left eye that required Bimstein's black arts to stem. Then in the eighth, blood coursing down his face, Ingemar landed two titanic rights to Richardson's jaw. The Associated Press: "Johansson sent Richardson slumping to the canvas for the count of eight. The big Welshman rose groggily and Johansson stormed in with another pulverizing right which dropped Richardson like a stone. The Welshman rolled onto his back, out cold."

Ingemar was no longer a fading memory from boxing's past. He was once again heavyweight king of Europe and back on the world stage. "I want Patterson or Liston, whoever wins the title in September," he told reporters after the fight.

* * *

Johansson's championship performance played to rave reviews. "Ingo is better now than he was in all three of his world title fights against Patterson," opined Bimstein.

Even Richardson was impressed. "What surprised me most was his speed," he said. "He moved like a middleweight. I have no excuses. Ingo was stronger and cleverer."

The sporting press, normally so critical of Ingemar, gushed in appreciation. "Did Johansson beat Richardson?" asked the *London Times*. "It was worse than that. Ingo shot him down, executed him in a guillotine, roasted him over a charcoal fire, and placed him in a refrigerator."

June 17, 1962: Ingemar regains the European heavyweight title with an eighth-round kayo of Dick Richardson (*Bilder i Syd*).

One Swedish newspaper declared, "With his victory Ingemar definitely returned to Göteborg hearts, forgiven for moving away from them."

Basking in post–Richardson afterglow, Ingo contemplated his timetable for repossessing Patterson's throne. "I've been training and fighting hard for the past year and I deserve a short layoff," he said. "Perhaps I will have one more fight before challenging for the world title."

One. More. Fight.

The lives of how many boxers have been unalterably transformed by *those* three words? To the list add Ingemar Johansson.

19

One More Fight

On the surface, taking on former British Empire champ Brian London hardly seemed risky, even after a 10-month layoff. Hadn't Ingo sat ringside in Indianapolis and watched the Blackpool Rock embarrass himself against Floyd Patterson? Hadn't Ingo publicly declared London no match for his kid sister? Hadn't Ingo already floored Britishers Bates, Bygraves, Cooper, Erskine, and Richardson? (The line was: the best place to buy advertising was on the soles of the feet of a British heavyweight.) Ingemar's newly won title wasn't even at stake, as the European Boxing Union, the continent's official sanctioning body, refused to recognize Brian London as a suitable contender. As a result the fight was reduced from fifteen rounds to twelve.

It should have been a quick and painless $50,000 payday, but Ingemar's prolonged layoffs and love of the Good Life had taken a toll. At the weigh-in he scaled an all-time high of 207 pounds.

The fight, held April 21, 1963, drew 10,000 fans to Stockholm's hockey arena. From the start it was a dreary, dispiriting affair. A pattern developed early: Ingemar, retreating, throwing only lefts, London pressing forward, looking in vain for an opening. In the sixth, clumsy infighting and a crash of heads opened a cut over Ingemar's eye. Once again Whitey Bimstein was there to work his magic.

But Ingemar was tiring, biding time, hoping to hang on for a narrow win via decision. In the twelfth and last round the fans turned on him and a chorus of jeers filled the hall. The final seconds were ticking down.

Then: *it* happened. London shot a vicious left hook to the jaw and Ingo dropped in a heap. At the count of four, a semi-conscious Johansson staggered to his feet—eyes glazed, arms limp, blood streaming from his nose. Referee Andrew Smyth was a breath away from stopping the contest and awarding London the TKO win when the final bell sounded. Ingemar had to be led to his corner.

Two or three more seconds and Ingo would have been toast.

Smyth, the sole judge, awarded the decision to Ingemar. In his corner, London wailed in anger and flailed his fists at the turnbuckle.

"Johansson was out and was in no position to defend himself," Smyth explained later. "I would have stopped the fight if the bell had not saved him."

Back in his dressing room, a still-dazed Ingemar admitted, "London was better, much faster, than I expected."

In the opposite dressing room, a distraught, unmarked London felt he'd been robbed twice, once by the bell ("I knocked him spark out and they rang the friggin' bell ... rang it *early*, I'd bet my life on it!"), again by the ref's decision. But Brian saved his best shot for last. When asked to assess Johansson's performance, he deadpanned: "His kid sister must be better than that."

*   *   *

The front page of Stockholm's *Dagen Nyheter* (*Today's News*) the morning of April 22, 1963, was a classic. Above a full-page photo of a helpless Johansson—bent in half, gloves dragging the canvas, struggling to regain cognizance and beat the count—appeared the following bold-font banner headline:

**Vakna Ingo,
DU VANN!**

In English, the headline read:

**Wake up Ingo,
YOU WON!**

*   *   *

The fallout from the London debacle was immediate. Within days the Swedish Boxing Board of Control withdrew Johansson's license for a month amid rumblings that the sport's cumulative concussive effects might be turning Ingo's brain to mush.

Ingemar dismissed it all as nonsense: "You know why the board withdrew my license? So they could get their names in the paper. They're old and have nothing to do and this gives them publicity and makes them feel important."

April 21, 1963, the last round: Ingemar hits the deck at the hands of Brian London (*Bilder i Syd*).

The dust-up caught the attention of the *Times* Robert Daley, who flew to Geneva to see for himself. Under the headline "Critics Call Johansson Punchy, But Swede Will Keep Fighting," Daley wrote: "Swedish sportswriters ... have been urging him to retire for his own good and for the good of boxing. [But] talking here today, he did not seem punchy at all. Speaking English, he is far more at ease and far more precise than he ever was as champion. Ingo is 30 years old. It is difficult to quit when you can earn so much money for fighting Brian London."

Ingemar may have intended to keep fighting, but a confluence of events conspired against him. For one, an imminent title shot now seemed improbable. Dreary rematches with Cooper or London seemed more likely.

More importantly, Floyd Patterson was no longer heavyweight champion. On the night of September 25, 1963—in the interim between

Johansson's bouts with Richardson and London—surly Sonny Liston turned Chicago's Comiskey Park into his own personal slaughterhouse, filleting Patterson in two minutes and five seconds of the first round. Ingemar witnessed the execution firsthand as he sat ringside and took a bow before the fight, along with fellow former champs Joe Louis, Rocky Marciano, James Braddock, and Ezzard Charles.

Ingemar had to be asking himself: did he really want to submit to the rigors of training in order to fight blokes he'd already beaten? Did he truly hunger to claw back up the rankings—he'd dropped to sixth—just for the opportunity to face the most feared man on the planet? Unnecessary risks, after all, were anathema to the Ingo Way. He didn't need the money, and fame was never his drug. So what was the point? Besides, he had a new family now, as Birgit bore him a son, Jens Patrick, on March 6, 1963. (Ingo liked to brag that ten days later the kid threw his first punch, a right to Daddy's jaw.)

On Sunday, May 26, 1963, Ingemar appeared on Swedish television and made it official: "I quit," he said, "and I won't change my mind." His tone brooked no uncertainty. "There's nothing left that incites me to go on boxing. I don't need to fight for fame anymore. I'm fed up with glory."

* * *

For a time, Ingemar, Birgit, and Patrick lived in a fifth floor apartment in Geneva, where they mingled with other members of the idle rich. (Patrick would soon be joined by a sister, Maria.) Here, even Ingemar's cream Porsche attracted no undue attention.

Among the millionaires attracted to the area were Swedish Formula One race driver Joakim Bonnier and wife Marianne, who lived in the tax-free municipality of Arzier, thirty minutes from Geneva. The Johanssons and the Bonniers had become close friends. On one visit, Ingemar and Birgit spied a nearby parcel of land along Arzier's Alpine slopes, 2,600 feet above Lake Geneva. It was here they would build their dream home, a 10,000 square-foot, five-bedroom log cabin.

The Johanssons hired a nanny and joined the jet set: London, New York, Paris, Mallorca, the Riviera—wherever there was action. Ingemar loved Formula One racing and he and Birgit followed the circuit around Europe. Ingemar formed tight friendships with many of the drivers, as if the boxer felt a bond that comes of meeting others whose notion of "sport" involves the risk of permanent injury and death.

"Every year someone was missing from the circuit," recalled Ingemar's friend, the Swedish journalist Sigurd Glans. "The accidents were not discussed. Life had to go on." For Ingemar and Birgit, that stoicism was tested in June 1972, when, during the running of Le Mans in Paris, Bonnier's car crashed into a concrete barrier and spun into a tree, killing him instantly.

* * *

To retire is one thing. To *stay* retired is quite another. Among heavyweight champions, only Rocky Marciano quit on top and managed to resist entreaties to return.

Like so many others before and since, Ingemar, too, heard the call of the ring.

In July 1963, Liston dispatched Patterson a second time via first-round kayo, then signed to fight the upstart kid from Louisville, Cassius Clay. The bout was scheduled for February 25, 1964. A week before the fight, an AP reporter called Ingemar for his slant on the fight and was surprised to learn: "Johansson has changed his mind and wants to meet the winner of the Liston-Clay fight." Ingemar claimed he'd need six months, tops, to get in shape. "I'd like to hear that my name is still on the list of possible challengers," Ingemar said. "Cassius Clay is my favorite opponent [but] the only chance for Clay to win would be if Liston tumbles on his shoelaces and knocks himself out."

Ingemar was hardly alone in underestimating Cassius Clay; it was practically a cottage industry in those days. Typical was veteran reporter Oscar Fraley's take in the days before the fight. "If Clay has the talent to capture the crown held by such as John L. Sullivan and Jack Dempsey," he wrote, "then the Rocky Mountains are a level plain."

But Clay did beat big bad Sonny, made him quit in his corner, his face a bloody pulp and his shoulder torn from its socket from swinging at air. For a time, nobody could quite believe that young Cassius, now going by the name Muhammad Ali, was heavyweight champion of the world—least of all Ingemar, still stinging from the butterfly/bee's antics during their 1961 sparring session.

"I don't regard Clay as a worthy champion," he told reporters the

190

day after the fight. "It wasn't Clay who won, but merely Liston who lost. I can't really understand why Clay is so happy. Sure he won the title, but in an unglamorous way." Ingemar was referring to Liston's quitting on his stool after six rounds.

Edwin Ahlquist mentioned holding an Ali-Johansson bout in Ullevi Stadium. "I told Ingo that it was my personal opinion that he had a good chance of beating Clay, who is not much of a boxer," Edwin said. Ingemar, holding up his right fist, added: "I've never liked braggers. It would be a pleasure to give Clay a treat." Obviously, Ali's showboating was an affront to Ingemar's Northern European reserve. When asked how he felt about Cassius/Muhammad holding the title that once belonged to him, Ingo responded: "I believe this means the end of the sporting spirit in boxing. I'm afraid there will be merely a big show in the future."

On this count, time would prove Ingemar wrong—and right. Ali's victory was not the end, but rather the beginning of a true new era in boxing; a new dawn, indeed. And yes, it would become a mighty big show.

* * *

In retirement, Ingemar indulged his famous sweet tooth and began to lose the battle to keep his weight under control. Even at his peak he was thick and broad *everywhere*—back, chest, neck, thighs—and now, without a daily training regimen, his weight ballooned precipitously. Getting back into fighting trim seemed increasingly unlikely, and before long Ingemar retreated from the headlines.

Every so often his name would bubble to the surface. There was a report in May 1964 that Ingemar had lost 350,000 krona (about $75,000 in today's dollars) when a business associate cashed some blank checks that Ingemar had signed. Two months later, when Edwin Ahlquist somehow convinced Eddie Machen to return to Sweden to face Floyd Patterson, Ingemar took a bow before the fight to wild applause. Then he shook the hands of the two men whose fates so determined his own. (Floyd would win via decision and, sixteen months later, challenge Ali, unsuccessfully, for the title.)

While Floyd was in Sweden, there was talk, briefly, of Patterson-Johansson IV. Edwin mentioned the prospect to both men and guaranteed each a $200,000 payday. Floyd was game, but Ingo was too out of shape.

In November 1964 the U.S. Federal Court of Appeals rejected Ingemar's claims that his Swiss citizenship exempted him from paying taxes on $1.1 million earned in 1960–61. During the period in question, the court claimed, he'd spent only 79 days in Switzerland, compared to 120 in Sweden and 218 in America. And the court didn't cotton to the "corporation" Ingemar had set up—he was its sole employee—calling it a "device used by Johansson to escape taxation." Not long thereafter, a court in Sweden ruled Ingemar had to pay taxes on the same amount there, too.

In March 1965, Edwin Ahlquist sent Ingemar to America to report on the upcoming Ali-Liston rematch for *All Sport* magazine. Ingemar watched Ali skip rope and shadowbox at Miami's 5th Street Gym. Afterwards, Ali told Ingemar: "You fight me and we'll draw $20 million. That ought to make you twice as rich as you are now." Ingemar laughed it off. "I have no intention," he informed The Greatest, "of returning to the ring."

Ingemar may have been done with fighting, but he was hardly through with boxing. He would soon team up with the unlikeliest of partners: Big Bad Sonny Liston.

20

Cutting Ties

For decades Edwin Ahlquist had commanded a virtual monopoly over boxing promotions in Sweden. Thanks to Ingemar, a nation preternaturally ambivalent about the fistic arts had suddenly gone bonkers for boxing. Edwin rode the wave and it made him rich.

As early as the 1958 Eddie Machen fight, however, Ingemar had begun privately questioning some of Ahlquist's financial decisions. "A severe rift developed between Ingo and Edwin," Swedish boxing historian Christer Franzen told me. "Ingo wrongly suspected that Edwin had shortchanged him."

Now in retirement, Ingemar wanted a piece of the promotional pie. He hooked up with childhood friend Bertil Knutsson and in 1965 the two men started their own promotional firm. "Ingo was more of a front man, the PR guy," according to Franzen. "When it came to business decisions, Knutsson ran the show."

All his life, Ingemar drew successful people to him, men like Bertil, who was born in Göteborg the same year as Ingo. As teens the two pals began boxing at the Redbergslids Boxing Club. Both boys achieved amateur success. But while Ingemar pursued his professional boxing ambitions, Bertil was building a multimillion dollar casino and gaming empire. The press dubbed him Sweden's "Roulette King."

As promotional partners, the two proved savvy businessmen, with an ever-ready eye for distressed merchandise they could resell at a profit.

* * *

After losing two fights with Muhammad Ali under suspicious circumstances, Charles "Sonny" Liston watched his life and career fall apart. The ex-champ was broke. He had yet to receive all his money from the Patterson fights, much less the Ali debacles, and was deeply in debt. Unfairly, perhaps, the scowling ex-con came to embody (white) America's notion of the black boogieman you'd hate to see walking toward you after dark. No promoter in America would touch him.

Sonny was just the sort of damaged goods Bertil and Ingemar were looking for. After a sit-down with Liston's manager Jack Nilon, they signed Sonny to a $150,000 contract for a four-fight series in Sweden. The first bout was scheduled for July 1966, in Stockholm, against German heavyweight champion Gerhard Zech.

Did Ingo extend a hand to Sonny out of friendship? Or was it strictly business? Most likely, a bit of both. No question, the deal represented a 180-degree change of heart for Ingemar, who, prior to the first Liston-Patterson fight in 1962, told reporters: "I wish with all my heart that Patterson wins. It would hurt boxing if Liston wins." After taking the title, Liston toured Europe, where he pocketed easy money for appearances and exhibitions. By the time the tour left Sweden, Ingemar and Sonny had become chummy. There was, Ingemar learned, another side to the man: away from the ring (and away from the bottle), Liston could be generous and affable.

Still, the reclamation of Sonny Liston got off to a bizarre start. The moment Sonny and wife Geraldine stepped onto the tarmac in Stockholm, they were greeted by a young lady whom Sonny befriended in Europe in 1963. At her side: a 3-year-old boy whom Sonny apparently had fathered. Eventually, the Listons would adopt the child and bring him back to America.

With Liston under contract, Ingemar began referring to Liston as "the best fighter in the world." It wasn't just hype. Ingo respected punching power. Marciano was his idol, after all, and Liston was Marciano and then some. One boxer, a prelim guy, recalled how Ingemar "talked about Sonny like he was a god."

The promotional plan was to humanize Sonny by opening his workouts to the public and making him available for interviews and public appearances. It didn't hurt that Sweden was a relative haven of racial tolerance at a time when the civil rights movement in America was seething. Sonny may have been despised in America, but Sweden embraced him as the gifted world-class athlete he truly was.

On Thursday nights, Liston agreed to appear at "Ingo's," the popular restaurant/tavern Johansson owned in downtown Göteborg, for a meet-

and-greet. At one joint appearance, Ingemar was approached by some-one he thought was a fan. When the man extended his hand, Ingemar, expecting a handshake, responded in kind. Instead, Ingemar was handed legal documents relating to his tax issues. Sonny watched the scene unfold. "That'll teach you to shake hands with strangers," he told Ingo.

* * *

Ingemar and Bertil had to have been pleased when 12,000 fans—more than had attended Liston-Ali 1 and 2 *combined*—flocked to the Stockholm hockey arena on July 1 for Liston-Zech. At first the fight seemed competitive. Liston, ten pounds above his normal fighting weight, looked fleshy and slow. At age twenty-eight, Zech was probably a decade younger than Sonny (whose true age remains a mystery). But Liston's heavy blows took their toll, and in the seventh round, with blood covering his face and shoulders, Zeck was felled by a short, lethal left-right combination.

Liston's second fight, against Amos Johnson, a California heavy-weight who had beaten Cassius Clay as an amateur, was six weeks away. In the interim, Ingemar led Sonny on a tour of western Sweden, where Liston fought four exhibitions a week at $2,500 a session, sometimes with Floyd Patterson's brother Ray as sparring partner.

On August 19, Liston-Johnson drew 20,000 fans to Ingo's old stomp-ing ground, Göteborg's Ullevi Stadium. Liston came out slugging. In the third round, Johnson went down twice before the referee stopped the slaughter.

With two fights left on Liston's contract, feelers were sent to con-tenders Oscar Bonavena, Karl Mildenberger, and George Chuvalo, among others, without success. "Nobody wanted to fight Charles," Sonny's wife Geraldine complained to reporters. "The managers holler like a pig on a fence. The public say he's through, and they base it all on the Clay fights. But nobody wants to fight him, so he can't be too through."

With no one to fight, Liston flew home to Las Vegas. Six months later he was back, so broke he had to borrow money to make the trip, putting up his green Cadillac Fleetwood as collateral. Ingemar and Bertil had lined up journeyman Dave Bailey, a Philadelphia heavyweight who had lost more fights than he'd won. On March 30, 1967, Sonny kayoed Bailey in one round before 5,000 fans at Göteborg's Masshallen arena.

For his fourth and final fight in Sweden, Sonny met Elmer "The Crush" Rush, a hard-hitting waterfront dockworker from San Francisco and former eighth-ranked contender whose 15–3–2 record included a draw against Eddie Machen. Five thousand fans showed up in Stockholm to watch Liston knock down Rush nine times before the ref stopped it in the sixth.

Sonny returned to America for good and fought twelve more times, losing only to Leotis Martin. His final fight was in June 1970, a TKO win over Chuck Wepner. Six months later, virtually penniless despite Ingo's best efforts, Sonny died of a heroin overdose at the reputed age of forty.

Liston's funeral was held Saturday, January 9, 1970. In death, at least, Sonny was a good draw: an overflow crowd of 700 mourners attended the service at Las Vegas' Palm Mortuary. Ingemar was there as an honorary pallbearer, along with Joe Louis, Archie Moore, Sammy Davis Jr., Wilt Chamberlain, and Godfrey Cambridge.

It had been merely half a decade since Jack Nilon tried to lure Ingemar out of retirement to fight Sonny, dangling a million-dollar payday under Ingo's famously snubbed nose. "I like money," Ingemar told him, "but not *that* much."

April 1967, Stockholm: If anyone could get Sonny Liston to loosen up, it was Ingo. At a news conference to hype Liston-Rush, Sonny plays air-sax to the tune "Night Train" (*Bettman/CORBIS*).

* * *

Promoting Liston had proved so profitable

that Ingemar and Bertil sought another American with name recognition to import. They found one in Buster Mathis, who, at 6'3" and 246 pounds was quite literally the biggest thing in professional boxing. An orphan from Grand Rapids, Buster, 23, had won the U.S. National Amateur Championship in 1964. That year he beat Joe Frazier—*twice*. By the time Ingemar and Bertil lured him to Sweden, Mathis was a highly touted up-and-comer, undefeated in twenty-one pro fights.

On November 18, 1967, Buster and Peruvian journeyman Roberto Davila drew a crowd of 6,000 to the Stockholm arena. Round after round, Mathis rained blows upon the helpless Davila, whose face was a mass of welts and cuts. After a while, the crowd began to boo the grisly mismatch. In the seventh, one mighty swing of Buster's massive arm floored his opponent *and* the referee. Only the ref got back up with his senses intact.

It was not a good time for an in-ring massacre. Sweden's Social Democratic Party, already in favor of banning professional boxing, used the Mathis-Davila affair to generate further discussions in the Swedish Parliament. It wouldn't be long before the Social Democrats would get their way.

Buster fought once more for Ingo, against South African Heavyweight Champion Gerry de Bruyn, on December 6 at Masshallen. Fewer than 3,500 fans dotted the vast hall. It took Buster just 36 seconds and five blows to knock out de Bruyn. The following day's AP story appeared in hundreds of American newspapers. It ran without a byline but was almost surely filed by a South African reporter. "This was de Bruyn's first defeat in 17 fights since 1963," it read, "and his first ever against a Negro." As if *that* were somehow relevant.

Ingemar and Bertil promoted a total of 22 fights, most of which featured home-grown boxers. Their final promotion was held on December 30, 1969, in Göteborg. Two days later Sweden banned professional boxing altogether, citing the likelihood of "severe and life-threatening injuries." Even sparring in a gymnasium could cost you six months in jail.

As it turned out, the man solely responsible for the biggest boxing boom in Swedish history was also responsible, at least in part, for the sport's demise. It would be thirty-six years before professional boxing returned to Sweden.

* * *

By the late 1960s, growing antagonisms were tearing apart the storybook life of Ingo and Birgit. Ingemar, who had always reveled in the company of others, now began spending more and more time hitting Swiss taverns and nightclubs and making the party circuit, a lifestyle the reserved Birgit, with two small children at home, increasingly rejected.

"I wanted to live life, have a drink now and then," Ingemar told a confidant. "Birgit did not like that. In the end, it was so she did not like anything I liked. We drifted apart. I constantly had the feeling that she taunted me and thought I was punchy."

Birgit had soured on her role as Ingo's appendage. She not only missed friends and family in Sweden, but desired a more fulfilling existence than that of Mrs. Ingemar Johansson. "I got bored with Switzerland, sitting on top of the Alps," Birgit said. "The whole glamorous, retired lifestyle wasn't for me. I needed something more."

Besides, Ingemar's behavior was growing increasingly worrisome. In December of 1968, he bought himself a convertible Mercedes 280SL for $14,000. (Average car price in 1968: $2,600.) Within hours of driving off the showroom lot, Ingemar crashed into a truck, leaving the Mercedes a mangled wreck. Inside the car were the kids, Patrick, 5, and Maria, 3. Fortunately no one was seriously hurt.

Six months later, Ingemar's car swerved off the road at a mountain resort in Switzerland's Jura Mountains. The vehicle overturned and landed upright but was totally demolished. Police called it "a sheer miracle" that Ingemar escaped with only minor cuts and bruises, while his companion, an unidentified young lady, received not a scratch.

Three weeks later, Ingemar got into a scuffle outside a nightclub in Göteborg. According to police, he knocked a man down, kicked him, and then drove off. Pulled over by the cops, Ingemar flunked a breathalyzer test, which resulted in a conviction for drunk driving and assault.

Early in 1969 Birgit informed Ingemar she was moving back to Sweden. It was one of the few ugly times in their lives. "Ingemar said he would take it to the Supreme Court, to fight for custody of the two kids. I told him, 'Of course you can have the kids.' I had legal custody, but Ingemar insisted he keep them. So I let them stay for a while."

And so Birgit moved back to Sweden, alone, into a studio apartment in Kungsbacka, an affluent suburb of Göteborg. She began her new life by taking a job as a receptionist at a hotel.

Three months later, Birgit's phone rang. "Dammit—this isn't working out," Ingemar told her. "You have to come get these kids!" Added Birgit: "I knew the whole time that would happen."

In March 1969 her status as celebrity-by-proxy landed her a plum assignment as Judy Garland's personal attendant on what would be the singer's final tour of Europe. Less than three months later, Garland would be dead of a drug overdose at age 47.

For a time, Birgit enjoyed a brief career as a singer as well, appearing

Mr. Mom, 1969: Newly separated Ingemar, in Göteborg, with Maria and Patrick. (*Kamerareportage*).

in local clubs accompanied by some of Sweden's finest musicians. "I have not just lived vicariously through Ingemar," she told an interviewer in 2005. "I've lived my own life. I earned a college degree. Now I am mostly retired, working in moderation, running my own law firm in Göteborg."

Birgit, who never remarried, remains unflinchingly unsentimental. "There is no point in looking in the past," she says today. "There is no future in it."

* * *

For Ingemar, the early 1970s constituted a lost weekend of late nights and high life. He and Birgit continued to see each other and spent extended time together with the children on the Bohuslän archipelago, in a gray house between the mountains and the sea. But things would never again be as they were.

Before long Ingemar grew tired of his fame and notoriety. Switzerland, France, Spain, Sweden—wherever he went in Europe, people pointed and stared and said there goes Ingo the fighter, the champ, the Hammer of Thor. Too often, however, it was there goes Ingo the

Clowning with The Greatest, 1977 (*Kamerareportage*).

bum, the one-punch wonder, the washed-up palooka. It all got to be too much.

Ingemar had always loved Florida, with its memories of his 1959 getaway with Birgit when they were young and beautiful, the title newly won and life still an endless path of possibilities. And so in 1974 he moved to a small bungalow at Lighthouse Point, an upper-crust enclave just north of Pompano Beach. Here he could stroll the beaches unrecognized and forget that he had once ruled the world. Days were spent on the golf course and tennis court. Come summer, Ingo escaped to his private island retreat, Goso, located among Sweden's western shore archipelagos. Ebba and Jens lived nearby.

* * *

In 1979, Ingemar purchased the Sea Cay Motel in Pompano Beach, Florida. It seemed a curious purchase. The place was a bit of a dump: fourteen small rooms on two floors, no office, and phone calls went to a phone booth by the pool. Worse, the motel sat on the wrong side of Ocean Boulevard, across the street from the Atlantic. From their rooms, Sea Cay guests could look to the east and see the parking lots of the gleaming high-rise luxury hotels along the ocean.

But the place suited Ingemar to the marrow, and he ran it as a virtual one-man operation where he served as maid, carpenter, painter, plumber, pool-cleaner, and desk clerk. His son Thomas (from his first marriage), then in his mid-twenties, spent summers there and pitched in.

Ingemar arranged a sweet deal with an overseas travel agency to book Swedes into the Sea Cay. For $25 a night they could soak up rays, frolic in the surf, and fawn over Ingo.

Ingemar enjoyed his role as tour guide, dispensing advice about the best eateries, watering holes, and golf courses. He loved talking tennis and golf. But boxing? Only if asked. Guests looking for fight photos or memorabilia were invariably disappointed. Nothing at the Cay spoke of the owner's previous life. Thomas suggested changing the name of the place to Ingo's, to capitalize on the champ's past, but his father would have none of it. Only a ring on the pinky of Ingemar's left hand betrayed his faded fame. It bore a small diamond with the words: "World Heavyweight Champion"; the underside was inscribed with his name and the date, "6–26–59."

Summer 1979: The proud new owner of the Sea Cay Motel in Pompano Beach, Florida (*Bilder i Syd*).

Once or twice a season, a journalist would stop by the motel for an interview. The results were predictable. An article would appear in a newspaper or magazine: former champ, down on his luck, reduced to motel handyman and chambermaid, the carpets worn, chaise lounges torn, two letters missing from the Sea Cay sign. Let us now pity once-famous men.

It couldn't have been further from the truth. Ingemar had plenty of money. At the Sea Cay he was free to create a domain over which he exerted complete control, a totally self-contained world free of expectations and criticism.

"I can't even explain to you what it is like to be Ingemar Johansson in Sweden," Thomas told a reporter one day at the motel. "The night my father won the championship is the only thing in people's lives that they remember exactly where they were, like when President Kennedy died. Here he doesn't have to live with that."

At the Sea Cay: handyman at work (*Bilder i Syd*).

Ingemar had no problem parrying reporters who questioned whether this jet-hopping globe-trotter could find contentment at the Cay. "I got tired of running around, tired of parties," he told them. "You can't be a swinger all your life. I've had my glory. Now it's over. Now it's time to go on to something else.

"I loved the old life and I love this one, too. I don't sit and dream of the old days. I never thought of boxing as my life … just some fun I had when I was younger.

"This is my life now. No more limelight."

21

Edna

Edna Alsterlund remembers the day she first laid eyes on Ingo: Sunday, November 4, 1979. Edna, 31, had been living in Stockholm, a well-known and respected journalist for a Swedish lifestyle magazine. Some months prior, the magazine had sent a reporter to Pompano Beach, Florida, for an article on the former champ. Johansson, 47, had just purchased his modest motel on the Florida coast, a curious career move that warranted much interest among Swedes. Now the magazine sent Edna to Florida for a follow-up.

She was looking forward to the assignment. She remembered sitting in front of her family's radio-gramophone one midsummer morning as an 11-year-old in Särö, 15 miles south of Göteborg on Sweden's west coast, listening to Radio Luxembourg, and feeling the tingle as the Hammer of Thor sent the nation into hysteria.

It was sunny with a hint of chill when Edna walked into the Sea Cay for her first face-to-face with the champ. It was instant magic, as if the Hammer of Thor had been replaced with Cupid's arrow. Edna describes herself, as being "totally overwhelmed by his personality." She was shocked to find this ex-pug "well-versed in art, music, poetry," his sly, subtle humor disarming, his shy, innate sweetness endearing in an old-world sort of way.

Ingemar asked Edna to dinner, to the nostalgia-themed sports bar Yesterdays, where the two supped on scallops and white wine. They reminisced about the old days and Ingo made Edna laugh—"so hard the tears ran," she recalled. Their age difference seemed to matter not. When it was time to say good night, Ingemar couldn't find the keys to his motel. Would you believe it? Locked out of his own place, darn the luck.

To the rescue came Edna with the proposal that Ingo spend the night at her lodging, in a spare bedroom. Within days the two were inseparable. Too soon, however, it was time for Edna to return to Sweden. If it was just a fling, so be it. Edna was devoted to her work. As one of the country's top journalists, she might interview a drug addict one day and Sweden's royal couple the next.

For Edna, who had never married, the idea of a long-distance relationship seemed out of the question. And certainly not with Ingo. Too old, she remembered thinking, plus too many ex-wives, too many children.

Apart, the two began a romance by phone. It wasn't long before Edna began making trips to South Florida. In early 1981 she packed up and moved to Pompano Beach, into a two bedroom apartment across from the Hillsboro Inlet lighthouse on the Intracoastal Waterway, and set up shop as a foreign correspondent for the Swedish newspaper *Expressen*.

These were idyllic times. Ingo taught Edna how to fish, swing a golf club, and cook Chicken a la King. Most of all, Edna remembers Ingo's unconditional love. As a child, Edna had been virtually abandoned by her parents and raised by relatives in an environment of uneasy silence.

So it pleased Edna when, following a lovers' quarrel, Ingo would typically respond, "Dearest, I not mad at you. I'm mad at what you said."

Ingemar sold the bungalow at Lighthouse Point and purchased a luxury condo atop of the 29-story Pompano Beach Club, with commanding views of both the Atlantic Ocean and the Intracoastal. It was a lair fit for a champ and his lady.

*   *   *

In the spring of 1981, Ingemar struck up a conversation with a Swedish tourist at the Sea Cay. A health nut, the guest

Edna selected this shot for the cover of her book *Den Länsta Ronden* (*courtesy Edna Alsterlund*).

205

planned to ingest only vegetable juice for 20 days in preparation for the Stockholm Marathon in August. He challenged Ingemar to run it with him.

On a whim, Ingemar accepted.

It was an insane idea. The 26-mile race was three months away and Ingemar, now 49, had ballooned to nearly 300 pounds. Two years earlier, Ingemar had portrayed Santa on a float in the annual Broward County Boat Parade ... and didn't require extra padding.

But one thing about Ingemar—the guy was headstrong. He started running ninety minutes a day in the Florida sun and limited food intake to vegetable juice and carrot juice. He walked 26 miles every morning for a week leading up to the event. When the former heavyweight champ arrived in Stockholm for the race he weighed a comparatively svelte 247 pounds.

Nearly 300,000 fans lined the route as 8,000 runners wound through the streets of Stockholm. The field was led by the legendary Bill Rodgers, who had won the Boston and New York Marathons four times each. He was trailed by 7,998 seriously slim-and-trim athletes. And then there was Ingo in super-short orange trunks and a sheer white V-neck T-shirt that accentuated his enormous chest and belly. He looked like a sumo wrestler who'd turned up at the wrong event.

Fans along the route roared with delight as Ingemar passed, the response so tumultuous that two motorcycle cops were forced to clear a path for him as he covered the final six miles. The finish line was inside Stockholm Stadium, where Rodgers was first across, to modest applause, in two hours and 13 minutes. Amazingly, 10,000 spectators hung around for another two and a half hours, and they stood and cheered wildly as Ingemar crossed the finish line in four hours, 40 minutes. One Swedish reporter, with just a dash of hyperbole, described the response as "the same insane amazement and unrestrained frenzy that greeted Charles Lindbergh after crossing the Atlantic."

Johansson was back in the spotlight, and for something positive for a change. It was a chance for the boxer to redeem himself in the eyes of his countrymen, to erase the image of the tax exile who had recently told an interviewer, "I'm a Swede but I don't like my country ... it's a bad country with a lot of babbling old men and women."

Now, improbably, he was a hero again, a role model for overweight, out-of-shape middle-agers everywhere.

Marathon Man, 1982 (*Bilder i Syd*).

"I'm more or less a guy for the people," Ingemar told the press afterwards. Touched by the crowd's embrace, he added: "I may have moved from Sweden but I am still a Swede." The ovation at the stadium, he said, was "almost the same feeling as when I came home from the United States with the title."

* * *

Emboldened by his reception in Stockholm, Ingemar entered the 1981 New York City Marathon on October 25. The winner was the defending champ, Alberto Salazar, in a time of 2:08. Ingemar, down to 235 pounds, finished in 4:30.

American sportswriters, it seemed, had rediscovered Ingemar, and they peppered him with questions post-race.

Why had he quit boxing? "I lost interest in training," he told them. "Sometimes I see what I could have done. But dreams are dreams. I decided to quit when I was young and in shape."

Someone mentioned the third Patterson fight, still a sticky subject after twenty years. "A world championship fight shouldn't be stopped," Ingemar snapped. "It makes me mad. The referee did everything he could to let Patterson get away from me. I'm sure with a different official I would have taken back the title."

Asked the difference between running and fighting, Ingemar explained, "In a marathon you may get sore feet, a sore body, but in a day or two you are all right. After a fight it might be forever."

* * *

For the 1982 Stockholm Marathon, a Swedish newspaper publisher hit upon a brilliant idea: a Patterson-Johansson rematch—not in a boxing ring, of course, but over 26 miles of asphalt. The newspaper agreed to cover Floyd's expenses and suddenly the upcoming race was the talk of Sweden.

Patterson had long since achieved folk hero status in his rival's homeland. "When I lost to Ingemar back in 1959," Floyd recalled in 1985, "I got more mail from Sweden than I did from my own country. Many of the letters read, 'We are happy Ingemar won, but very sorry he won it from you.' So I said that if I could regain the title I'd celebrate my victory in Sweden." True to his word, within weeks of regaining the title in 1960, Floyd sailed for Sweden for a series of charity exhibitions and received "the greatest reception I've ever gotten." Each time he left his hotel he was mobbed by fans who kissed his hand and offered him gifts. "Everywhere I went in Sweden," Floyd told a reporter, "I saw there was no color line." In 1964, after a second straight humiliating defeat to Sonny Liston, Floyd returned for another dose of solace, telling *SI*: "I feel a closeness with the Swedish people that I have never felt anywhere else."

The news that Floyd had agreed to compete in the Stockholm Marathon ignited Ingemar's competitive fire; that Floyd, 47, had remained a youthful 182 pounds had not escaped his attention. A month before the race Ingemar flew to Ft. Eustis, Virginia, the site of Operation Lifestyle, the U.S. Army's newly formed 10-week physical fitness boot camp, especially designed for obese middle-aged soldiers. He arrived with just a toothbrush, jogging suit, and sneakers, and was assigned living quarters and a uniform—"just like any other soldier in the program," according to Warren Kemph, a camp trainer.

Days began at 4 a.m. with a march to the field house, where campers were met by a drill sergeant and put through an excruciating series of squat jumps, pullups, pushups, knee bends, arm twists, and other assorted tortures. Afternoons consisted of weight lifting, cross-country runs, and more calisthenics.

The men subsisted on 1,500 calories a day, everything sugar- and salt-free. Good thing recruits were not issued firearms. Ingemar would have killed for pastry and shortcake.

One evening, Ingemar sat down with fellow recruits for a Q&A, during which he blamed his weight gain on business worries and the breakup of his marriage. "I consoled myself with eating and drinking," he told them. But completing the Stockholm marathon, and his joyous reception, had revived his competitive fire. "As a child, if someone said, 'Let's see who's first to that tree,' I would give everything to be first there. It's the same with this program. I have a determination to win ... or get knocked out trying."

Asked for tips on getting into condition, Ingemar revealed: "There's no secret to it. It's simple: a little eating, a little drinking, a little flirting. It's an old Swedish custom."

*   *   *

Held on June 5 in record 88-degree heat, the 1982 Stockholm Marathon produced the first home-grown winner of the event in Kjell-Erik Ståhl. But that news paled in comparison to fan interest in Patterson-Johansson IV. Unfortunately, Ingemar's trip to the Ft. Eustis fat farm was all for naught, as his weight was back up to 246 pounds. It didn't help that, the night before the race, he attended a downtown Spaghetti Festival for some pre-race carb-loading.

The rematch was no contest. Floyd the Swedish Folk Hero finished in 4:22 and beat his rival by 33 minutes. The two didn't cross paths during the race but had a chance to catch up when they met that evening for dinner, Floyd with his Swedish wife Janet, Ingo with Edna. "The first time my wife met him," Floyd told a reporter, "we sat in a hotel hospitality room until four in the morning, he and my wife and me, and I'm telling you, I was laughing so much I was crying at some of the things he was saying ... my wife, too." Gene Kilroy remembered seeing them together in Las Vegas, "laughing like a couple of high school students." Just as he had with the sullen Sonny Liston, Ingo, with his innate conviviality, brought out the sunny side of the congenitally sober, buttoned-down Patterson.

Over the next half-decade, Ingemar and Floyd became something of an item on the running circuit, showing up together at races both in America and Europe. Less important than the outcome was the fact that competitive running had cemented a profound bond between the two, a warmth and respect renewed many more times in the coming years at big fights, banquets, and memorabilia shows.

*   *   *

Fame, money, love, good health—Ingemar had it all.

Privately, however, he

The champ is back in the limelight after completing the Stockholm Marathon in 1982. This headline reads, "Incredible Ingo!" (*courtesy Aftonbladet*).

October 1986: Ingo and Floyd train for an upcoming 8K road race in Griffith Park, Los Angeles (*photo/Nick Ut*).

still fumed at having been denied a silver medal at the 1952 Olympics. After all, he'd legitimately finished second by beating Illya Koski in the semifinals, and there was no rule prohibiting a boxer who lost via DQ from receiving a medal. Clearly, the emotionally charged decision to deny Ingemar, made at the insistence of Finland's Erik Von Frenckell, organizing chairman of the 1952 games, was unwarranted and unjust.

"Over the years," recalled journalist and friend Olof Johansson, "Ingemar always said publicly that he didn't give a damn about the medal. But I knew how much it bothered him inside."

At various times, Olof and *Göteborg Posten* sports editor Sven Ekstrom and others lobbied the International Olympic Committee to reconsider, but it was to no avail, not as long as Von Frenckell remained an IOC member. It didn't help Ingemar's cause that relations between Finland and Sweden had been historically frosty for centuries—the Norwegian Von Hatfields and McCoyquists. And Von Frenckell had a powerful ally in IOC President Avery Brundage, an old-guard potentate who ran the Olympics as if it were his personal fiefdom.

Brundage stepped down in 1972, Von Frenckell in 1976, and by the early 1980s the IOC began to soften toward Ingemar's claim under the leadership of its new president, Juan Samaranch, who happened to have been ringside that night in Helsinki when Johansson met Sanders. Ekstrom helped prepare a ten-page brief outlining Ingemar's case, which he presented to Samaranch in 1981. In the fall of that year, the IOC announced its decision: 30 years after the fact, Ingemar Johansson would be getting his medal. (A year later, the IOC would reinstate two more medals: the gold won in 1912 by the legendary Jim Thorpe, whose first-place finishes in the decathlon and pentathlon had been stripped for equally dubious reasons.)

And so the 1952 Olympic silver medal for boxing, heavyweight division, was presented in May of 1982 at a special ceremony at Göteborg's Aby Racetrack. The day broke gloomy and rain-soaked, but by the time the ceremonies began a radiant sun had burned through the gloaming, and thousands of fans gathered for the event.

There were trumpets and a parade of Olympic flags. Sweden's Prince Bertil and Princess Lilian were there, along with members of the Swedish and Finnish Olympic Committees and past Swedish gold medal winners. Jens and Ebba attended, of course, along with Rolf, Annette, Eva, and

Ingemar's children Jean, Patrick, Thomas, and Maria. Even Birgit was there, although previous commitments prevented Edna from making the trip. A cheer arose at the sight of an aging Edwin Ahlquist—the two men, mentor and protégé, together again, their past disputes forgiven. (Edwin would die two years later, at age 86.)

Ingemar was called to the stage, to the traditional 1–2–3 medal-winners' podiums. Holding a small Olympic flag, he stepped onto the Number Two box as Samaranch himself placed the medal around the fighter's neck. There were no formal speeches. Samaranch

May 1982, Göteborg, at the Olympic medal ceremonies (*Bilder i Syd*).

simply said, "It is easier to make mistakes than it is to correct them. Now it is done and I congratulate Ingemar."

* * *

Through the mid–1980s, Ingemar and Edna traveled frequently but not always together. Story assignments kept Edna globe-trotting, while Ingemar provided boxing commentary for the Nordic network TV1000, a gig requiring weekly flights to a London studio. For Ingemar there were also marathons, promotional tours, charity events, and memorabilia shows where fans paid to meet the champ and get his autograph. From time to time, Ingo and Floyd would be booked into the same show and the two old rivals would sit together at a long table filled with memorabilia waiting to be bought and signed.

It was a profitable sideline. Ingemar always made it a point to write his entire name, careful not to miss a letter lest fans get the impression he'd gone punchy. "It's OK for a tennis player to miss a letter," Ingo told Edna, "but never a boxer." Few things in life were more important to

Ingemar than protecting the image of boxing, and he detested the notion that the sport he loved left a bunch of punch-drunk stumblebums in its wake. At restaurants, on the street, at public events, Ingemar was unfailingly polite to fans, especially to autograph-seekers. "It takes longer to say no," he told Edna once, "than it does to sign my name."

In September 1986 the couple flew to Las Vegas to watch their friend Steffan Tangstad challenge Michael Spinks for the latter's IBF heavyweight crown. Tangstad, a Norwegian and reigning European titleholder, proved no match for Spinks, who won by TKO in the fourth round. Also on the bill was a 20-year-old boxing history buff named Mike Tyson, who stopped his opponent, Alfonso Ratliff, in two. At festivities following the fight, Edna spied the shy, socially awkward Tyson standing alone. Edna offered to introduce him to Ingemar. "Mike was in awe," Edna remembers. "He didn't just shake his hand, he actually bowed to Ingemar. He had such respect for him. 'I know all your fights,' Mike told him. 'I've watched them over and over. Left jab, left hook, right ... *incredible!*'"

To Edna, Ingemar was an incurable and chronic romantic. When Edna would leave on assignment, Ingo's parting words were always the same: "I miss you already." Sometimes Ingemar would miss Edna so badly he'd hop a flight and join her on assignment.

Eventually the constant travel grew tiresome. In late 1986 Ingemar sold both the Sea Cay Motel and his condo (purchasing instead a smaller unit off the ocean in Pompano Beach as a sunny getaway) and the pair flew back to Stockholm, where Ingemar blended effortlessly into Edna's circle of writers and artists.

That fall Ingemar bought an apartment in Puerto Portals in Mallorca, an exclusive island paradise off Spain's east coast in the Western Mediterranean. Exclusive? Think mini-Monte Carlo, where Jags and Bentleys pulled into marinas awash with super-yachts. Casa Johansson featured a roomy terrace overlooking the sea. This was the good life.

Mallorca was a fall retreat. What about the rest of the year? Ingemar decided he preferred Sweden's east coast to the Göteborg of his youth and bought a plot of land in Dalarö, a luxury seaside community of fewer than 2,000 inhabitants in the Stockholm archipelago. Here, in 1989, the couple built their dream house. Ingemar painted it himself, a rich deep blue with white trim. First, though, he had to put together the scaffolding. It required the keen touch of a mechanical mind, and Edna marveled at her husband's handiwork.

Edna's favorite room was an upstairs office overlooking a blue-gray sea dotted with tiny green islands. Here she found the solitude to write. Occasionally Ingemar would appear with tea and a plate of graham crackers—the perfect host. At night Ingo the Cook would prepare the evening's repast.

To Edna, her big Swede seemed a living contradiction: a hulking thick-bodied ex-fighter, yes, but socially at ease among well-heeled swells. A man of old-world values, sure, but also a champion of women's rights.

Ingemar and Edna, 1988 (*Bilder i Syd*).

"His confidence in me was copious," she remembers, "and was convinced I could do anything."

Ingo also proved quite the homemaker. "When the zipper of my jeans broke," Edna said, "it was Ingemar who picked up the sewing machine and fixed them." Ingo was a virtuoso with needle and thread. He even sewed his own shirts. And like Momma Ebba, Ingo loved to cook.

Edna called Ingemar her *oppfinnar-jocke*, or gyro-jockey, someone adept at jerry-rigging—"an emergency solutions sorcerer," in Edna's words. In January 1985 the couple was invited to Ronald Reagan's second inaugural gala in Washington. Edna was getting dressed for the event

With Jens and Ebba, 1992 (*Kamerareportage*).

when she noticed the decorative buckle on one of her shoes had broken. Edna freaked. Ingemar strolled over, whistling a tune. No problem, he insisted. Within minutes he found a paper clip and fashioned a matching buckle out of it.

Their 16-year age gap would only occasionally surface. Someone might ask Ingo, "Is this your daughter?" Ingemar had a ready reply: "No, it's my girlfriend's mother." Edna liked listening to Bruce Springsteen, the Rolling Stones, and Rod Stewart. Ingo preferred jazz, big band, and Sinatra. Over time, the couple's tastes cross-pollinated. Ingemar even learned to appreciate rock and roll.

In the early 1990s, with the relationship on solid footing, Ingemar expressed his desire to father a child with Edna, but she wasn't so sure. Edna wasn't the motherly type, her maternal drive quashed by an unhappy childhood. Still, Ingemar persisted. And why not? They were financially set and in perfect health. Why, look at Pappa Jens, Ingo would say, I've got good genes, I'll live to 100. The two visited a specialist who determined that their best hope lay in *in vitro* fertilization. The couple decided to wait.

22

Troubling Times

The fall of 1993 was especially rainy, the Dalarö sky a perpetually gloomy blanket. Normally the couple would be gone, to Mallorca or Pompano Beach, but Edna's work kept them homebound. In October came news of the unexpected death of Ulf Björlin, 60, the Swedish-born conductor of the Palm Beach Symphony Orchestra. Björlin's dealt a blow to Ingemar and Edna. Ulf and his wife had been two of the couple's closest friends in Florida.

A few weeks later Ingemar and Edna flew to their Pompano Beach abode. One night, at dinner with friends, the topic turned to Ulf's passing. "What's that you say?" Ingemar asked. "Ulf is dead? I had no idea!" He seemed truly devastated, as if hearing the news for the first time.

When Ingemar left the table for a moment, a puzzled Edna tried to pass off the incident as an example of his increasing forgetfulness. Don't we all get that way as we get older?

Other incidents seemed equally puzzling. Ingemar had always been a whiz at crossword puzzles, and the couple worked them daily. For the first time, Edna noticed Ingemar struggling with the simplest of clues. She wondered, how could this be?

By 1995, traveling solo had become increasingly difficult for Ingemar: flight numbers and times, hotel reservations, car rentals, phone numbers. It was suddenly becoming too complicated, and TV1000 executives began asking Edna to accompany Ingemar on broadcast gigs.

There were other troubling signs. Ingemar, never more than a social drinker, had begun consuming more heavily. By the mid 1990s the alcohol was turning the once cheery Ingo increasingly glum.

As Ingemar began relying on Edna to manage his daily affairs, she gradually accepted fewer and fewer writing assignments. Still, Edna remembers thinking: A bit of rest was all Ingo needed, and life could be as it ever was.

The turning point in the post-fight life of Ingemar Johansson occurred in mid–1996 with the death of Jens. "Ingemar's love for his father was endless," Edna explained. "Every opportunity, every interview, he told how his father toiled and sacrificed for his family, so they would have everything."

Every spring, no matter where Ingemar was living, he rented a nearby apartment for his folks. Mallorca, Pompano Beach, Dalarö— Ebba and Jens were always close by. When Jens died, according to Edna, "Ingemar's grief was bottomless and solidified into something more lasting."

* * *

On April 19, 1996, Ingemar and Edna attended an event in Tulsa, Oklahoma, called "Fight Night '96," a charity gala featuring some of boxing's biggest stars of the past, all of whom gathered at the city's Marriott Hotel for a black-tie dinner where donors could mingle with their heroes. Chief among the feature attractions: Ingemar Johansson and Floyd Patterson.

After the event, Ingemar and Edna retired to their rooms for the night. It was one year to the day since Timothy McVeigh had carried out the Oklahoma City bombing which claimed 168 lives. Suddenly, in the middle of the night came the piercing shriek of the hotel's fire alarm.

Considering the date and concentration of celebrities, a sense of panic began to spread as guests spilled out of the stairwells and into the hotel parking lot. Finally, the source of the alarm proved to be cigar smoke from the VIP lounge. Guests trudged back to their rooms.

The next morning, at breakfast, Ingemar and Edna bumped into Patterson. Ingemar asked Floyd if he was as frightened by the alarm as they were. "What alarm?" Floyd asked. Edna remembered how she and Ingo "exchanged astonished glances." It would be another year, Edna recalled later, before Floyd's dementia would become public knowledge.

Back home, in Mallorca, the normally taciturn Johansson began to display flashes of temper. He refused to attend one party because he was convinced that the host had fallen in love with Edna. Was Ingemar simply working through his grief?

That summer the Johanssons watched on television as Muhammad Ali, his hands trembling, lit the torch to open the Games of the XXVI

Surrounded by memorabilia, 1996 (*Kamerareportage*).

Olympiad. Ingemar was horrified. "It's appalling to show him so sick," he told Edna. "People will blame everything on boxing."

*   *   *

In November of 1996, Ingemar and Edna flew to Las Vegas for the Mike Tyson-Evander Holyfield heavyweight title fight. Longtime friend Gene Kilroy, a casino executive who famously served as Muhammad Ali's aide-de-camp, suggested the time had come, after 16 years together, for Edna and Ingo to tie the knot.

Why not, indeed? Ingemar had packed his tux. Edna had brought a nice little off-white Donna Karan number. Kilroy set the event in motion, booking Las Vegas' Treasure Island resort for the occasion. The night before the wedding, Ingo called Floyd Patterson, in town for the

November 1996, Las Vegas: Ingemar and Edna exchange wedding vows (*courtesy Edna Alsterlund*).

fight, with an invitation to attend. There was no answer, so Ingo left a message on the answering machine.

TV1000 arranged for the wedding to be broadcast on Swedish television as a prelude to the big fight. The ceremony took place at midnight, Swedish time. Ingemar's best man was Steffen Tangstad, like Ingo a former European boxing champ-turned-broadcaster. Artist LeRoy Neiman and writer Budd Schulberg served as witnesses. Following the nuptials, Ingemar joined the broadcast team as color man.

The fight ended in the eleventh round with Mike Tyson out on his feet. Evander Holyfield was now the proud owner of a crown once worn by Sweden's own Smorgasbord Smasher. It would be Ingemar's last broadcast.

The next day, Edna and Ingemar bumped into Patterson's wife Janet, who was surprised to learn of the wedding invitation. Floyd must have heard the message and forgotten about it. "Floyd is hopeless these days," she said. It would be a while yet before Edna understood what that meant.

* * *

Ingemar and Edna celebrated Christmas 1996 in Florida. Rolf, who wintered in a nearby apartment, visited each afternoon. It was clear that Ingemar was changing. He drank too much, argued needlessly, at times fell asleep mid-conversation. Edna asked Rolf if he thought Ingo had become an alcoholic. "Come on, Edna," Rolf responded. "Can't you see he has Alzheimer's? We have two cousins who've died from it. I recognize the signs." Edna had heard the term but was unfamiliar with the disease. "What's Alzheimer's?" she asked.

On New Year's Eve, Ingemar and his bride welcomed 1997 at the exclusive Brazilian Court in Palm Beach. In the coming weeks Edna resolved to find out more about this disease. She knew some things, naturally—that Ronald Reagan suffered from it, that it was a disease of forgetfulness. How bad could it be?

Some days, the champ seemed like Ingo of old. He and Rolf would get together three days a week for tennis, just as they had always done. Gradually, however, Ingemar's behavior grew increasingly strange. He began peppering Edna with the same questions, over and over: What is today? Is our money safe? When are we leaving? Are you sure no one is living in our home in Dalaro while we're away? What day is today? Is our money safe? In the evenings Ingemar began watching the same three movies night after night: *The Godfather, Death Wish*, and *Dirty Harry*. Ingemar would ask Edna how Jens was doing, as if he were still alive.

Ingemar and Floyd would see each other one last time, in late summer of 1997, at a fundraising banquet in Washington, D.C. Months earlier, Mike Tyson had bitten off a piece of Evander Holyfield's ear in the ring during their championship bout. The fundraiser was uneventful, but Edna remembers the dessert. "Everyone was served chocolate in the shape of an ear, with a chunk missing, and the whole thing was covered in red raspberry sauce."

*   *   *

The Johanssons returned to Dalarö in time to celebrate Ingemar's sixty-fifth birthday on September 22, 1997, a milestone the Swedish press planned to cover in depth. In the days before the 22nd, the Johanssons' phone lit up with journalists wishing to schedule an interview with the champ. No way would Edna allow that to happen. No one knew of Ingemar's plight, and Edna intended to protect her husband's dignity. She and Rolf settled on a cover story. Reporters would be told that Ingemar planned to spend the day with his mother in Göteborg, no press invited. In fact, he did just that.

At nine that evening, a reporter and photographer from the *Göteborg Post* managed to pierce the family's privacy. They needed just one photo, so Edna relented, but cut conversation short when Ingemar began talking about Jens in the present tense. A photo and a brief article appeared the next day. The reporter hadn't caught his *faux pas* and to readers all seemed well in the life of the city's most fortunate son.

In 1998 a new drug, Aricept, was approved in Sweden for treatment of mild to moderate Alzheimer's. No miracle pill, Aricept might slow a patient's deterioration by one year at best. After clinical evaluation Ingemar was approved for the drug. The official diagnosis: "Alzheimer's-*like* disease, with additional deterioration of the frontal lobe." The ambiguous diagnosis left open the question: was boxing to blame?

If Edna entertained second thoughts about keeping mum on Ingemar's declining mental state, they evaporated in the spring of 1998 when the *New York Post* outed Floyd Patterson with tabloid relish: "Heavyweight Heartbreak: Boxing Legend Cannot Remember Career Triumphs or Secretary's Name." In truth, Ingemar's great rival inadvertently outed himself. Patterson, who had served competently for years on the New York State Athletic Commission, was giving a deposition at a commission hearing in April 1998. Questioned by attorneys, he suddenly couldn't remember winning the heavyweight title from Archie Moore, much less his secretary's name.

To a sweet, sensitive soul like Floyd, the public nature of his embarrassment cut especially deep. He immediately resigned his post, withdrew to his home in New Paltz, New York, and disappeared from public view.

"I would do my utmost," Edna vowed, "to prevent Ingemar from being outed in the same cruel way. Ingemar would never have to read about his disease in headlines. I would not allow it." Edna decided on a pre-emptive strike, making a series of phone calls to Ingemar's children, relatives, and best friends. She informed them of Ingemar's sad turn and swore them to silence.

The Johanssons flew to Pompano Beach in October of 1998 in what would be their final winter in Florida. Ingemar was becoming increasingly disoriented. At times neighbors would find him wandering the Pompano neighborhood, lost. Rolf no longer stopped by for tennis.

Only two things seemed to have a calming effect: riding in the car, and shopping for clothes. Edna would drive Ingemar to Marshalls or TJ Maxx when the stores were not busy and Ingo would spend hours picking out polo shirts and sweaters. He had to buy one in every color and style, eight or ten at a time. Edna would take him back the next day, and the day after that. At the apartment in Pompano the shirts and sweaters piled up in great unopened stacks.

Their Florida days at an end, Edna packed their belongings for the last time in preparation for a permanent move back to Sweden.

*　*　*

Once back in Dalarö, Ingemar began taking Aricept. Like most Alzheimer's sufferers, Ingemar had no inkling anything was wrong, so Edna administered the meds hidden inside a pastry. After a couple of weeks Ingemar seemed calmer, less easily agitated.

From time to time one of Ingemar's children would stop by, allowing Edna to sneak away for a doctor's appointment or to get her hair cut or … any of the countless other day-to-day doings that once comprised life with a healthy Ingo.

Running errands *with* Ingemar could prove dicey. If she brought him into a store, he would make offensive comments to other shoppers. Once, Edna left Ingemar in the car while she dashed into a shop to buy thread. When she came out, he was chasing a skinhead down the street.

Soon it became necessary for Ingemar to take a sedative each day, which Edna crushed and spread into blueberry jam atop crackers and cream cheese. That was one thing that never changed: Ingo's sweet tooth.

There were frequent trips to a state-run coffee shop in the area that employed the mentally challenged—towards whom Ingemar displayed infinite patience—where he and Edna could grab a snack without being recognized.

There were days spent at Stockholm's magnificent Rosendal Gardens, a vast expanse of fruit trees and blossoms surrounding a fully restored royal palace originally occupied by Swedish King Karl XIV Johan in the 1820s. Edna and Ingemar strolled the grounds, picked bouquets, and stopped at the café for pastry and people-watching.

In September 1998, Momma Ebba, 87, suffered a stroke at her home in Göteborg. She was rushed to the hospital, but died before Edna and Ingemar could arrive. Thomas broke the news to his father, who seemed, briefly, to understand. Minutes later, Ingemar asked Thomas: "How are mother and father feeling?"

Ebba's funeral was scheduled for September 24, Edna's 50th birthday, which she had planned to celebrate with friends. Instead, she and Ingemar bade farewell to Momma Ebba. While in Göteborg, Edna and Ingemar spent nights at Ebba's apartment, where Ingemar paced from room to room, searching for his parents.

* * *

In the spring of 1999, Edna welcomed a new member to their Dalarö home: a white wire-haired Jack Russell terrier with brown ears. They named her Dixie, in remembrance of their halcyon Florida years. Ingemar and Dixie took to each other immediately.

As summer approached, the Johansson home was deluged with phone calls from journalists seeking to interview Ingo about the upcoming 40th anniversary of his title win over Patterson at Yankee Stadium, which had occurred June 26, 1959.

Edna took charge of the situation. She scheduled only one interview a day and sat nearby, ready to intervene if Ingemar began to drift. It didn't hurt having Dixie around, either, as a strategic diversion. Fearful her husband's empty gaze would betray his secret, Edna brought Dixie into every photo. Sure enough, in shot after shot, the little terrier stole the limelight.

The articles and photos appeared, the anniversary passed, and Ingemar's dementia went unnoticed—mostly. A reporter for the Swedish newspaper *Expressen* asked Ingemar point-blank if he was ill. Ingemar looked shocked. "No, I feel good in every way," Ingo answered. When the reporter mentioned Muhammad Ali's Parkinson's disease, Ingemar held out his hands. "See," he said, "steady as a rock."

* * *

Later that year Ingemar received a phone call from Eddie Henriksson, 48, of Göteborg, a name which meant nothing to Ingemar. Not until Henriksson told him, "I'm your son."

This was Ingo's forgotten child, conceived out of wedlock during his wild teenage years. "I was afraid he would tell me to stay away," Eddie remembered, "but he immediately said, 'Oh my God, come visit.'"

Eddie drove to Stockholm and met his father for the first time. He and daughter Paula, 28, spent a weekend with Ingemar and Edna. "It was tense at first, but then it went well," Eddie said. "We never talked about why things turned out the way they did, why he never contacted me when I was younger."

The reunion was short-lived. They kept in phone contact for a short time, and Eddie even spoke with Edna about getting back together so Ingemar could meet his great-grandson, Paula's two-year-old boy Lion. But as Ingemar's illness progressed, the calls stopped coming, the reunion never happened, and Eddie never saw his father again.

23

Changes

The year 2000 would mark the professional boxing debut of Maria Johansson. Women's boxing, banned in most of the civilized world for much of the 20th century, was, by the late 1990s, suddenly in vogue as a novel way to spice up undercards. But the sport needed a twist, a gimmick, to break through to a skeptical public.

When J'Marie Moore—daughter of legendary former light heavyweight champ Archie (The Ol' Mongoose) Moore—turned pro in 1997, it offered up a whole new construct.

J'Marie's entry into the pro ranks was followed by Laila Ali, Jacquelyn Frazier, Freeda Foreman, and Irichelle Duran. Promoters were swift to seize on the concept. Nicknames were bestowed. J'Marie was dubbed Lady Mongoose, Jacquelin was Lady Smoke, and Laila became Madame Butterfly—or, if you prefer, the She Bee.

Perhaps this was the spark the sport needed, the pugilistic version of Take Your Daughter to Work Day. Might we see Ali-Frazier IV? (In fact we did, on June 8, 2001, at Turning Stone Casino in Verona, New York; Ali won on a majority decision).

It was brother Patrick—he and Maria are the only two offspring of Ingemar and Birgit—who sensed the opportunity to wring cash out of the Johansson cache. He convinced Maria to start training, and offered to serve as manager. Patrick's goal was to steer Maria into big money fights against Ali and Frazier.

When Ingemar first heard about his daughter's career plans, Maria recalled, he wasn't pleased, even in his diminished capacity. "Do you have rocks in your head? Do women do this?" he asked. Maria, after all, was 35 and the mother of two with no prior fighting experience save for a brief gig as a bar bouncer at a tavern in Göteborg. After earning a drafting degree, she'd spent most of her adult life raising and training horses on a small farm in a forest, 60 miles north of Göteborg.

Edna was equally displeased, and grew angry when Patrick called and insisted that Ingemar fly out to Las Vegas for Maria's first fight, sweetening the offer with the promoter's promise of a $10,000 stipend. A million dollars, Edna told Patrick, won't make your father well again. The family divide was deepening, and it would only get worse.

Billed as the "Daughter of Thor," Ingo's *filia* made her pro debut on Sunday, June 18, 2000—Father's Day—at the Regent Las Vegas.

Maria, at 5'9" and 168 pounds, was to face Karrie Frye, 27, a six-foot, 166 pound tattooed ex-cook with a record of 4–1. Two of Frye's previous opponents lasted less than one minute, and no wonder: Frye was a natural athlete who had played on her high school baseball team—the *boys* team. She excelled at basketball, track, and martial arts as well.

The fight, televised nationally on FoxSports, was scheduled for four rounds. At the opening bell, Maria came out throwing jabs, body shots, and quick combinations. "The crowd screamed '*Maria!*' while Johansson edged, steely-eyed, around the ring," the press reported. In the second round, a ferocious Frye bloodied Maria's nose and floored her for a nine-count. At fight's end, two judges scored the bout for Frye while one judge favored Maria.

The loss did nothing to discourage Maria, who received $10,000 for the night. (Frye received $1,500, but then her father wasn't a former world champ.) "Hey—I'm OK," Maria told reporters afterwards, her face still bloody and swollen with welts. "It's what I expected. I plan to keep on fighting."

Maria was back in the ring barely a month later, on July 21, against Karen Bill, a 33-year-old Penn State alum who joined the army after graduation and set military records in discus, javelin, and shot put. Her claim to fame was a second round knockdown of undefeated Laila Ali in April 2000 at Detroit's Joe Louis Arena, the only fighter ever to floor Ali.

Maria was no match for Karen. The referee stopped the contest 38 seconds into the second round. After just two pro fights, Maria was done with boxing. She returned to the small farm in a forest north of Göteborg and to her job as a draftswoman, the only Johansson offspring with actual in-ring experience. (Ingemar steered his sons away from the sport. Today, Thomas is a municipal recreational director in Göteborg, while Patrick works construction in Thailand.)

23. Changes

Ingo in 2000 (*Bilder i Syd*).

*   *   *

By the fall of 2000 Ingemar was sleeping 14 to 18 hours a day, would go days without shaving, weeks without showering. His diet dwindled to Danish pastry, blueberry jam, and milk. For the first time, Edna tried explaining to Ingemar the nature of his affliction. Ingemar shrugged her off.

In November, Edna received word that the last of her aunts had died, leaving behind a cozy cottage on a wooded lot in Vishult, a rural community in southern Sweden. The surviving cousins wanted to sell the property, but Edna, looking for just such an isolated retreat, agreed to buy it.

The cottage was a time capsule, a portal to the past: creaky hardwood floors, an old-time radio, wood stove, antique clocks, wooden utensils. Ingemar loved it, as if he'd returned to a childhood home of his own. He spent hours wandering the grounds, plucking currants and filling bowls with them, the woods mostly silent save for the soothing chirp of starlings and leaf warblers, wagtails and larks. Afternoons might find Ingo in the attic, plundering through Auntie's boxes of old photos, vintage clothes, and nicknacks.

For brief moments life seemed almost normal. There were delight-
ful day trips by car, for example, to a nearby quaint fishing village. But
each time they returned, Ingemar wanted to know: Who lives here?

While Ingemar slept, Edna used the free time to work on articles,
conducting interviews by phone. Once, Ingemar awoke while Edna was
interviewing a weight-loss guru. Edna to guru: "What other weight loss
methods have you tried?" Ingemar, interrupting, on the other line: "Have
you tried going to the toilet occasionally?"

Often Ingemar talked in his sleep, mostly just incoherent babble.
But Edna remembers more than one night when Ingemar held a press
conference in his sleep, answering reporters' questions patiently, in
English, as he did in his salad days. And some nights, just before falling
asleep, he whispered to Edna, "Goodnight, Mother."

* * *

Ingemar had become mostly sedentary, his days spent in bed with
the television on, the sound off. Only occasionally could he be aroused
for short, pajama-clad walks through the woods of Vilshult. Edna noted
how the disease had begun to affect, "not just memory, but fitness, moti-
vation, initiative, desire and pleasure." Once, Ingemar awoke in a panic
and thought he was late for school.

By the summer of 2001 the Johansson family divide had widened.
Ingemar's siblings and children rarely visited or phoned. Edna felt she
was shouldering her burden alone, that the others failed to understand
how far Ingemar had deteriorated, how difficult he had become to manage. Rolf and Eva began to question Edna's motives. Why was she keeping
Ingemar tucked away in a remote cabin in the woods?

Clearly, a battle for control was beginning to boil. Ingemar had
always been solid as sediment, the alpha planet around which his siblings
and children revolved, held in place by his gravitational force. Now,
Ingemar's affliction-induced absence left a black hole that filled with
suspicions, accusations, recriminations. It was a scenario, no doubt,
played out among the elderly and their families all over the world. But
several factors separated this case from the ordinary. For one, Ingemar
wasn't particularly elderly; his mental decline had been evident since
his early sixties. And he was the former heavyweight champion of the
world.

*   *   *

At 4 a.m. on a Friday in July 2001, a fierce thunderstorm pounded the cottage in Vishult. Suddenly: a deafening explosion and a blue glow. Edna got out of bed to investigate while Ingemar slept. Sure enough, the house had been struck by lightning. The bolt had literally melted their phone. Right away, the journalist in Edna grasped the real sizzle to this story: *Lightning strikes the Hammer of Thor. What are the odds?* But she kept the incident to herself. The last thing their unraveling life needed was publicity.

In the fall of 2001 a desperate Edna arranged for a dementia-trained nurse named Anna to come two days a week. On Thanksgiving, Edna marked the American holiday with a new mantra: "It is best not to remember Ingemar as he was," she pledged, "but to learn to love him as he is."

*   *   *

In early January 2002, Edna received an email from Edward Brophy, executive director of the International Boxing Hall of Fame in Canastota, New York, informing the Johanssons that professional boxing's highest honor had been bestowed upon Ingemar: election into their esteemed Hall by their select panel of sportswriters and boxing historians.

Brophy wanted Ingemar in New York on January 10 to attend a news conference announcing the honor. Furthermore, Brophy needed the Johanssons in Canastota for Induction Week in June, a four-day celebration that would include a parade, banquet, and golf tournament.

Edna responded by borrowing a bit of the ol' Floyd Patterson peek-a-boo—covering up, mostly, but exposing just enough to get the job done. Paraphrased, Edna's reply went thusly:

Dear Mr. Brophy,

Please keep the following information in strictest confidence. Ingemar suffers from dementia, and it would be cruel to expose him to the media, which would blame his affliction on boxing just to sell papers. Actually we don't know enough about his disease right now to make that determination. We are extremely proud to accept this honor but must decline your invitation. Thank you for appreciating the delicate nature of our situation.

Sincerely, Edna Johansson

Edna's apprehension grew as the January 10 press conference approached. Would Ingemar's affliction leak to the press? Edna imagined worst-case scenarios involving stories about how Floyd and Ingo were devastated by the beatings they inflicted upon each other, an angle that would have horrified Ingemar.

On January 10, the Swedish newspaper *Aftonbladet* reported that Ingemar Johansson was seriously ill ... with cancer. It was actually a break, as it allowed Edna to legitimately deny the report. "What a perfect time," she said, "for a false rumor to arise."

* * *

Throughout his adult life, Ingemar had remained Sweden's golden boy, never mind the troubled teen, the military miscreant, the Olympic blackguard, the tax-dodging émigré. In his homeland, at least, Ingo would always be forgiven—their once and forever tousle-haired boy-king.

The occasion of Ingemar's 70th birthday, Sunday, September 22, 2002, should have warranted a national observation, a marker in time for all who revered the Hammer of Thor in his brief hour upon the stage.

For Edna, the days leading up to Ingemar's 70th presented a familiar challenge: how to keep a prying media at bay. For help she turned to the only members of Ingemar's immediate family who remained in her corner, Ingemar's son Thomas and his wife Susanne.

The couple took Ingemar into their home for the weekend, to Ingarö, an isolated archipelago community 40 miles east of Stockholm. There was no mention of Ingemar's 70th birthday. In the recent past when asked his age, Ingemar usually responded with a number between 35 and 45. In his mind, he was perpetually in the prime of his post-fight life. Edna, meanwhile, spent the weekend alone at the cottage and placed a sign at the driveway entrance. "Birthday Boy not home," it read.

Monday morning, September 23, 2002, Edna and Anna drove Ingemar to Huddinge University Hospital for his first complete physical exam by specialists in the field of dementia. Their diagnosis, "atypical Alzheimer's with frontal and temporal attacks," included a suggestion that Ingemar be placed in a group home as soon as possible.

Edna recoiled at the thought. Ingemar is not ready for that yet, she remembered thinking. Inside, she roiled with emotion. All her life she had dealt with feelings of abandonment by her mother. Was she now abandoning her beloved Ingo?

Doctors suggested that Edna at least put Ingemar on a waiting list. Clearly, not just any facility would do. There was the matter of Ingemar's celebrity status plus his relatively young age. Finding just the right place could take a year or two. Edna reluctantly agreed, and sent Anna on a tour of possible locations.

Still, every so often, the old Ingo would emerge from behind the veil. That spring Edna was driving Ingemar to the dentist when they passed a gaggle of geese landing in a nearby meadow. To the tune of Nat King Cole's "There Goes My Heart," Ingemar sang, *"There goes my goose/There goes the goose I love/There goes the goose I am not worthy of/There goes my happiness..."* The humor was pure Ingo, and for an instant, against all logic, Edna found herself thinking he might become well again. In her memoir, *Den Länsta Ronden*, Edna compared the moment, and others like it, "to standing outside an abandoned house where a dear friend lived long ago, looking up and seeing a curtain move, asking—Is that my friend peeping out?—knowing the friend cannot possibly be there."

Back in Vishault, Ingemar dozed away the days in an apathetic haze, rarely bothering to eat, subsisting on the nutritional drink Ensure. Weak and short of breath, he could no longer sit up in bed without help. For Edna, Christmas 2002 came and went with "silent melancholy," knowing it would be Ingemar's last holiday at home.

* * *

In January 2003, Edna received word that a unit was available in a group home in Saltsjöbaden, a swank community of luxury hotels and private mansions on the Baltic Sea, twenty minutes from downtown Stockholm and 300 miles west of Göteborg. Ingemar was scheduled to move January 21, to a spacious room with a bed and sitting area overlooking a forest.

In the days leading to Ingemar's arrival, Edna brought in his favorite recliner and stacked his favorite CDs on a shelf—Sinatra and King Cole, mostly. On one wall she hung paintings by his friend, the renowned Swedish realist Yrjo Edelmann; on another, scenes from the western archipelago of his youth. Come move-in day, Ingemar was surprisingly compliant. He was told he was being treated for ulcers.

"How long will I be here?" Ingemar asked.

"We'll see," Edna said. Ingemar drifted off and began to doze and Edna slipped silently out of the room.

* * *

Ingemar adjusted quickly to his new life. Edna visited nearly every day and invariably found him freshly shaved, showered, and in good spirits. He had even begun eating regularly. The vagaries of Ingemar's affliction were such that he had no idea how long Edna had been away. Each time she arrived, it was as if mere moments had passed since he'd seen her last.

An old friend, retired tennis pro Uffe Schmidt—Wimbledon doubles champ in 1958, and winner of the Swedish Open in 1957 and 1961—dropped by occasionally. Thomas and Susanne and their three sons visited often, sometimes taking Ingemar back to Ingarö for the day. Never did Ingemar seem happier than when Edna brought Dixie to Saltsjöbaden. The little jack terrier would leap to her master's lap while Ingo gushed: "Daddy's girl, how's Daddy's girl?"

Team Rolf, meanwhile, had no idea Ingemar had been moved to Saltsjöbaden. They weren't around to help before, Edna reasoned, so why would I need their permission now? When Edna informed Rolf and the others by letter, their reaction was predictable. "They went mildly insane," Edna said.

In the summer of 2003, on a visit to Saltsjöbaden, Rolf had Ingemar sign an application requesting a move to a municipally run group home just outside Göteborg. "My brother is unhappy at Saltsjöbaden," Rolf told the press. "He mostly sits in his room. In the Göteborg area are four of his children and friends from before he was famous. Here he would live a more normal life." The application was then filed by Birgit, who lived in the municipality. Now it became clear to Edna: her husband's ex-wife, who had been apart from Ingemar since the late 1960s, was in league with Rolf. Their goal, Edna knew, "was to engineer a divorce over our heads and against our will."

The internecine battle for control, which now included a signed public document, convinced Edna to go public with Ingemar's dementia, before the media could turn this sordid mess into tabloid fodder. Edna phoned a trusted friend, a journalist for *Aftonbladet*, whom she felt could handle the story with sensitivity. The next morning, the story was front-page news. Edna was suddenly inundated with calls from morning shows and magazines. She declined them all.

*   *   *

On August 12, 2003, Edna and Dixie were headed out the door for a morning walk when the phone rang. It was one of her closest friends. "Are you sitting down?" her friend asked. "The headline in today's paper reads, 'Ingo Applying for Divorce.'" Edna slumped to the floor.

The anti–Edna faction had scored a knockout blow. The fact that Ingemar could scarcely have understood the complexities of whatever documents he was signing seemed lost in the noise and clutter.

Edna consulted a trusted counselor. After studying the various filings and weighing arguments on both sides, he delivered the bad news. She could contest the divorce, certainly, but the case would undoubtedly drag on for years, their private lives played out in open court and sensationalized by the press, none of which would benefit Ingemar in the least. Edna was beaten.

Saturday, December 13, 2003, was "a crude, dreary, gray morning," Edna remembered. She and Thomas sat with Ingemar as he slept in his bed at Saltsjöbaden. The room was empty now, stripped of his belongings. The recliner, paintings, CDs, family photos ... all gone now. Rolf had taken everything to the facility near Göteborg. Maria would be arriving soon to carry her father to his new home. Edna leaned in and kissed Ingemar gently on the cheek. Just before she left, she pressed her lips to his ear. "I will always love you," she whispered. It was the last time she would see Ingemar.

24

There Is Only One Ingo

In the fall of 2005, a Swedish television documentary became the centerpiece of a raging war of words between the two factions battling for Ingemar's soul. Well, if not his for soul, then for control of his legacy, which is pretty much the same thing. On one side, Edna and Thomas. On the other, Rolf, Eva, and Birgit.

The controversy began in late 2004 when Birgit was approached by celebrated Swedish filmmaker Tom Alandh, who wanted to shoot a documentary about Ingemar, part retrospective, part where-is-he-now.

Birgit declined. Alandh persisted. After consulting with Rolf and Eva—"do it for Ingemar," they pleaded—Birgit agreed to the project. The result was *There Is Only One Ingemar Johansson*, a 90-minute special that aired on Swedish national television in September 2005.

Birgit serves as the film's de facto narrator as she recalls their early romance, the Patterson fights, the retirement years, the marital problems, their split and eventual reconciliation. Eva is seen sorting through a trove of old family photos and providing wistful captions to each. Rolf is interviewed, as are a half dozen of Ingemar's lifelong friends, mostly members of the Redbergslid Boxing Club. Floyd's brother Ray Patterson and boxing historian Bert Randolph Sugar share their thoughts as well.

But it was the scenes in which Ingemar appeared that caused the ground to quake.

Birgit is shown leading her frail, doddering ex-husband through the Göteborg Sports Museum, where an entire section is devoted to his life and career. Magazine covers, trophies, signed contracts, photos, boxing gloves, Olympic medal—they're all here. But as Ingemar shuffles past each display he appears oblivious to the fact that these trophies and medals and memories were once his.

They stop to gaze upon the magnificent world championship belt Ingemar won in 1959. "You're going to need that to hold up your pants,"

Championship belt (*courtesy Goteborg Sports Museum, Sweden*).

Birgit jokes, referring to Ingemar's gaunt appearance. Ingemar maintains a blank countenance. In fact, he says almost nothing throughout, just an occasional "Yes," or "Yes, exactly."

The image of a fragile, addlepated Ingo shocked Swedish viewers. After all, the champ had been kept out of the public eye for years and his illness hidden by his well-meaning wife Edna. To the general public, the impact of Alandh's documentary felt like an overhand right to the chin.

* * *

Former WBC world welterweight champ Paolo Roberto, a close friend to Edna and Ingemar, fired the first shot. As Edna's unofficial spokesperson, Roberto had plenty to say:

> This was Humiliation TV, an insult to Ingemar. I am convinced he would not have have participated had he been in his right mind. Edna nursed Ingemar at their home until he became too ill and had to enroll him in a nursing home. Then suddenly other members of his family show up who were largely absent during his long illness.
>
> Over the last few years newspapers wanted Edna to do a story but she refused. She protected him. Then he moves to Göteborg and a year later he's on TV.

They should have called the film *There is Only One Birgit Johansson*. I found it deeply offensive when he stands in front of the championship belt he fought his whole life for, and doesn't know what it is, and Birgit jokes about it. My God, Ingemar Johansson is dying, that's why he is so skinny! I cried when I saw it."

Speaking for Birgit and Rolf, Swedish entertainer Stig Caldeborn, a lifelong friend of Birgit and Ingemar, offered this rebuttal: "Roberto's disparaging statements about Birgit are abusive. She has never sought the spotlight. Tom Alandh came to her. Ingemar is receiving the best possible care and daily visits from family and friends."

Caught in the crossfire, Alandh defended his work: "I am surprised at Paolo's reaction. I think we described Ingemar's disease in a very gentle, loving way. Would it have been better if I had just shown Ingemar as our Golden Boy? Or should I show the whole person? A documentary's obligation is to show reality. It would be a fraud not to."

Ultimately, *There Is Only One Ingemar Johansson* brought Ingemar's life and accomplishments back into public consciousness and focused

Ingemar and Birgit at the Göteborg Sports Museum in 2005, during the filming of *There Is Only One Ingemar Johansson* (*Sveriges Television AB*).

attention on the dangers of any sport where blows to the head are commonplace. Viewed objectively, the documentary neither exploits nor sensationalizes, and Birgit, Rolf, Eva, and Ingemar's friends come across as loving and sympathetic people dealing with the tragic consequences of dementia.

In its review of the film, one Swedish publication called it "thorough and harrowing, a heartbreaking record of an epic life meeting an inevitable end."

And yet...

In one of the final scenes, Ingemar is shown sitting on a couch at his nursing home, shoulders slumped, head down, his dull eyes glazed and unfocused. In the background, a tune begins to play, softly, over the loudspeaker. It's Sinatra. Ingemar suddenly raises his head, thrusts back his shoulders, and his feet tap the rhythm as he sings along with Frank:

> *I've got the world on a string,*
> *and I'm sitting on a rainbow,*
> *I've got the ring around my finger,*
> *What a world, what a life, I'm in love....*

* * *

Ingemar spent his last years in a nursing home on Sweden's west coast, in Kungsbaka, a few kilometers from his childhood home. "Ingemar was physically a very strong man," friend Olof Johansson said, "which allowed him to fend off the illness. It bought him more time."

But time is an opponent no man can best, and when Olof visited in the fall of 2008, Ingemar's inexorable decline was evident: "He got up from a chair and took one step and froze. The doctors said it was because his brain did not remember how to tell his body to move the other foot."

In mid–January 2009, Ingemar required hospitalization for pneumonia and a urinary tract infection. "When he got home from the hospital he went downhill quickly," Ingo's son Thomas said. Mostly, Ingemar slipped between sleep and increasingly brief moments of consciousness. Normally, the staff would greet him with "Good morning" and Ingemar would reply. Now he was unable to utter a word. On Saturday, January 24, the nursing home staff informed family members that Ingemar's condition had turned critical.

Maria arrived on Wednesday and stayed with him all morning. "It

In 2008, Swedish journalist Tommy Holl snapped the last published photograph of Ingemar, at his nursing home in Kungsbaka (*Tommy Holl*).

was a calm and beautiful day," she said. "I talked a lot to him, about the old memories. He looked at me but I don't know how much he understood."

Thomas arrived at 2 p.m. and knew the end was near. Ingemar was comatose. Thomas lay down on the bed next to his father and thanked him for all that he had done for his children and for his family. "I know you are so very tired," Thomas told him, "and we will understand if you must leave us now."

Thomas: "About 11:30 that night his breathing was very changed. Then everything went very quickly. I sat there with him and held his hand the whole time."

Five minutes before midnight on Friday, January 30, Ingemar Johansson, 76, slipped out of this ring and into the next. "He took three deep breaths," Thomas said, "and then it was as if he fell asleep. There was no pain. I felt peace. He was beyond his misery."

* * *

The death of Sweden's iconic national hero was front page news in Sweden. No, correct that: it was the nation's *only* news on January 31, 2009. On television and in newspapers it was as if a head of state had passed.

The funeral, planned for Friday, February 13, at Vasa Church in Göteborg, reopened family fissures that had begun with the onset of Ingemar's illness.

Patrick and Rolf wanted a small, family-only ceremony. "He should be honored for who he was," Patrick told reporters, "and to me he was just Dad." Thomas and Edna favored opening up to the public. "Ingemar had great respect for his fans," Edna said. "I'm sure he would want those who wish to say goodbye to do so." Thomas agreed: "He had a great many friends from around the world who want to follow him to his last resting place."

The decision was made, finally, to hold an open funeral. The only question was whether or not the service itself should be televised. Göteborg mayor Anneli Hulthen argued in favor, saying, "He was not only a Göteborg personality, he was a sportsman for the whole world. I firmly believe many Swedes want to see him on his final journey." Ultimately, the family decided to prohibit cameras inside the church.

Even the selection of pallbearers fell victim to the family schism, as finding six non-feuding Johanssons seemed unlikely. "From the beginning there was the idea of trying to find family members who could carry the coffin, but they have declined," funeral director Tommy Atkins told the press. "They say they would rather carry him with them in their hearts than to carry him with their arms that day." Instead, at 9:45 a.m. the simple brown casket was borne into Vasa Church by representatives from Ingo's old Redbergslids Boxing Club.

Inside the church lay a multitude of wreaths with banners. *"You Made an Entire Nation Proud,"* read one. *"Once a Champ, Always a Champ,"* read another. Among the mourners was Raymond Patterson, representing his brother Floyd, who had passed away in 2006 from complications resulting from boxing-induced dementia.

* * *

It was a ceremony, the newspaper *Expressen* reported, "marked by a sense of hope and light rather than tears and sorrow." Funeral director

February 13, 2009: Ingemar's coffin is carried by past and present members of the Redbergslid Boxing Club (*Kamerareportage*).

Atkins added: "It is the family's wish that their father be buried, not the boxer."

Swedish pop star Sofia Fris, a friend of Ingo's daughter Jean, sung "Amazing Grace," followed by a traditional Swedish hymn.

The pastor looked upon the sea of mourners—all 1,200 seats were taken—and said: "We see in this church today how many have been touched," and evoked laughter when he recalled a conversation with Ingemar many years before, when he asked the champ: "How can someone who hits so hard be so nice?"

The service concluded with Fris singing "Invitation to Bohuslän," the unofficial anthem of Sweden's western province. "It is the family who chose the song, a song Ingo liked very much," Sofia said. She sung:

> *Between its bare primeval hills*
> *Is fertile soil and old peasant country ...*
> *And torrents clear as crystal*
> *And leafy stands with birch and arrows*
> *And ash and oak at barn and stables.*

242

Yes, come and see our Bohuslän in spring
See our burgundy heather, black sheep
And pink clouds over mountain.
Here you will be healthy ...
Here you thrive, I promise!

The coffin left the church accompanied by Frank Sinatra's "My Way," Ingo's personal favorite, a song Sinatra himself had sung to Ingemar on several occasions.

The body was cremated and the ashes buried at Göteborg's Western Cemetery. Here, Ingemar lies for all time in the family plot, where a single headstone reads:

JENS JOHANSSON
1907–1996

EBBA
1911–1998

SON HENRY
1931–1962

SON INGEMAR
1932–2009

Side by side two brothers lie, one a frail, mentally handicapped epileptic, the other, boxing's twenty-first heavyweight champion and lineal descendant of John L. Sullivan. In death, reduced to ash, the king and the knave are one and the same; Ingo would have appreciated that.

*   *   *

Present-day visitors to Göteborg's Ullevi Stadium will encounter Ingemar Johansson in his prime, the way he must have looked to poor Eddie Machen in the chill of a Sep-

Johansson grave site, Göteborg (*courtesy Stig Skogstedt*).

September 2011: Sculptor Peter Linde, left, supervises installation of *Ingo the Champ* (*Kurt Durewall*).

tember eve in 1958. Unveiled in 2011, a life-sized, half-ton bronze statue called *Ingo the Champ*, by sculptor Peter Lindes, sits on a meter-high granite plinth at the arena's entrance. The facial features are spot-on, but Lindes can be forgiven if the musculature seems a bit exaggerated. This is, after all, the mythopoetic Ingo, the Ingo we wish him to be, forever—all athletic grace and power, and throwing the right that made weather happen.

Epilogue:
The Hammer of Thor

Not long after Ingemar Johansson shot to international attention in 1958, sportswriters quickly settled on the term "Ingo's Bingo" to describe the Swede's lethal right-hand punch. But it took the wry wit of *Newsweek* columnist John Lardner to bestow upon Ingo one of the great sobriquets in sports history: "The Hammer of Thor." The name stuck.

No way that Lardner, son of legendary sportswriter Ring Lardner, could have realized how insanely apt a nickname he had loosed upon the world, nor did he live to find out. He died on March 24, 1960, during Ingo's championship reign, from a heart attack at age 47. But if sportswriters go to heaven—a dicey supposition, at best—then no doubt John is looking down with sardonic amusement at the cosmic ways in which Thor mythology relates to the life of Ingo.

*   *   *

The most famous god of the Northmen, Thor is the mythological deity associated with lightning, thunder, and prodigious strength. He is known for his three possessions: the mighty hammer Mjölnir, which, when thrown, caused lightning to flash; his iron gloves, needed to handle his powerful hammer; and a magic belt, which, when strapped around his waist, doubled his might. *Clear parallels are found in Ingo's mighty right, his boxing gloves, and his championship belt.*

Ferociously savage though he was, Thor was worshipped by the common man as his protector against the forces of evil. *Göteborg's son-of-a-street paver became the idol of millions while battling the underworld for control of his sport.*

Thor was also a bit of a rogue, known for his hearty appetite for food and drink, and he kept a mistress with whom he fathered children out of wedlock. *Sounds about right.*

Thor's archenemy was the sea serpent Jormungand. In an epic struggle, Thor vanquished his adversary but, alas, ultimately died from its poison. *Although seemingly vanquished in 1959, Floyd Patterson— Ingo's Jormungand—returned to finish off his foe.*

Nineteenth century Swedish chemist Jons Berzelius was the first to identify a critical radioactive element, which he named Thorium in honor of the Norse god. According to the World Nuclear Association, thorium is "a silvery metal which quickly tarnishes." *A tarnished silver medal!*

Norse mythology lives on in the modern world. The English-speaking word for the fourth day of the week is "Thursday," a literal translation from Old English for "Thor's Day." *For the record, Ingemar was born on September 22, 1932—a Thursday.*

Professional Boxing Record

Height: 6 feet; Career record 26–2 (17 KOs)

05–12–52	Robert Masson, France	W, KO 4	Göteborg
02–06–53	Emile Benz, France	W, KO 2	Göteborg
03–06–53	Lloyd Barnett, England	W, pts	Göteborg
03–12–53	Erik Jensen, Denmark	W, pts	Copenhagen
12–04–53	R. D'Innocenti, France	W, KO 2	Göteborg
11–05–54	Werner Wiegand, Germany	W, KO 5	Göteborg
01–06–55	Ansel Adams, Trinidad	W, pts	Göteborg
02–13–55	Kurt Schiegl, Austria	W, TKO, 5	Göteborg
03–04–55	Aldo Pellegrini, Italy	W, DQ, 5	Göteborg
04–03–55	Uber Bacilieri, Italy	W, pts	Stockholm
06–12–55	Gunther Nurnberg, Germany	W, KO 7	Dortmund
08–28–55	Hein Ten Hoff, Germany	W, KO 1	Göteborg
02–24–56	Joe Bygraves, England	W, pts	Göteborg
04–15–56	Hans Friedrich, Germany	W, pts	Stockholm
09–30–56	Franco Cavicchi, Italy	W, KO 13	Bologna
	(*European Heavyweight Championship*)		
12–28–56	Peter Bates, England	W, KO 2	Göteborg
05–19–57	Henry Cooper, England	W, KO 5	Stockholm
12–13–57	Archie McBride, USA	W, pts	Göteborg
02–21–58	Joe Erskine, Wales	W, KO 13	Göteborg
07–13–58	Heinz Neuhaus, Germany	W, KO 4	Göteborg
09–14–58	Eddie Machen, USA	W, KO 1	Göteborg
06–27–59	Floyd Patterson, USA	W, KO 3	New York
	(*World Heavyweight Championship*)		
06–20–60	Floyd Patterson, USA	L, KO'd 5	New York
03–13–61	Floyd Patterson, USA	L, KO'd 6	Miami Beach
02–09–62	Joe Bygraves, England	W, TKO 7	Göteborg
04–15–62	Wim Snoek, Netherlands	W, KO 5	Stockholm
06–17–62	Dick Richardson, Wales	W, KO 8	Göteborg
	(*European Heavyweight Championship*)		
04–21–63	Brian London, England	W, pts	Stockholm

Bibliography

Books

Ahlquist, Bo. *Guld i Nävarna.* Göteborg: AB Cirkelförlagets, 1965.

Ahlquist, Edwin. *Må Bäste Man Vinna.* Stockholm: Askild & Kärnekull, 1981.

Alsterlund, Edna. *Den Länsta Ronden.* Stockholm: Forum, 2010.

Cosell, Howard. *Cosell.* Chicago: Playboy Press, 1973.

Dundee, Angelo, with Bert Sugar. *My View from the Corner.* New York: McGraw-Hill, 2007.

Edwards, Robert. *Henry Cooper: The Authorized Biography.* London: John Blake, 2012.

Fitzgerald, Ed. *Heroes of Sport.* New York: Bartholomew House, 1961.

Fried, Ronald. *Corner Men, Great Boxing Trainers.* New York: Four Walls Eight Windows, 1991.

Gallender, Paul. *Sonny Liston: The Real Story Behind the Ali-Liston Fights.* Pacific Grove, CA: Park Place, 2012.

Giller, Norman. *Henry Cooper: A Hero for All Time.* London: Robson Press, 2012.

Glans, Sigurd. *Tungviktaren.* Stockholm: Askelin & Hägglund, 1982.

Goldstein, Ruby, with Frank Graham. *Third Man in the Ring.* New York: Funk & Wagnalls, 1959.

Grossinger, Tania. *Growing Up at Grossinger's.* New York: Skyhorse, 2008.

Heinz, W. C. *What a Time It Was.* Cambridge: Da Capo Press, 2001.

Heller, Peter. *Bad Intentions: The Mike Tyson Story.* New York: New American Books, 1989.

Johansson, Ingemar. *Seconds Leave the Ring.* London: Sportsmans Books, 1961.

Kahn, Roger. *A Flame of Pure Fire.* New York: Houghton Mifflin Harcourt, 1999.

Keiter, Les. *Fifty Years Behind the Microphone.* Honolulu: University of Hawaii Press, 1991.

Kelley, Kitty. *Elizabeth Taylor: The Last Star.* New York: Simon & Schuster, 2011.

Levy, Alan. *Floyd Patterson: A Boxer and a Gentleman.* Jefferson, NC: McFarland, 2008.

Liebling, A. J. *A Neutral Corner.* New York: North Point Press, 1990.

Linet, Beverly. *Ladd: A Hollywood Tragedy.* New York: Berkley Books, 1980.

Marsh, Irving, and Edward Ehre. *Best Sports Stories, 1960.* New York: E. P. Dutton, 1960.

McCallum, John. *The World Heavyweight Boxing Championship.* Radnor, PA: Chilton Books, 1974.

Mercante, Arthur, with Phil Guarnieri. *Inside the Ropes.* Ithaca: McBooks Press, 2006.

Newcombe, Jack. *Floyd Patterson: Heavyweight King.* New York: Bartholomew House, 1961.

Pacheco, Ferdie. *Tales from the 5th Street Gym.* Gainesville: University of Florida Press, 2010.

Patterson, Floyd, with Milton Gross. *Victory Over Myself.* New York: Scholastic Books, 1962.

Pomeranz, Joel. *Jennie and the Story of Grossinger's.* New York: Grosset & Dunlap, 1970.

Porter, Darwin, and Danforth Prince. *Elizabeth Taylor: There's Nothing Like a Dame.* New York: Blood Moon Productions, 2012.

Remnick, David. *King of the World.* New York: Vintage, 1998.

Ribowsky, Mark. *Howard Cosell: The Man, the Myth, and the Transformation of American Sports.* New York: W. W. Norton, 2012.

Schulberg, Bud. *Ringside: A Treasury of Boxing Reportage.* Chicago: Ivan R. Dee, 2006.

Skehan, Everett. *Rocky Marciano: Biography of a First Son.* Boston: Houghton Mifflin, 1977.

Stratton, W. K. *Floyd Patterson: The Fighting Life of Boxing's Invisible Champion.* New York: Houghton Mifflin Harcourt, 2012.

Sullivan, Russell. *Rocky Marciano: The Rock of His Times.* Urbana: University of Illinois Press, 2002.

Sumner, Andrew. *Be Lucky, the Story of Brian London.* Bloomington: Trafford, 2008.

Well, Glokar. *Född till Boxare.* Stockholm: Christophers, 1959.

Newspapers

Baltimore Afro-American
Boca Raton News
Bonham Daily Favorite
Brandon Sun
Calgary Herald
Clearfield Progress
Daytona Beach Morning Journal
Edmonton Journal
Eugene Register Guard
Fredericksburg Free Lance Star
Gainesville Sun
Göteborg Post
Lethbridge Herald
Meridan Journal
Miami News

Milwaukee Sentinel
Montreal Gazette
Modesto Bee
New York Herald Tribune
New York Journal American
New York Times
Ottawa Citizen
Pacific Stars and Stripes
Palm Beach Post
Pittsburgh Courier
Pittsburgh Press
Reading Eagle
St. Joseph Gazette
St. Petersburg Evening Independent
St. Petersburg Times
Sarasota Herald Tribune
Saskatchewan Leader Post
Saskatoon Star Phoenix
Schenectady Gazette
Spokane Daily Chronicle
Spokane Spokesman Review
Stockholm Aftonbladet
Stockholm Dagens Nyheter
Stockholm Expressen
Sumter Daily Item
Victoria Advocate

Magazines

Ahlquist, Edwin. "Millions Tempt Johansson." *Ring,* December 1963.

_____. "Vem av Utmanarna om VM Slår Ingemar?" *Record,* April 1962.

Bellew, Mike. "From the Past: Ingemar Johansson." *Fight Beat,* April 1985.

Bimstein, Whitey, and Barney Nagler. "My Wacky Life with Ingo." *Sport,* August 1961.

Breslin, Jimmy. "I Can Beat Patterson." *True,* June 1959.

_____. "Johansson and the Mighty Right." *Boxing Yearbook,* 1960.

Bromberg, Lester. "Confidence Misleading?" *Ring,* December 1960.

"Can Johansson Do It Again?" *World Boxing,* March 1970.

Casey, Mike. "Ingo's Bingo: The Mightiest Right?" Cyberboxingzone.com.

Cohn, Howard. "Epitaph for a Promoter." *True,* December 1960.

Conrad, Harold. "Going Down with Muhammad Ali." *Rolling Stone,* February 4, 1982.

Daniel, Dan. "Ingemar Johansson: Will Patterson Fight Him?" *Ring,* December 1958.

_____. "Ingemar Marking Time." *Ring,* November 1959.

_____. "Fighter of the Year." *Ring,* February 1959.

_____. "Patterson-Johansson Brings Big Time Boxing Back to New York." *Ring,* May 1959.

_____. "Patterson Sweats it Out." *Ring,* January 1960.

_____. "Ring Staff Picks Johansson to Repeat," *Ring,* July 1960.

_____. "This Big Fight Like No Other in Ring History." *Ring,* April 1961.

_____. "Top Heavies Are Banned by D'Amato." *Ring,* December 1957.

"Easy Workout for the Champ." *TV Guide,* December 19, 1959.

Eidmark, Henry. "Ingo Spanjor, på Deltid." *All Sport,* November 1964.

Ekström, Sven. "Den Dramatiska Returen." *All Sport,* July 1960.

"Events and Discoveries of the Week." *Sports Illustrated,* June 27, 1960.

"Events and Discoveries of the Week." *Sports Illustrated,* July 11, 1960.

Fleischer, Nat. "IBC Loses Fight." *Ring,* September 1957.

_____. "Johansson Second Choice Now?" *Ring,* September 1959.

_____. "London's Long Stay Encouraged Johansson." *Ring,* July 1959.

_____. "Nat Fleischer Says." *Ring,* May 1960.

_____. "Where Will It All Lead?" *Ring,* December 1959.

"The Fun of It All." *Sports Illustrated,* June 1, 1959.

"Går det Likadant för Clay?" *Rekord,* September 1963.

Greene, Bob. "After the Last Knockout." *Esquire,* April 1983.

Greene, Lee. "Europe's Heavyweight Hope." *Sport,* April 1959.

Hamilton, Bill. "Johansson Tops Challengers." *Ring,* November 1958.

_____. "Ingemar Johansson: Many Sided Character." *Ring,* July 1959.

Heinz, W. C. "A Visit with Ingemar Johansson." *Saturday Evening Post,* June 20, 1959.

Hennesey, Hal. "Johansson: Big Question Mark for 1961." *Boxing Illustrated,* February 1961.

_____. "Root for Johansson to Win, Boys—It's the Best Thing for Boxing." *Boxing Illustrated,* August 1959.

_____. "What's Next for Johansson?" *Boxing Illustrated,* September 1961.

"Ingemar Johansson, Fighter of the Month." *Ring,* November 1958.

"Ingo Is Man of the Year." *Sport,* February 1960.

"Ingo, Please Come Back!" *International Boxing,* January 1969.

"It Was a Victory for Us!" *Ebony,* August 1960.

Jansson, Bertil. "Göteborg's Gentle Giant," *World Sports,* June 1959.

Jones, Jersey. "Marciano's Own Odds on Comeback." *Ring,* November 1959.

_____. "Seen and Heard in New York." *Ring,* July 1959.

Kane, Martin. "Big Punch, Small Chance." *Sports Illustrated,* May 9, 1960.

_____. "Boxing Greets its New Dawn." *Sports Illustrated,* July 6, 1959.

_____. "Ingo Is the Man for 1959." *Sports Illustrated,* January 26, 1959.

_____. "Ingo Out and then...Ee-Yah!" *Sports Illustrated,* June 27, 1960.

_____. "Ingo's Right and Floyd's Peekaboo in Collision." *Sports Illustrated,* June 22, 1959.

_____. "Labyrinthine Plans Laid in Indianapolis." *Sports Illustrated,* April 13, 1959.

_____. "The Man and the Plan." *Sports Illustrated,* January 4, 1960.

_____. "New Ingo with a New Left." *Sports Illustrated,* February 13, 1961.

_____. "A Real Crown for Floyd." *Sports Illustrated,* July 4, 1960.

_____. "The Two Faces of Cecil Rhodes." *Sports Illustrated,* April 29, 1959.

_____. "What It All Means." *Sports Illustrated,* August 10, 1959.

_____. "When Millions are at Stake." *Sports Illustrated,* August 17, 1959.

_____. "Why Ingo Is Champ." *Sports Illustrated,* July 13, 1959.

_____. "Why Ingo Will Do It Again." *Sports Illustrated,* June 20, 1960.

Loubet, Nat. "Floyd Patterson, Jinx Breaker?" *Ring,* May 1960.

_____. "Ingemar Johansson, Pride of Sweden." *Ring,* October 1958.

_____. "Patterson and Johansson Swap Places in Prestige." *Ring,* September 1960.

Mulliken, John. "Ingemar Fingers the Fight Mob." *Life,* August 24, 1959.

_____. "Mr. Anderberg's Odyssey." *Sports Illustrated,* July 6, 1959.

"Några Sparringronder med Ingemar." *All Sport,* April 1963.

"Old World's New Heartthrob." *Sports Illustrated,* June 20, 1959.

"Patterson Pulverized," *Boxing News,* July 3, 1959.

Rogin, Gilbert. "The Big Four Meet in Paris." *Sports Illustrated,* August 17, 1959.

_____. "The Drama in Miami." *Sports Illustrated,* March 20, 1961.

_____. "Handsome Johansson Pays a Secret Visit." *Sports Illustrated,* December 1, 1958.

_____. "The Invisible Champion." *Sports Illustrated,* January 16, 1961.

_____. "Man with Fight Seeks Site." *Sports Illustrated,* March 2, 1959.

_____. "Meet Mr. X." *Sports Illustrated,* August 31, 1959.

_____. "Will the Tiger Be Back?" *Sports Illustrated,* March 13, 1961.

Salak, Johnny. "TV and Boxing." *Ring,* November 1958.

Schaap, Dick, and Martin Siegel. "What Ingo Wants." *Sport,* December 1959.

"Success at the Summit." *Sports Illustrated,* July 4, 1960.

"Swedish Hurrah for Hero Ingemar." *Life,* July 20, 1959.

"Ticket to a New Era, Maybe." *Sports Illustrated,* June 8, 1959.

"We Told You So," *Boxing Illustrated,* October 1959.

Weston, Stanley. "Marciano Will Fight Again." *Boxing Illustrated,* October 1959.

"World Is Stunned by Swedish Punch." *Life,* July 6, 1959.

Documentaries

En Dag med Ingo (1959)
Med Krut i Nävarna (1960)
Det Finns Bara en Ingemar Johansson (2005)

Interviews

Edna Alsterlund, Robert Daley, Paul Gallender, Joe Gallison, Maria Johansson Gregner, Olof Johansson, Patrick Johansson, Rolf Johansson, Thomas Johansson, Gene Kilroy, David Ladd, Birgit Lundgren Johansson, Paolo Roberto.

Index

Page numbers in **bold italics** indicate pages with illustrations.